For Dummies
BESTSELLING BOOK SERIES

Coaching Hockey For Dummies
Cheat Sheet

Coach's Checklist

Keep this checklist on your clipboard and review the list before or after practices, meetings, or any encounter with the athletes you coach. All these steps will become second nature in time. Then you'll be a great coach.

- **Set your goals.** Spend time before the season starts to consider your hopes, expectations, and priorities for yourself and your team. Write them down.
- **Be prepared.** Use your goals to plan your overall season including what you want to accomplish monthly, weekly, and daily in practices and games.
- **Carry a positive attitude.** Every day, bring an upbeat attitude to the team and to each player you deal with on the team.
- **Dispense positive reinforcement.** Catch players doing things right. When you do, you reinforce the behavior and performance you want.
- **Provide motivation.** Motivation comes from within the individual players, not from your "Rah! Rah!" speeches. Fun and praise pave the most direct route to motivated players.
- **Instill pride.** You want your players to wear your team jersey with pride every day. Develop a team reputation that they can all feel proud of.
- **Show confidence.** Confidence comes from knowing what you're doing and that you can do it. Educate yourself; become knowledgeable about the game. Ask questions. Learn.
- **Cultivate good work habits.** Lead by example on this one. Do your homework; come to practices and games prepared. Work tirelessly with the kids and help them discover that a little hard work pays off in spades.
- **Cultivate positive self images.** Help players believe in themselves so that they can feel great about themselves as players and as people.
- **Provide great practices.** Have players moving, participating, succeeding, learning, and laughing.
- **Balance game coaching.** Make games fun and positive at the same time as players learn from their experiences.
- **Be safety conscious.** Be medically informed about those you're working with. Check equipment and facilities. Know emergency procedures.
- **Show respect.** Everyone you work with deserves to be shown some respect. That includes the players, parents, officials, and your assistants. Respect sets a tone for the team.
- **Teach and challenge.** Start simple. Progress step-by-step. Know where the kids are in their skills so that you can lead them a little further forward and reward them for getting there.
- **Pay attention.** Every kid wants to feel valued in some way. Talk to the kids. Know their names. Find out something unique about them. Point out something they do well, daily.
- **Set a great example.** Lead by example in attitude, enthusiasm, and sportsmanship. Your team, and even most parents, will follow.
- **Control the parents.** Lead. Set rules and consequences. Clearly communicate those rules and consequences. Do not waver from what you set and communicate. But have fun with them as much as possible.
- **Dispense discipline.** Make sure all players know that the team comes first. Anything that disrupts or hurts the team or individual team members is *not* acceptable. Make sure that they know the consequences of unacceptable behavior and dole it out when necessary, with consistency.
- **Use your creativity.** Be adaptable and creative when things don't work out as you expected. Design your own drills. Find tricks to help kids learn. Adjust in lousy facilities. You'll all get more out of the experience.
- **Have fun.** Coaching should be a great experience for you too!

For Dummies: Bestselling Book Series for Beginners

Coaching Hockey For Dummies®

Drills Legend

⟶	Forward skating
∿∿∿	Backward skating
∿∿⟶	Skating with the puck
- - -➤	Pass/path of puck
⟹	Shot
‖‖‖‖‖‖‖	Sidestep
X X X X	Cross-overs
ℒ	Pivot
⌒➤	Turn
‖	Stop
X	Player
○	Opponent
F	Forward
C	Center
W	Winger
D	Defenseman
G	Goaltender
©	Coach
•	Puck
✓	Stick
▲	Cone
⌣	Net

For Dummies: Bestselling Book Series for Beginners

Coaching Hockey

FOR

DUMMIES®

Coaching Hockey FOR DUMMIES®

by Don MacAdam and Gail Reynolds

John Wiley & Sons Canada, Ltd.

Coaching Hockey For Dummies®

Published by
John Wiley & Sons Canada, Ltd
6045 Freemont Boulevard
Mississauga, Ontario, L5R 4J3
www.wiley.com

Library and Archives Canada Catologuing in Publication

Reynolds, Gail, 1949-

    Coaching hockey for dummies / Gail Reynolds, Don MacAdam.

Includes index.

ISBN-10: 0-470-83685-7

ISBN-13: 978-0-470-83685-9

    1. Hockey–Coaching. I. MacAdam, Donald Joseph, 1950-

II. Title.

GV848.25.R49 2006   796.962'077   C2006-902222-4

Printed in Canada

1 2 3 4 5 TRI 10 09 08 07 06

Distributed in Canada by John Wiley & Sons Canada, Ltd.

For general information on John Wiley & Sons Canada, Ltd, including all books published by Wiley Publishing, Inc., please call our warehouse, Tel 1-800-567-4797. For reseller information, including discounts and premium sales, please call our sales department, Tel 416-646-7992. For press review copies, author interviews, or other publicity information, please contact our marketing department, Tel 416-646-4584, Fax 416-236-4448.

For authorization to photocopy items for corporate, personal, or educational use, please contact in writing The Canadian Copyright Licensing Agency (Access Copyright). For an Access Copyright license, visit www.accesscopyright.ca or call toll free, 1-800-893-5777.

WILEY

About the Authors

Don MacAdam grew up playing ice hockey on a river in Prince Edward Island on the east coast of Canada. Players there had to be quick to avoid losing pucks down eel holes chipped in the ice by the local fishermen. Since then, Don has coached hockey for over thirty years. He has worked with kids who stepped into skates for the first time and has coached players at most levels on the way up to and including Olympians and NHL players in the Detroit Red Wings, Edmonton Oilers, Ottawa Senators, and Columbus Blue Jackets organizations.

In addition to coaching, Don has been an educator in the hockey field. He helped develop Canadian Amateur Hockey Association (now Hockey Canada) materials for their coaching certification programs and conducted coaching seminars at all levels for the association. Don has also co-authored five books on hockey.

Gail Reynolds started out with an affinity for the softer side of water, as a competitive swimmer and eventual swimming coach. Swimming awakened a general love of sport that ultimately saw her coach a variety of sports and athletes, including wheelchair track and field.

At the same time, Gail became an exercise physiologist and started developing training programs for athletes in all types of sports. Hockey came into focus when Don, who was coaching the University of New Brunswick Red Devils hockey team (where Gail was a professor), asked whether she'd develop a training program for his team. That evolved into the writing of five hockey books together. Gail also worked with the Coaching Association of Canada to develop materials for their coaching certification program and conducted their coaching workshops for all levels of coaches for all sports.

Dedication

We dedicate this book to the coaches who started us off in pursuit of sports and who left us with only good things to say about them:

From Don,

To Reg MacAdam, who drove us to games, coached us, cheered us on, and did everything for us in such a positive way.

To A.J. MacAdam, an inspiring coach and sports administrator, who opened my eyes to the fact that you could actually make a living as a coach.

From Gail,

To Buck Billings, whose instruction methods and patience always made you feel like you were a winner.

To Al Clark, who gave as much as he demanded and made you better than you thought you might be.

Authors' Acknowledgments

Thank you, Derek Reynolds, for being our "go-to" guy throughout this project. When Derek's young son wanted to play hockey and the league said, "We need coaches," Derek stood up. He'd never coached hockey before. In fact, he'd hardly played; he was a competitive rower. Derek picked many brains as he started out, including ours, and then he gave a lot of kids a great hockey experience. Thanks for sharing your lessons.

Thank you, Frank Hubley and Bruce Elliot, for the brainstorming sessions at the outset of this book. Your minor hockey experiences and coaching wisdom helped us focus on some important themes for this book, such as Frank's persuasive insistence that minor hockey has to be for the kids, not the parents, and Bruce's reminder that minor hockey coaches will coach a lot more old timers than NHLers.

Thank you, Robert Hickey, our editor at John Wiley and Sons Canada, and Mike Kelly, our developmental and copy editor, for your patience and confidence in guiding a couple of coach-authors through a new approach to book writing. You're great team players. A special thanks goes out to Zoë Wykes for her Dummies style prowess.

Publisher's Acknowledgments

We're proud of this book; please send us your comments at canadapt@wiley.com. Some of the people who helped bring this book to market include the following:

Acquisitions, Editorial, and Media Development

Editor: Robert Hickey

Copy Editor: Mike Kelly

Cartoons: Rich Tennant
    (www.the5thwave.com)

Composition

Publishing Services Director: Karen Bryan

Publishing Services Manager: Ian Koo

Project Manager: Elizabeth McCurdy

Project Coordinator: Lindsay Humphreys

Layout and Graphics: Wiley Indianapolis Composition Services

Proofreaders: Laura Bowman, Dwight Ramsey, Techbooks

Indexer: Belle Wong

John Wiley & Sons Canada, Ltd

  Bill Zerter, Chief Operating Officer

  Jennifer Smith, Publisher, Professional and Trade Division

Publishing and Editorial for Consumer Dummies

  Diane Graves Steele, Vice President and Publisher, Consumer Dummies

  Joyce Pepple, Acquisitions Director, Consumer Dummies

  Kristin A. Cocks, Product Development Director, Consumer Dummies

  Michael Spring, Vice President and Publisher, Travel

  Suzanne Jannetta, Editorial Director, Travel

Publishing for Technology Dummies

  Andy Cummings, Vice President and Publisher, Dummies Technology/General User

Composition Services

  Gerry Fahey, Vice President of Production Services

  Debbie Stailey, Director of Composition Services

Contents at a Glance

Drills at a Glance

Table of Contents

Introduction

*I*ce hockey is the only game in the world in which players use a crooked implement to control a half-round, half-flat implement while standing on meager support and moving over a slippery surface. Think of all the coaching challenges!

We take that back. Think of how hockey's many unique characteristics make for such a fast, challenging team sport. It can't help but be exciting to coach, whether you're a beginner or a pro.

If you are about to coach this amazing game of ice hockey, or you've dabbled in hockey coaching and want to get better, you've picked up the right book. This book provides the technical information you need to teach hockey skills and strategies to beginner- to advanced-level recreational players of all ages and of both genders. It provides step-by-step plans to help you meet all your hockey coaching challenges with confidence. *Coaching Hockey For Dummies* gives you the tools to create a great hockey experience for you and for your players.

About This Book

This book is written for moms, dads, and part-time hockey enthusiasts who take on — or get drawn into — the role of volunteer coach. Whether you know much or you know little about the sport, whether you have ever coached a day of anything in your life, whether you coached mites last year and enjoyed it so much you wanted to move with them to the next level, this book provides you with all the tools you need to do the job well.

As you embark on this adventure, you may be asking yourself a few questions:

- ✔ What do I need to know to give these kids a great hockey experience?
- ✔ How do I do a good job teaching the skills the kids need?
- ✔ What hockey rules do I need to know?
- ✔ Do I have to be able to skate?

You find answers to these questions and more throughout this book, with easy-to-use tips, diagrams, and explanations that provide the information you need to coach an entry-level hockey team, intermediate-level players, and more advanced youth teams. You find information to help you design good practices, help you coach effectively on the bench, and help you deal with off-ice problems that may arise. Beyond all these tools and information, you discover how you can enjoy the challenge of coaching one of the most unique sports in the world.

You also find a few true stories of coaches' experiences throughout the book. Details have been altered to maintain privacy, but hundreds of coaches could tell a similar story. We even include one story that came to us over the Internet, whose authenticity we can't vouch for, but that leaves many coaches nodding in empathy.

You don't have to read this book from front to back — or in any other order — to benefit from its contents. You don't even have to read the entire book! Simply go to whatever chapter contains what you want to know and take what you need from its content, diagrams, and tips. Or check out the Table of Contents and you may discover some topic listed there that you didn't realize you wanted to know about. Who knows, you may discover more fun things to coaching hockey than you ever thought possible.

Foolish Assumptions

We assume you know that every kid who comes under your charge believes that he or she will become the next Wayne Gretzky or Jarome Iginla, or Cammi Granato or Hayley Wickenheiser. We assume you also know that you could coach kids for 50 years and never encounter the next Iginla or Granato. So we assume you realize that you're coaching kids who want to learn, play, and improve as though they are headed somewhere important. And they are — toward having a fun, positive, life experience with one of the best sports in the world. The end result for most players should be that they will have made friends and developed activity habits and social skills that they will use for the rest of their lives.

We assume that you'll let the kids have their dreams and help them along that road with the full realization that they'll learn more from the journey than the end point. Know that you are coaching mostly future moms and dads who will want to pass some valuable lessons on to their kids eventually. Remember too that you're coaching future old-timers who will want to enjoy hockey for the rest of their lives. Coach with the full awareness that you will have an impact on each life you touch.

How This Book Is Organized

This book is designed to provide quick and easy access to the tools a hockey coach needs. The first few chapters cover topics of use to all coaches. The middle chapters provide information specific to the skill level of the team you're coaching: beginners, who are usually under 8 years old; intermediate players, who are often 9 and 10 years old; and advanced players, who are likely 11 years and older. Of course you can have a 10-year-old beginner or a highly skilled 7-year-old, so you should use the teaching tools and drills according to ability, not age.

The final chapters of the book provide coaching information that you may or may not need to know to coach your team effectively. In Chapter 21, for example, if you're already trained in first aid and cardiopulmonary resuscitation (CPR), there won't be much new for you in the section on dealing with emergencies. However, you may want to consider using something from the sections on nutrition or conditioning for your team, which are in that same chapter. Pick out what you need when you need it.

Hockey coaches are always looking for drills — and you can find thousands of drills out there. We have organized drills into three separate chapters, one in each of the beginner-, intermediate-, and advanced-level parts, and matched the drills to the skills taught in those parts. Of course, you'll have times when you may wish to choose drills from a lower level to brush up on players' skills. For example, at the beginning of a season, an intermediate-level team may benefit from using some beginner-level skating and puck-handling drills to reinforce skills that went unused during the summer layoff. Or if you have an older player who is playing hockey for the first time, definitely start with beginner-level drills and work him or her up. These players will advance more rapidly this way and will soon catch up to their peers. So select drills from the part that reflects the skill level you need to work on.

Here's where to go for all the tools you'll want in your coaching bag.

Part 1: The Puck Drops Here: Coaching Hockey 101

The five chapters of Part I walk you through the steps you need to take in preparing for your hockey season. You find out what rules you need to know for each level of player, how to put an overall coaching plan in place, and what items to gather to run practices and games. You establish a coaching philosophy and communicate it to the players and their parents so that you're all taking the same steps toward creating a positive hockey season. You discover how to design and run great practices and coach games with confidence. The more items in this part you use, the better prepared you'll be to meet the challenges and joys of coaching hockey.

Part II: Coaching Beginners

In this part, we present a list of the fundamental skills and strategies that provide a good start for beginner-level hockey players. The chapters here provide specific techniques for teaching these skills and drills for practicing them. We also include tips about what a coach at this level should focus on.

Part III: Coaching Intermediate Players

This part of the book presents techniques and drills for teaching skills, and coaching players who have some skills and hockey experience but still have much to learn. At this level, players have sufficient skating and puck-handling skills to begin focusing on offensive and defensive skills. Goaltending skills also begin to emerge. So in this part, we present teaching techniques and drills that help build skills specific to these positions and strategies. Coaches at this level can also refine their strategies by objectively evaluating individual players, their team, and their own strengths and weaknesses.

Part IV: Coaching Advanced Players

This part presents techniques for teaching the rest of hockey's fundamentals — the finer skills and the more advanced offensive, defensive, and special team strategies. We provide teaching tools and practice drills to help fine-tune your team's game, as well as tips for fine-tuning your own game, that is, your coaching abilities. From this level, both players and coaches will have the tools to comfortably enjoy hockey for the rest of their lives, or to move on to more highly competitive amateur hockey.

Part V: Common Coaching Conundrums

The topics in this part apply to many coaching situations but not equally to all skill levels. Health and injury topics are obviously important to all teams on some level, but they become more crucial as players get older and more physical in their play. Unique coaching situations may arise, such as girls and boys playing on the same team, parents presenting challenges, or ice-time being limited. In this section, we present some possible approaches to resolving such issues.

Part VI: The Part of Tens

This part contains lists of some of the most important elements in coaching hockey. They are the coach's "aha" moments in looking back, the signs you've done a great job. Therefore, they are the keys to keep in mind throughout the season regardless of what level you coach.

Icons Used in This Book

You'll find little pictures in the margins throughout this book. These icons point out specific types of information that you can use as a quick hit. Here is what each icon means:

This icon highlights practical ideas for all coaches.

The information included with this icon contains ideas to keep in mind that you'll likely use throughout your coaching tenure.

We notate common trouble spots — as well as some possible solutions — with this icon.

This icon directs you to significant teaching points, particularly for helping your players improve hockey skills.

We offer suggestions on coaching principles that you should consider establishing as priority items within your coaching style and personality. This icon highlights those suggestions.

In case you need a little reminder about certain hockey-specific terms, this icon leads the way.

Where to Go from Here

You can head straight to the sections that answer questions you already have swirling around in your head. Or, if you picked up this book after you were already knee-deep in coaching, you can go straight to the practice-planning and drill chapters for immediate help. If you bought this book for summer reading, you can begin at Chapter 1 and proceed to read in an orderly fashion from start to finish, circling and underlining the passages that particularly appeal to you.

We advise that, at some point, you do read Part I. You get some valuable tips there for getting off on, and staying on, the right foot (or, should we say "skate"?) as a coach.

Now, go coach some hockey — you're in for a great experience!

Part I

The Puck Drops Here: Coaching Hockey 101

The 5th Wave   By Rich Tennant

RICHTENNANT

HOCKEY UNIFORM OFFICIAL NHL!

"Yep, the coach will think you're a real pro. This kit even comes with a jar of tooth-black for that 'just checked' look."

In this part . . .

This part gives you, as a hockey coaching neophyte, the package of tools you need to coach a season of ice hockey, regardless of the level. We offer you guidelines for establishing your coaching frames of reference and a chapter to help you understand the game and its rules. We also give you the tools you need for developing your plans for the season, month, week, and for practice sessions. Finally, we provide practical information for coaching a real game.

Chapter 1

Jumping In with Both Skates

In This Chapter

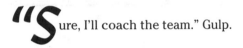 Discovering what it means to be a coach

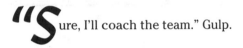 Setting goals for yourself and your team

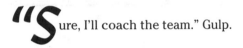 Establishing expectations for yourself, your players, and their parents

"**S**ure, I'll coach the team." Gulp.

Perhaps that was your reaction when you got carried away at your son's minor hockey league meeting when they said they were having a hard time finding enough coaches for all the teams. Or maybe it was the look on your daughter's face that haunted you from last year when she and her friends suffered with a deprecating coach and you repeatedly thought, "I may not know a lot about hockey, but I could give the kids a better experience than this." Or maybe you just love hockey and would like to share your enthusiasm with some kids who need a coach.

We can think of lots of reasons for starting to coach hockey. Whatever yours may be, congratulations! You're about to leap off the bench into one of the most rewarding jobs you'll ever experience. You have an opportunity before you to help a bunch of kids discover what it means to have teammates to count on, to get better at something every day, to work hard and accomplish something big, to fly down a sheet of ice and score a goal, to catch up to another player and stop him from scoring, and to win and to lose and to deal with the aftermath.

As the coach, you're bound to be asked to be a lot of different things. You'll be great at some of those things and some others won't end up being your favorite way of spending time. However, if you keep foremost in your mind that you are there for the kids, you'll juggle the demands of coaching hockey in fine style.

Your impact as coach

Some time ago, a group of researchers decided to see who had the most significant, lifelong influence on kids as they grew up. They ranked all the people they could identify as having influenced the kids. In the end, *coach* topped the list, way ahead of parents, pastors, and peers.

Think about that. You may be about to exert more impact on some kid's life than his or her parents, a favorite teacher, a wayward uncle, or a best friend. That's huge!

The good news and the bad news is that your influence can be positive or negative; it's up to you, coach.

We think that you should keep this nugget of information in mind during every moment spent coaching kids. And now is a good time to make a deliberate choice to impart a positive impact on the life of every kid you coach.

Understanding Your Job Description

And you thought you were just volunteering to help out!

Coaches spend time teaching, leading, motivating, communicating, being a hockey technician, organizing, checking safety factors, administering first aid, and doling out discipline. At the same time, you may be a parent — and you may become a friend.

Coaching is obviously a job in which you wear many hats. The key to wearing each of these hats well is to set them at a tilt that sits entirely in tune with your beliefs and your personality. If you are a quiet and steady person, teach, communicate, and administer that way. If you are rah-rah and outgoing, toss your hat in the air with that flair.

The following list discusses key coaching duties that you want to blend with your personality and belief system to establish your unique coaching style:

✔ **Teacher:** Your priority as a hockey coach of beginner to advanced players is first to teach — or re-teach — kids the fundamental skills of the game. If you yourself need a refresher on the rules, check out Chapter 2. In Chapter 6 we cover the basic skills beginners should know, in Chapter 9 we get to some finer skills for intermediate players, and in Chapter 15 we get to some fancy stuff for advanced players.

Only when the kids master the appropriate skills for their level can you effectively teach your team to use the skills to execute appropriate offensive and defensive systems. Kids learn by hearing, feeling, seeing, and doing, so stimulate all their senses in your teaching. Break down complex skills into simple, doable pieces, and then gradually add the pieces back together to get the whole skill.

✔ **Team leader:** You set the example; you call the shots. You may consult with parents, assistants, and league officials on various issues, but in the end, you are the one who accepted the responsibility to coach, so you are the one who must take the lead. The kids will look to you for leadership on all issues from work ethic to attitude; the parents must look to your leadership for everything from expectations to behavior.

✔ **Motivational speaker:** Different kids have different motives for playing hockey. Some are just out for a good time; some are highly competitive; some are there because their friends signed up and could care little about hockey or winning. Your job is to motivate each child to learn, to improve, and to contribute in the best way they can to the team effort. You do that by being good at wearing the other coaching hats and by being positive in your approach.

✔ **Master communicator:** The best way to get optimum performance out of a child is to make him or her feel important and valued. You do that by communicating with the child often and at a meaningful level. Learn each player's name and use it at every practice. Discover something unique about each player and refer to it on occasion. Praise each player for something done well at every practice and game. In Chapter 4 we offer some tips on running great practices, and in Chapter 5 we cover what it takes to be a great game coach.

Your other target group for communication is parents. Be organized and clear in your own thinking so you can communicate what is important, such as your goals and objectives. You can pre-empt many potential problems by communicating your expectations up front and by remaining consistent in your approach thereafter. But we know that some parents can be challenging to deal with, and we talk more about that in Chapter 22.

✔ **Liberal listener:** When an issue arises, stop talking long enough to hear what a player or parent wants to say. When the person is finished, re-phrase the issue back to them in your own words but using their perspective. That makes the person feel understood and defuses many agitated situations. Then, if you have an immediate solution, state it, simply and concisely. If not, or if the issue needs some thought or cooling time, say something like, "I'm going to take a few days to consider this." Then do so, but make sure you do get back to them with your solution after a few days.

✔ **Hockey technician:** You don't need to know everything there is to know about hockey to coach young kids well. But you need to be willing to find out what you need to know. This book provides the information you need to become an accomplished hockey technician quickly. In this part we cover the basic rules of the game and fill you in on how to run excellent practices and fun games. In Part II we deal with what you need to know to coach beginners; Part III is for coaches of intermediate players; and Part IV is for coaches of advanced players. Master the art and technique of teaching fundamental skills and hockey sense. Then understand the fundamental strategies of offense and defense and you will give players a sound technical base for playing hockey.

✔ **Wily organizer:** You can't do everything yourself. It takes a lot of effort by a lot of people to give kids a good minor hockey experience. Kids need affordable equipment. They may need help with transportation and accommodations. You may need a coaching assistant. Somebody needs to throw a team party. And so it goes. You have to decide what to delegate and then stay out of the way, aside from requesting that you be kept apprised of progress. A good organizer is a coordinator; that leaves you free to focus your time on the kids. Chapter 3 is all about getting organized.

✔ **Safety inspector:** Kids are likely to get hurt in hockey if they wear poorly fitting equipment, if ice-surface doors are left ajar, if glass is improperly installed around rink boards, or if a variety of other preventable conditions are allowed to exist. Your job is to inspect any possible sources of danger and have them corrected *before* even a chance of injury occurs. Don't let kids, parents, or officials talk you out of this. In Chapter 4 we take you through the safety checks you should run before practices.

✔ **First-aid worker:** Kids do get hurt playing hockey. They get cut by wayward sticks and pucks; they break arms by falling wrong; and, in spite of the equipment, they may whack their heads on the boards or ice hard enough to suffer a concussion. You must be capable of jumping into the emergency situation quickly and doing the right thing. All that's needed may be a pat on the shoulder and a shift on the bench for recovery time. Or you may need to call 911 fast. You need the confidence to know which is required. In Chapter 21 we provide hints on how to prevent injuries from happening, and offer advice on what to do in the unfortunate event of an emergency.

✔ **Disciplinarian:** Normally, you set out to have a fun and positive experience with the players and their parents. To ensure that happens, you need to establish some guidelines for behavior. Of course, any time you have rules, you must have consequences, and that means someone must impart those consequences. That somebody has to be you. You're the leader.

The most effective way to wear the disciplinarian hat is to determine your rules and consequences before you start the season. Then communicate those rules clearly to everyone at the outset. After that, all you have to say is, "You know what the rules are." End of issue.

✔ **Parent:** Treat all kids on the team the same. If you favor your son by giving him more ice time, you compromise his relationship with his teammates, which ultimately reduces his hockey experience. If you are harder on your daughter by demanding a higher level of performance from her because she's the coach's daughter, you run the risk of damaging her self esteem — and you set her up for not fitting in with her friends. Overall, you lose the kids' and parents' respect for you as a coach, thereby making your job harder, and you leave the kids with a sour hockey experience. That's the antithesis of the job you have set out to do.

✔ **Friend:** You don't need to be everybody's best friend to be a good coach. But you will be more effective as a coach if you seem human, approachable, and you appear to care about the players as people. Talk to the kids about hockey and non-hockey things in their lives, such as what music they listen to, how school is going, what their favorite video games are. Organize a team social or outing, perhaps to a professional or junior hockey game. Remember that hockey is just one small segment of this broad, interesting thing we call life.

Coaching constants

No matter how you blend your coaching duties into a coaching style that feels comfortable, these truisms will help you keep things in perspective as you go about your job as coach:

✔ Kids want to play; parents want to see their kids play.

✔ Winning is not a primary source of satisfaction for most kids.

✔ Kids go off in their own little mental world, and they make mistakes. They're kids.

✔ Praise is the quickest and most effective technique for helping kids learn and behave. Constantly pick on the positives. If you need to state a negative, finish with a positive: "I know you can change that. It'll really help the team."

✔ Odds are you'll never coach a future NHLer or Olympian. You may coach one or two future college prospects; you *will* coach numerous future old-timers; and you *are* coaching a whole cast of kids who are looking for a good time with their friends today.

The business world has a phrase that can be paraphrased for coaches: coach by walking around. This saying simply means to be out there and involved with those in your charge. For example, make a habit of saying something to each player each day. You can make what you say as simple as, "Hi Joey."

Setting Goals

A team without goals is like a boat without a compass — you can go miles out of your way trying to get where you want to go. The same holds true for coaches. If you establish goals, actions, and solutions, then, if communicated to all involved, results flow quite easily from there.

Your minor hockey association may determine some general goals and objectives for teams, such as having every player get equal ice time. Beyond those, you determine where you want your team journey to take you over the course of the season.

In setting goals, begin by considering the following:

- **Sport-specific goals and objectives:** For example, with a beginner team that rotates position, you may determine that every kid should score at least one goal over the season, thereby encouraging teamwork.

- **Non-hockey goals:** For example, you may decide that every player on your beginner team will tie their own skates by the end of the year, a subtle lesson in taking responsibility.

- **Individual player goals:** For example, you may identify the two worst skating players on your team and set goals for each that they will rise to the middle of the pack in their skating ability by the end of the season.

- **Overall team goals:** For example, you may set a goal to have every member of the team honestly say at the end of the season, "I had a great time!"

- **Your own goals:** For example, you may make laughing daily with the kids one of your goals.

Goals for yourself

Considering yourself first isn't selfish. After all, you've agreed to take on an important assignment; you're the leader. You need to know what you want to get out of it.

Pick goals that fit for you. Write the goals on a piece of paper and then file the paper at the front of your coach's binder. Add other goals that are important to you. Be sure to state your goals in measurable terms so that you can monitor your progress. For example, if you list a goal to learn more about coaching hockey, the measurable statement may read, "To attend one coaching seminar and read two hockey coaching books over the season."

The following list offers some goals that many youth coaches consider:

✔ Enjoy my coaching experience; I will have fun.

✔ Believe in myself and my abilities and pass that confidence on to the kids.

✔ Gain a solid understanding of the art and science of coaching.

✔ Gain a solid understanding for the sport of hockey.

✔ Develop communication and teaching skills so that every player improves.

✔ Be a better coach on the last day of the season than I was on the first day.

✔ Have no child quit for the wrong reasons, such as being disgruntled, having a negative experience, or receiving no attention. If a player discovers she would rather play basketball than hockey, that's okay. Similarly, it's okay if a parent pulls a player because I'm not giving her star treatment at the expense of the team.

✔ Have a positive and constructive relationship with parents and assistants.

✔ Go to every practice and game prepared with a plan.

Some coaches target a .500 winning percentage as a goal. We offer a word of caution about where that percentage should rank in your priorities when coaching kids: Although winning does feel good — even when it happens at least half the time — playing well, scoring goals, and getting lots of ice time feel better for kids. The kids' goals need to come first.

Goals for your team

Team goals should reflect specific things you want the kids to walk away with at the end of the season. Once again, you can make general statements, but go that extra step and list measurable outcomes so that you can honestly determine whether your goals are being met. Here's a list of some team goals you may want to consider: Strive to ensure that every player

- ✔ Has fun daily
- ✔ Improves his or her hockey skills
- ✔ Gets fair practice and play time (nearly equal time)
- ✔ Develops a solid knowledge of the basic skills and rules of hockey
- ✔ Gains an understanding of team dynamics: discipline, team play, team rules, goals, and sportsmanship
- ✔ Has a positive team and hockey experience
- ✔ Has a positive social experience, such as making new friends, that develops cooperative social skills

Determining Rules and Consequences

After you decide on your goals (refer to the preceding sections), your next step is to establish an environment that is conducive to the achievement of those goals. You do that by setting guidelines or rules that circumvent destructive behaviors that would compromise your chances of achieving those goals. For example, if one of your goals is that all players on your team improve their game sense, you can't let a small group of parents convince you that their kids should get more ice time in games because they are better players than the other kids.

The most common troublesome issues that arise within a team usually have to do with sportsmanship, commitment, and team play. These, unfortunately, are the same issues that may arise with some parents. You must decide what rules are important at the outset, and then communicate those rules clearly to players and to the parents at the beginning of the season so that they know exactly what you expect.

The consequences of your rules must also be pre-determined, and they must be the same for everybody, whether the perpetrator is your son, the star of the team, or a parent who donates the most time. For example, if someone argues with a referee, that person misses the next game — assuming that's the rule and consequence you put in place at the outset — regardless of their talent.

We suggest three categories of rules to consider to help create a positive hockey experience for the whole team. Setting these rules lets you focus on hockey and not on the distractions of disciplinary problems. Some rules are more relevant as age and ability increase. Consider the following rules and others that may be important to your situation. Then list your rules with their consequences on paper so that you have a handout for your first team meeting.

Rules for you

If you're going to make rules for others to follow, you have to have rules by which you abide as well. Otherwise, you command no respect. The following three rules help to put you in a position to establish rules for others:

- **Stick to your convictions.** Have a credible reason for setting each rule, communicate that reason, and then be consistent. The consequences of not doing so are that parents and players will constantly lobby you to make exceptions.

- **Play only by the rules.** If you are prepared to bend the rules in some situations, you send a message to all involved that rules are not to be respected.

- **Lead by example.** Be on time. Don't argue and swear at officials. Be a team player. In other words, demand of yourself what you want to demand of others. The consequence of not doing so is a lack of credibility and respect.

Rules for your players

Discipline is a necessary part of the smooth running of a team. Kids especially need to know limits and expectations. If players are free to do as they please, the divergence and disruption of their behaviors will compromise your ability to accomplish all you can as a coach.

Consider setting some of the following rules for players to help minimize team disruption. The consequence for any of them may be being benched for a specified amount of time during the practice or game.

- Be on time for practices and games. "On time" may mean in the dressing room ready to go on the ice ten minutes before practice or game time (to give you time for the pre-game or pre-practice talk).

- Give full attention when getting instructions: assemble quickly; no talking; no horseplay.

- Work hard in drills and throughout practices and games.

- Show respect for teammates, opposing players, and officials.

- Don't play for individual glory at the expense of teammates.

- Play fair: no cheap shots or intent to injure.

- Show commitment to the team: take responsibility for what you contribute to games and practices.

- Put the team first: praise your teammates; use your teammates; go for team goals ahead of your own.

- Call at least 24 hours in advance if unable to attend a practice or game.

Rules for parents

Unfortunately, you may encounter the odd parent who disrupts the positive environment you are trying to establish for the team. You can wait until an incident occurs and deal with it then. However, if you set and communicate rules at the outset, you can eliminate many distracting incidents. In addition, you usually get other parents on your side, which helps deter negative incidents. (We talk more about challenging parents in Chapter 22.)

Following are some rules for parents you may want to consider. The consequence that has been effective for other coaches is to ban the offending parent from being in the building for practices and games.

✔ Accept that every player gets treated fairly and equally.

✔ Cheer for the team, not just your favorite player.

✔ Be a team-building block, not a stumbling block.

✔ Realize that team rules are for everyone, all the time.

✔ Do *not* use profane language; do not argue with coaches or officials; show respect for other players and their parents.

Take the time to set rules and consequences, and then communicate them clearly to players, parents, and staff. The time and hassles you save will be your own.

Chapter 2

Knowing the Basics of the Game

In This Chapter

▶ Getting to know the basic principles of hockey

▶ Understanding rules and referees' signals

You don't need to be a master of the game of hockey to help kids have a positive experience. You should, however, be able to explain the gist of the game to beginners, and you should know enough about the rules of the game to guide play and to minimize negative incidents. Similarly, you don't need to teach beginners everything at the outset. Start them off with a few principles of play and some basic rules along with the signals that referees use to call those rules so that they know what to do when a call is made.

If you're coaching intermediates, you can get more specific about the principles of play and introduce the remaining basic rules. Advanced players are ready to learn the intricacies of the game that build on the principles, such as how to beat a forecheck (don't worry if you don't even know what a forecheck is — we cover that in Chapter 11). At this stage, both you and the players need to know the rules well so that you can understand the officials' calls, and so that you can explain unusual calls to players and know what implications the calls have for your team.

Some rules are league specific, such as how long a game lasts, how many periods are played, and whether the periods run on *stop time* (the clock is stopped for every whistle) or *running time* (the clock runs on regardless of whistle stops). Eventually, games will be 60 minutes long, divided into three 20-minute periods of stop time, and may be followed by overtime if necessary. Kids won't care much about time as long as they're getting lots of it on the ice while the game is on.

Popular hockey wisdom suggests that hockey coaching in North America places too much emphasis on teaching plays and positions when compared to the European model, which focuses on individual skill development and principles of play. The result is that North American players are not well versed at reading the play, nor do they have the skills to react appropriately to it. From the coaching perspective, that means that your most important challenge is to help kids learn the principles and concepts of playing hockey and to give them skills to react appropriately, not just to teach them hockey plays.

Kids learn by doing. So your job is to teach skills and to set up mini-game situations where players can become comfortable with principles. Once players develop their skills and understand a principle such as moving to an open space, they can more easily grasp the finer intricacies of reading the play and can then apply what they've learned to prescribed plays.

Even though you may coach an intermediate- or advanced-level team, you may have some individuals who never learned the principles of play. In that case, you'll have to introduce those basic principles to the players by using plenty of mini-game and game-sense drills before they become consistent at performing the more intricate plays.

Presenting Principles of Play in a Nutshell

Ice hockey is a team game in which five skaters and a goalie work together to accomplish two things: put the puck in the other team's net and prevent the other team from putting the puck in your net. The keys to coaching your players to do this successfully are the following:

✔ When your team has the puck, help players find all ways possible for your team to keep control of the puck until somebody on your team can get a good shot on the opponent's goal.

✔ When your team does *not* have the puck, help players learn to do everything legally possible to try to get control of the puck and, failing that, make it as difficult as legally possible for your opponent to move the puck where they want it to go.

If you present these simple concepts to players and provide on-ice experience that supports these concepts, the players will figure out how best to play the game. For example, if your team is trying to keep control of the puck, a player will soon realize that he can't control the puck alone — he's a sitting duck to be checked. Because hockey is a team game, he can look for a passing opportunity to keep one step ahead of the opposition. Other players who want to help their team keep the puck soon figure out that they need to get clear of their opponents. By doing so, they're free to receive a pass and thereby help their team keep the puck.

Conversely, if your team is trying to stop the other team from doing good things with the puck, but your players get in the way, cut off passing opportunities, or knock the puck free, they make it more difficult for opposition players around them to receive a pass. The principle they learn is to eliminate space between the puck and the free opponent, which is a defensive skill that is transferable to all sorts of eventual plays.

Young players typically start out chasing the puck wherever it goes and they all end up wherever it goes together. If you teach your players the principle of helping their team keep the puck, they automatically let the nearest player go for the puck. Then, the next closest player skates to open ice to be free to receive a pass.

You can help young players discover the following key principles:

- ✔ With or without the puck, keep moving so that you remain a difficult target for the opposition.

- ✔ On offense, get away from opponents and move in the direction your team wants to go.

- ✔ On defense, stay between your opponent and your goalie.

- ✔ Use your stick to limit space between your opponent and the puck carrier.

- ✔ Use your teammates at every opportunity.

- ✔ Spread out as teammates so that it is more difficult for opponents to cover all of you.

One of the best ways to teach these fundamental hockey concepts to players is to have mini-scrimmages and simple games in which everyone gets plenty of ice time. Focus on a specific principle, then let a drill lead players to discover and use the principles. For example, you could have them play "Monkey in the middle" (see Chapter 7) in which two players on the outside of a face-off circle play keep-away passing across the circle while a player in the center tries to interrupt the passes. The players outside the circle learn where to move and pass to avoid having passes picked off, and the player in the center learns how to cut off passes. All three players may learn these basic concepts better from this simple game than you could explain in a lesson. Look for other game drills you can use for any age in Chapter 7.

Hey, Ref! Hockey Rules Made Easy

The most important rule in youth hockey is to respect the officials. This goes for players, parents, and coaches. Just as you are learning as a coach, the officials of youth hockey are also not yet NHL caliber. So let the officials make their mistakes just as you and your players will also make your own mistakes. Work with it. That means no yelling, no complaining, and no confrontations. If you run across a particularly weak or consistently biased official, notify the league with specifics. Tutoring the officials is up to your league.

You do not need to teach all the rules of hockey to players all at once. This chapter divides the most common rules of the game into those that beginner players should learn, those that intermediate players should know, and those that advanced players should know. Rather than being hard and fast divisions, this system is a progression for your focus on rules. If you coach at a highly competitive level, you may want to explore additional hockey rules, which are not discussed here. For that information, consult an elite league rule book. Remember that rules change yearly, so consult your league to confirm changes.

Referees and linesmen use different signals to indicate the various rule infractions on the ice. Coaches and players should recognize which signals indicate which penalties. We provide illustrations of the signals in the sections that follow, along with explanations of the rules.

Pick up a rule book and spend some time getting to know the rules. Have the rule book with you at games and use referees at your games as resource people to help you get to know the rules. Ask the referees questions after the game and cite game examples to provide clarity.

Rules beginners should know

Little kids need to know how to line up for face-offs. They also need to know a few things about what they *can* and *can't* do to move the puck and what they *can* and *can't* do with their stick. Finally, they can begin to learn a few technical rules about passing the puck up ice. Beyond these few basic rules, direct young players to listen to the officials, who will indicate to the players such things as where the puck will be dropped for a face-off.

The price of a penalty

When hockey players or coaches do something that goes against the rules of the game, referees or linesmen blow their whistles to stop play and penalize the offending team. The more serious the breach of the rule, the more severe the penalty, as described here:

✔ **Neutralizing an unfair advantage:** For example, if a team passes the puck ahead over too many lines, the puck is brought back for a face-off *behind* the point of the illegal progress, to where the pass started.

✔ **Minor (two minutes) penalty:** For example, when called for tripping, the offending player must sit in the penalty box for two minutes of play, and his team must play short a player. If the opposing team scores during that time, the penalized player can return to the ice. Occasionally, the referee may assess a *double minor* (two consecutive two-minute penalties). Also, occasionally, a player from each team may be penalized at the same time (coincident minors). In this case, each player serves the full two minutes regardless of goals scored, and teams play with an equal number of players.

✔ **Major (five minutes) penalty:** This penalty is for more serious offenses such as a dangerous check at the boards. When a player gets a major penalty, he must serve the whole five minutes in the box, even if goals are scored against his team.

✔ **Misconduct (ten minutes) penalty:** Misconducts are given for even more serious rule breaches, such as abuse of officials. The offending player must sit ten minutes in the box and can't come out until the *first whistle* (stop of play) after the ten minutes is up. The team does not play short-handed on a misconduct.

✔ **Game misconduct:** When a player gets a game misconduct for a very serious offense, such as fighting with an opposing player, he is immediately ejected from the game. The offending player does not sit in the penalty box and his team does not play short-handed.

✔ **Penalty shot:** When a player hinders an opponent by, for example, grabbing, tripping, or throwing her stick, when that opponent otherwise has a clear path to the net, the referee will stop play and call a penalty shot. This gives the opponent a chance to skate in from center ice on the goalie for a free shot on goal. No one on the penalized team can try to stop her except the goalie.

The bottom line on penalties is to get as few as possible. Penalties put your team at a significant disadvantage. Teach players that, if an opponent does something frustrating or illegal to you, they need to get even by scoring.

Lining up for a face-off

Face-offs are used to start play at the beginning of a period or at any time a whistle is blown to interrupt play, such as when a goal is scored or when a penalty is called. One player from each team faces his opponent's net at a *spot* or *dot* designated by the official. If the official designates a dot on the ice, the face-off circle will be marked. Sometimes, however, the official will pick a spot on the ice that's unmarked, such as the place where the puck left the ice surface on its way over the boards. In those instances, the face-off circle must be estimated by the players and officials. The teammates on the ice must stand facing the opponents' goal anywhere outside the real or imaginary face-off circle, and behind a real or imaginary line that runs across the rink through the middle of the dot, until the official drops the puck on the spot. See Figure 2-1 for the proper face-off alignment.

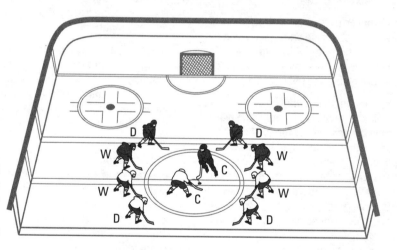

Figure 2-1:
Lining up for a face-off.

The two players facing each other at the dot try to direct the puck to someone on their team, while their teammates can move anywhere to get control of the puck. Most leagues require that the visiting team player taking the face-off put his stick on the ice first, followed by the home-team player, before the official will drop the puck. If players don't follow procedures, the official can order a substitute player to take the face-off.

The location of the face-off is indicated by the official who blows the whistle. For example, when a goal is scored, the referee points to the puck in the net signifying a goal, then to the dot at center ice where a face-off will restart play.

Moving the puck

Kids need to know two key concepts about puck movement rules: They should pass the puck and shoot on net using their stick and they have to keep the puck moving. That means they can't fall on the puck and stay on it, and they can't cover it with their hands, as shown in Figure 2-2. Players can pass the puck with their hand by pushing it to a teammate, if they fall on it, as long as they don't close their hand over it or push it forward if they are outside their defensive end. If a player's stick is being held or she's dropped her stick, a player can kick the puck to a teammate but she can't kick it into the net for a goal.

Figure 2-2:
Keep the puck moving — by hand if you must!

Using the stick

The stick is for passing, shooting, stealing, and otherwise moving the puck. The stick *cannot* be used against other players; it cannot be thrown to stop the puck; and if a player breaks his stick, he must immediately drop it to the ice away from the play without throwing it. See Figure 2-3 for an example of inappropriate stick work.

Figure 2-3:
Use the
stick on
the puck
only —
and hang
on to it.

Avoiding offside passes

Once beginners start to pass the puck, they need to understand that rules of progression apply to moving the puck up ice. *Note:* Passes that move the puck back toward your own net are legal from anywhere on the ice. Only forward passes may be called "offside."

The two blue lines and center red line that go across the ice surface are the lines that matter in an offside call. A puck can cross only one of those three lines per pass to be legally onside. For example, if a player is approaching his own blue line, he can pass the puck forward to a teammate who must receive the puck on the defensive side of the red line. If the receiving player is right at the red line, one skate must stay in touch with the red line until the puck crosses the red line to stay onside. If the receiving player is already over the red line, the passing player must skate across his blue line before releasing the puck so that the puck crosses over only one line. See Figure 2-4 for an example of an *offside* pass and an example of a legal or *onside* pass.

Figure 2-4:
An onside pass crosses one line at a time.

Offside

Figure 2-4:
Continued.

Onside

The rule is the same for a player approaching the center red line wanting to pass to a player near the opponent's blue line, with one addition: No player from the offensive team can skate over that blue line into the opponent's end of the rink ahead of the puck. That means the pass receiver must carry the puck across the blue line or keep one foot on the line until the puck precedes him across the line. Similarly, his teammates must have at least one foot on the line until the puck crosses the line.

The officials will blow the whistle for an offside pass and indicate a face-off near where the pass originated.

Preventing icing

Players cannot shoot the puck from their own half of the ice all the way into the opponent's end just to get the puck down ice. See Figure 2-5 for an example. If a player sends the puck down ice and no one on either team touches it before the puck crosses the goal line, without going in the net, "icing" is called and the puck is brought back to the passing player's defensive end for a face-off. You can send the puck down ice, however, if your team is short-handed or if the puck is sent directly off a face-off.

Figure 2-5:
This pass
has crossed
way too
many lines.

Intermediate rule know-how

After players become more adept at skating and puck handling, they begin to discover that the stick is a useful tool for more than just moving the puck. However, most such stick work is illegal in hockey; so most of the rules in this section have to do with stick infractions that result in two-minute penalties. We also discuss here a few other illegal defensive actions that players may be inclined to try at this level of play.

Tripping

A player cannot use his stick to hook the feet out from under an opposing player (see Figure 2-6). If "tripping" happens accidentally, however, no penalty should be called. This is a judgment call for an official when a player from each team is going for the puck at the same time. To make these calls go mostly in your favor, make sure that your players make every effort to touch the puck first. The intention to touch the puck first is the fine line officials use to determine whether the trip was accidental or intentional.

Figure 2-6:
Can't take a
player's feet
out from
under.

Advise players never to trip an opponent on a breakaway. If they do, they give the opposition a *free shot on goal* (penalty shot) or automatic goal if the goalie is off the ice.

Hooking

If a player uses the blade or shaft of her stick to restrict the progress of a puck-carrying opponent, she will be called for "hooking" and get a two-minute penalty. See Figure 2-7 for an illustration of this infraction. The call is the same whether the opponent is simply slowed down or falls.

Figure 2-7:
Keep your stick on the ice, not on a player.

Holding

Players are not allowed to grab an opponent, his sweater, or his stick to prevent him from going where he wants to go or to prevent him from making a play that he wants to make with the puck. Doing so is called "holding," as shown in Figure 2-8. Players can, however, push off or block an opponent who is carrying the puck, if they have "established a position" on the puck carrier first. This means that in order to be legally permitted to push off or block the opponent, the defender needs to be standing in the path the puck carrier wants to take before the puck carrier gets there. Players are allowed to grab an opponent's stick momentarily to protect themselves if the stick takes an errant path.

Figure 2-8: No grabbing on.

Slashing

Slashing is when a player takes a swing at another player with his stick, as illustrated in Figure 2-9. Slashing is not allowed. Whether contact is made or not, a penalty is warranted and may be two or five minutes or more according to the severity of the intent or the result (injury) of the slash.

High sticking

Coaching your players to keep their sticks on or near the ice at all times makes sense not only for moving the puck but also for keeping your players out of penalty trouble. If a player's stick contacts an opponent above the waist, she will be penalized for "high sticking" for two or five or more minutes depending on the severity of the contact. See Figure 2-10 for an example of a high stick. If the contact is accidental during the windup or follow-through for a shot, no penalty is called.

Figure 2-9:
No whacking an opponent either.

Figure 2-10:
High sticks are dangerous.

Occasionally, you see a player with good eye-hand coordination knock down a high-flying puck with her stick. This play is legal up to the height of the player's shoulders, as long as nobody gets hit. Teaching players to use their gloved hand to knock down the puck is usually more effective and is safer.

Kicking

A player can *kick* the puck in any direction to pass it to a teammate or away from an opponent, but he can't kick it into the net for a goal. If the puck accidentally rebounds off a non-directed skate blade into the net, however, the goal will count.

Kicking another player, as is illustrated in Figure 2-11, is not allowed under any circumstance. This act is considered a serious offense and is penalized accordingly.

Delay of game

Players cannot do things to deliberately stall the game. Actions such as holding the puck on the back of the netting or along the boards so that it can't be played are penalized as a "delay of game," as is a player who deliberately pushes the net off its moorings (shown in Figure 2-12). Any player who deliberately shoots the puck out of the playing surface will also receive a delay-of-game penalty.

Figure 2-11: No kicking allowed.

Figure 2-12:
No stalling
for an
advantage.

Goalie interference

Coach your players to try to avoid any contact with the opponent's goaltender, known as *goalie interference* (see Figure 2-13 for an example). This goalie interference applies whether the goalie is in or out of his *crease* (the area enclosed by the lines in front of the net) and whether the body or the stick makes the contact. Even if a player is pushed toward the goalie, he must attempt to avoid contact. Only when a player could *not* avoid contact will he *not* be penalized.

Figure 2-13:
Stay
away from
contact with
goalies.

Know-it-all rules

Only by studying the official rule book can you become familiar with the dozens of fine points about the rules of hockey. Coaches who work with advanced players or elite or travel teams must acquaint themselves with the finer points of the rules. Most recreational hockey players must simply abide by the officials' decisions without argument. The rules listed in this section arise when body checking is introduced, and games and players generally become more competitive.

Interference

One principle of hockey is to stop the other team from doing what they want to do on the ice. However, rules limit how far players can go to do this, and going too far will result in a two-minute interference penalty. For example, players can't

- ✔ Block the progress of, check, or force offside a player who does not have the puck.

- ✔ Knock the stick out of an opponent's hands or prevent him from retrieving his stick when he drops it.

- ✔ Shoot anything, such as a glove, at the puck carrier.

- ✔ Interfere with a player or the puck from the bench, or throw anything onto the ice, such as a water bottle.

See Figure 2-14 for an example of an interference penalty.

Elbowing

A player who extends an elbow (called *elbowing*) to contact an opponent, like the player in Figure 2-15, gets a two-minute penalty unless the infraction is malicious, in which case the player could be penalized for five minutes.

Figure 2-14:
Go for the
puck; not
the player.

Figure 2-15:
Keep your
elbows to
yourself.

Kneeing

Players who make a distinct thrust with the knee, known as *kneeing*, to
contact an opponent, as does the player in Figure 2-16, get a two-minute
penalty — five minutes if the action is deemed malicious.

Cross-checking

Players must not place two hands on their stick and extend their arms to
thrust the stick against an opponent's body, commonly referred to as *cross-
checking*. This action is illustrated in Figure 2-17 and usually results in a
two-minute penalty — but if done to a goalie in his crease, the offense war-
rants a minimum five-minute penalty.

Figure 2-16:
Knees can't become weapons.

Figure 2-17:
You can't use your stick to check a body.

Boarding

A player can be legally *checked* (or have his progress stopped) along the boards, but he cannot be pushed or checked into the boards with any degree of roughness (called *boarding*) without being penalized. See the example in Figure 2-18. If a player is blindsided into the boards, the penalty rises from two to five minutes because the action creates too much risk of injury. Coaches should clearly instruct players on the difference between legal and illegal checks. (We offer suggestions on coaching checking in Chapter 15.)

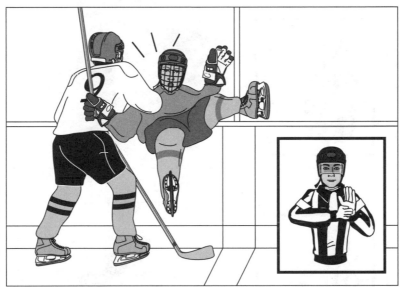

Figure 2-18:
Check firmly but safely along the boards.

Checking from behind

Pushing, cross-checking, or charging into a player from behind, especially when the player can't brace or otherwise defend himself, is a very serious infraction because of the high risk of injury. See the example in Figure 2-19. Players are severely penalized and, depending on the league, may get a game misconduct. Coaches should make clear to their players that this playing behavior is completely unacceptable.

Charging

Players are expected to make some body contact when trying to get the puck away from an opponent, and that is legal. However, a player cannot take two or more deliberate strides before ramming an opponent nor can his feet leave the ice to leap at an opponent. See the example in Figure 2-20. In either case, he will be penalized for "charging." The penalty is more serious if the offense is against a goaltender whether he is inside or outside his crease.

Figure 2-19:
Never, ever
check from
behind.

Figure 2-20:
Knock him
off, not out.

Clipping

Clipping is a more serious form of tripping. When *clipping,* a player throws his body across or below the knees of an opponent from any direction. See the example in Figure 2-21. The risk of knee injury with this action is significant, and coaches must stress that players never execute such actions.

Figure 2-21:
Don't risk injuring a player's knees.

Spearing and butt-ending

Any use of the stick to strike an opponent is illegal in hockey. *Spearing* is when a player uses the blade of the stick to stab at an opponent. See the illustration in Figure 2-22. *Butt-ending* is the same action except that a player uses the top end of the shaft to stab at an opponent. Both acts have a high risk of injury and are penalized severely whether the player actually makes contact or not. Coaches need to forbid these types of stick work.

Figure 2-22:
Spearing
can cause
serious
injury.

Roughing and fighting

"Roughing" is called when a player goes beyond what is considered accept-able physical contact and exerts unnecessary roughness in attempting to get a player off the puck. See the example in Figure 2-23. Such aggressiveness usually results in a two- or four-minute penalty. If a player gets even more aggressive and punches another player, he will be penalized for fighting. In amateur hockey, the player throwing the punch is ejected from the game.

Coaches should instruct players in acceptable and unacceptable levels of roughness and in how to avoid being drawn into fights, such as turning away when provoked and heading straight for the bench. That's not backing down; it's staying in the game. Players will be penalized further if they *head-butt* (use their forehead to strike the face of an opponent) in a confrontation. Coaches should never condone such high-risk action as an anger release or anything else.

Figure 2-23:
Leave
sparring to
boxers and
wrestlers.

Unsportsmanlike conduct

Hockey has a list of actions that are penalized as unsportsmanlike. For example:

- Neither players nor coaches are to argue or protest an official's call.
- No one can throw something on the ice in frustration or send the puck away from the official who is about to retrieve it.
- No one is to use profane language or disrespectful names directed at officials or make deliberate, physical contact with an official.

Such actions can be penalized from two minutes to a game ejection.

Coaches must instill in players a respect for officials that will allow them to survive poor calls and frustrating situations — that's sportsmanship. "Get even" by scoring.

Odds and ends

In this section, we include a few "can't do's" that you may encounter if coaching more-skilled and competitive players. In addition, coaches at these more competitive levels may want the opportunity during a game to use a strategic pause, otherwise known as a *timeout*.

More no-no's for competitive players and coaches

Here's a list of behaviors to avoid when the competition heats up:

- A player cannot deliberately shoot the puck over the boards.
- A player can't delay lining up for a face-off (she has five seconds) after the official blows the whistle to start a face-off.
- A player can't bring a message off the bench from the coach to a player on the ice, and then go back to the bench.
- A player can't leave the players' or penalty bench at any time during the game except to go on the ice to change players. At the penalty box, the player will be told when he can leave the box. If a player does go on the ice and no player comes off immediately, his team will be penalized for having too many players on the ice.
- A coach cannot leave the bench at any time without the official's permission.

Timeouts

Most sports allow some opportunity for coaches to call a strategic break in the action. Players may need clarification on a strategy they are executing poorly, or they may be playing uptight and need a joke to loosen up. Hockey is no exception when it comes to using timeouts, but the timeouts come few and far between — so use them wisely.

Most leagues allow one 30-second timeout per game, and it must be requested during a stoppage in play. However, when games are not the standard three 20-minute, stop-time periods, coaches should check with their league to confirm the timeout rules.

Chapter 3

Getting Organized: Your Keys to Success

In This Chapter
▶ Pulling together everything you need for a great season, from plans to volunteers
▶ Communicating your expectations to parents and players

Some hockey coaches fly by the seat of their pants all season long with the attitude that coaching's all old hat to them. But veteran NHL goalie and coach, Glen Hanlon, once put things something like this: Proper preparation prevents poor performance. For both coaches and players, Glen's "five Ps" hold true — you will always be more effective if you plan ahead.

This chapter offers some approaches to getting your hockey season off on the right skate.

Getting Yourself Organized

As coach, you come first. After all, a coach has league rules to check out, a whole season of practices and games to organize, other people to organize, equipment to gather, and a whole host of other plans to put in place. You have to figure out what you want to do with each of these tasks, and then you have to communicate what is necessary to parents, players, and assistants so that they will be organized as well. If you spend time planning before the season starts, your season should run fairly smoothly. If you don't plan ahead, you may feel like you're being pulled in several directions at once when things get busy during the season.

On a practical level, planning ahead provides the opportunity to avoid potentially unpleasant incidents that can otherwise arise, such as having a parent threaten to pull a child off the team because the parent feels the child isn't getting enough ice time. If you inform parents at the outset that you'll be playing all kids equal time all season, you shouldn't have an issue.

Acquainting yourself with league rules and regulations

Your first step to getting organized for the season is to find out what your league wants from you and what plans it has for your team. Don't rely on the hearsay of parents and previous coaches. They may be able to provide some sound advice, but you need to get regulations direct from the source. Rules change.

You need to become clear about your responsibilities and what your league expects of you. The league may provide a code of conduct regarding such behaviors as a positive approach, fair play, and no discrimination. In addition, you may find it useful to know what the officials see as being important in administering the rules of the game. For example, at the beginner level, officials may not bother to call offside; at the advanced level, they may choose to be extremely judicious about clean hits.

To get acquainted with your league and what's required, you can contact the head of your hockey organization — or the organization's assigned coaching coordinator — and the supervisor of officials. The following list includes some of the items your league and its officials may prescribe for you:

- **Player selection:** Some leagues assign players randomly to teams, but at some levels, coaches have a range of input into who will be on their teams. Most minor hockey leagues limit the number of players per team and have restrictions on player movement between teams.

- **Scheduling games and practices:** Some leagues provide a game schedule, but you have to book practice times yourself. Other leagues have all practices and games scheduled, but if you want to hold off-ice sessions, you are responsible to schedule those.

- **Providing facilities and equipment:** Check ahead to know whether your practice and game rinks have change facilities, particularly if you need special arrangements because you're coaching a mixed team of guys and girls. Some rinks provide pucks and pylons — some don't. Does the league both provide and clean jerseys, or do players look after their own?

- **Keeping the league informed:** Leagues usually prescribe specific lines of communication to report problems, scores, finances, and other league matters, such as procedures for injuries, complaints, suggestions, or changes.

- **Planning for rules variations:** Official playing rules are often modified for different skill levels in leagues, with variations such as no hitting or equal ice time.

✔ **Knowing officials' priorities:** Find out what the league and its officials feel is important for players at your team's skill level. Ask what the three most common problems are for officials at your level that coaches can help circumvent.

Adopt an attitude of working with officials. Both of you are there to help provide a great experience for the kids.

✔ **Keeping your players safe:** Safety issues, such as not wearing jewelry and wearing only certified equipment, are usually dictated by the league.

✔ **Understanding punishment policies:** The league usually prescribes the consequences of their rules, such as a player not being allowed on the ice without a proper face shield.

Drawing up your master plan

The next step in getting organized is to sit down and begin to plan your whole season. If that sounds daunting, remember that the process is straightforward, and the exercise will make your season progress more smoothly and effectively than if you don't establish a plan.

The easiest way to approach the planning process is to break it into four segments:

✔ A seasonal plan

✔ A monthly plan

✔ A weekly plan

✔ A daily practice plan

The seasonal plan provides the overall picture. Each subsequent segment expands on the previous plan, providing the detail that is necessary for the coach, parents, and players. We explain the first three segments in this chapter, but the daily practice plan deserves its own chapter. Go to Chapter 4 for those details.

Making a seasonal plan

The seasonal plan is your worksheet for the year. Everything that should be scheduled goes on this master plan: games, practices, business meetings, holidays, exams, and parties. Include anything that impacts your hockey season.

To make things easier, the season is typically organized into five successive planning phases, each with specific coaching priorities:

- ✔ **Preliminary season:** Use this time for coaching preparation and attending clinics and league meetings.

- ✔ **Pre-season:** This period is when you select and organize your team. Take this time to have your parent and team meetings. In addition, you can run practices and *shinny* (informal games with no officials, body contact, or puck lifting) or exhibition games, which give you a chance to get familiar with your players' skills and talents.

- ✔ **Regular season:** For planning purposes, divide this phase into thirds: early season (approximately the first third of your season's practices and games), mid-season (the middle third of your games and practices), and late season (the final third).

- ✔ **Post-season:** This period includes playoffs or significant end-of-season tournaments.

- ✔ **Off-season:** This phase is when hockey is done for another year. Only at very advanced levels would you require players to participate in off-ice training programs. Kids typically switch to soccer or lacrosse or guitar lessons, and maybe attend a summer hockey school if they really want to.

Take seven blank pieces of paper and mark columns on them as shown in Figure 3-1 and Figure 3-2. Identify each page by one of the seasons previously outlined, using a page each for the three regular season segments. Then write in the months and weeks that correspond to each season for your league, as we've done in Figures 3-1 and 3-2.

Gather all significant dates from your minor hockey association and the players' school systems, keeping in mind seasonal holidays and your work commitments. Write these in the Date/event column. Include events you may want to do with your team, such as a holiday outing or year-end party. Record as much information as possible so that you avoid overlooking or double-booking important events.

Following is a checklist of events to consider including in your master plan:

- ✔ Minor hockey league dates, such as the annual meeting, coaches' clinics, information sessions, and parent and team meetings.

- ✔ Team information, such as team tryouts, practice dates, game dates, tournament schedules (apply early to play in these — good ones fill up fast), off-ice training sessions, all-star activities, and travel commitments. Include facility locations (rinks, gyms, and so on) and times for each item as available.

 ✔ School information, such as holidays, exam periods, and field trips.

 ✔ Personally significant dates, such as mandatory job seminars or meetings, holidays, family commitments, and travel plans.

In the last column (the Focus column), develop your plan for your team's skill and ability development over the course of the season. You need to have a plan for what you hope to teach them at each point along the way, including having some logical progression toward a reasonable goal or level of accomplishment. For example, if you're coaching an unskilled team, your team's pre-season focus may simply be fun and social interaction on the ice so that the kids learn to stand up and progress forward while they get to know their teammates. By early in the regular season, you may want to progress to forward and backward skating, starting, and stopping. By contrast, an advanced team's pre-season focus may be team selection and conditioning, with a quick review of skating, passing, and puck-handling skills.

'06-'07 Cougars		Master plan	
Preliminary		Season segment	

Month	Week	Date/event	Skills/strategy/conditioning focus
Sept.	10–16	Tues. 11/League meeting	
	17–23	Sat. 23/Coaches' clinic	
	24–30		Master plan prep week
Oct.	1–7	Sat. 7/Parents meeting	Philosophy/rules/schedule
	8–14	Sat. 14/11 a.m. First team meeting and skate	Rules Fun/social

Figure 3-1:
An easy way to plan your year.

Sometimes you may find it easier to fill in this Focus column by working from both ends toward the middle. For example, with an intermediate team, you may decide that, by the end of the season, you want your players to be able to make deliberate plays offensively and to have a good understanding of defensive position, all of which you would put under the Focus column for the post-season. You may know that you need to review skating and puck-handling skills in the pre-season, which means that early in the season you have to focus on teaching passing, shooting, and stickchecking skills so that you have time during the mid- and late seasons to work on the offensive and defensive lessons that you need in order to reach your post-season goal.

For a checklist of skills and strategies to include in your seasonal focus plan, use the list of skills covered in Chapter 6 for a beginner team, Chapters 9 to 12 for an intermediate-level team, and Chapters 15 to 18 for an advanced team.

If you decide on a focus for a practice, you can't simply practice that element of play all session. You should first review something you previously covered. For example, your focus may be to work on shooting instruction, but you may find it useful to first do a combination drill that reviews skating, puck handling, and passing. Remember that basic skills continue to improve with practice and are best repeated all year long.

If you make a skills-and-strategies focus plan for the season, your team is likely to progress further in skill development and run less risk of missing important elements during the season than if you just practice what you feel like working on each day. You've no doubt heard a coach lament after losing a playoff game, "I wish I'd worked more on face-offs," or "I just ran out of time to work on defensive positioning." Having a good seasonal plan helps you to avoid this scenario.

Look at Figure 3-1 and Figure 3-2 again for some ideas on how to put your own skills-and-strategies seasonal plan in place. Figure 3-1 is a typical preliminary plan for coaches of any level. Figure 3-2 is more typical of a mid-season plan for a beginner-level team.

Keep your master plan updated as things change or are added during the year. You may also want to adjust your focus plan periodically. Game play may point out a weakness that needs immediate attention, or your team may progress more quickly or more slowly than you anticipated. Regardless, with a good seasonal plan, you always have a snapshot of what lies ahead in coming weeks and months and you also have a good yardstick for monitoring progress.

Filling in your monthly plan

The monthly plan provides the scheduling information that you want to make available to the players, parents, and team assistants at the beginning of each month. Add specific details to items from the seasonal plan — what, where, and when. For example, your master schedule may include a date when try-outs start, but the monthly plan would add a time and location.

___'06-'07 Cougars___	Master plan
___Mid-season___	Season segment

Month	Week	Date/event	Skills/strategy/conditioning focus
Dec.	3-9	Tues. 5/practice	Stopping with puck instruction
		Sat. 9/game	Fun
	10-16	Tues. 12/practice	Forehand passing instruction
		Sat. 16/game	Passing
	17-23	Tues. 19/practice	Forehand receiving instruction
		Fri. 22/start Christmas vacation	
		Sat. 23/game	Passing and receiving
	24-30	Mon. 25/Christmas	
		Tues. 26/Boxing Day/practice	Backhand passing instruction
		27-31/Family ski trip	
		Sat. 30/game *need sub coach	Passing and receiving
'07 Dec.	31-6	Tues. 2/school resumes + practice	Backhand receiving instruction
		Sat. 6/game	Passing and receiving
	7-13	Tues. 9/practice	Passing/receiving combo drills
		Sat. 13/game	Passing and receiving

Figure 3-2: Planning for when things get busy.

Use a regular monthly calendar, provided it has large writing spaces and is easy to copy for distribution. Make one chart for each month of your hockey season. See Figure 3-3 for an example of an intermediate team's late-season monthly plan.

| February | | Schedule for | | '06–'07 Bears | | |

Sunday	Monday	Tuesday	Wednesday	Thursday	Friday	Saturday
				1 8p.m./WA practice/game	2	3
4	5 6p.m./MA practice/game	6	7	8	9 8p.m./WA practice/game	10
11	12 1p.m./MA practice/game	13	14 Valentine's Day	15 8p.m./WA practice/game	16	17
18	19 6p.m./MA practice/game	20	21	22	23 8p.m./WA practice/game	24
25 Week of March Break	26 1p.m./MA practice	27	28 Buffalo – work presentation	1	2 Horvath Minor Hockey Tournament – Toronto 2-3rd	3

Figure 3-3: A monthly handout so players know your plan.

MA – Memorial Arena   WA – Wilson Arena

Check the Internet or other tools, such as a personal digital assistant (PDA), that have ready-made formats available for drawing up monthly plans. In addition, these tools may provide for easy e-mail distribution, if that would work for your team.

The next step in planning is to make a second copy of blank charts for each month of your hockey season for your exclusive use. Fill these in with your focus for every practice and game you have scheduled that month. Figure 3-4 shows a sample of focus plans that may be used for an advanced team.

Use your seasonal plan as your guide and expand on the details of what you need to do to meet your skills development plan. For example, if your seasonal plan for your beginning team is to focus on passing and shooting in November, then you might specify the approach shown in Table 3-1.

November   Schedule for   '06–'07 Cougars Practice/Game Focus

Sunday	Monday	Tuesday	Wednesday	Thursday	Friday	Saturday
			1	2 7p.m. practice Aerobics/ stretching Body checking instr	3	4 10a.m. game Checking
5	6 9p.m. game Passing	7	8	9 6p.m. practice Aerobics/ stretching Breakouts	10	11 8a.m. game Breakouts
12	13 10p.m. game Shot opportunities	14	15	16 7p.m. practice Aerobics/power/ stretching Offensive zone play	17	18 9a.m. game Offensive zone play
19	20 9p.m. game Team scoring opportunities	21	22	23 8p.m. practice Aerobics/power/ stretching Neutral zone play	24	25 8a.m. game Transition to attack
26	27 10p.m. game Transition to attack	28	29	30 7p.m. practice Aerobics/power/ stretching Winning face- off strategies		

Figure 3-4:
Planning a focus for each practice and game.

Table 3-1	Seasonal Practice Plan for November
Session	*Focus*
First	Forehand passing instruction
Second	Easy passing drill(s)
Third	Backhand passing instruction
Fourth	Combo passing drill(s)
Final	Forehand and backhand shooting instruction

This gives you a smooth progression in skill development.

Remember that this design is for planning the focus for a practice and is not exclusive. In the example practice plan, you would also want to include at least one skating drill to review the focus skill of the previous month.

If your team is at an advanced level, be sure to include training plans, such as aerobic or power training, in this monthly plan, as well as skill and strategy plans. Also include specific drills in your monthly plan if you already have some favorites. You'll take less time later to draw up your weekly plans.

Your monthly plan adds detail to your seasonal plan. Do the monthly plans before the season begins, then update them monthly before handing them out, in case you have any last minute changes. The monthly plans keep everyone on schedule, as well as keep you tuned to your own coaching goals. Monthly plans also allow you to add new items that may come up as the season progresses, such as the opportunity for a team outing to see a touring celebrity hockey game in your area.

Detailing your weekly plan

Pick a consistent time each week as the season progresses to sit down and draw up a weekly plan, such as Sunday evening after dinner. Plan a week in advance of the actual week you are about to start so that you can distribute copies to parents, players, and assistants a week ahead of time.

You want to include every detail of the hockey week in this handout. For example, if the monthly plan provides the date, time, and location for team tryouts, the weekly plan for tryout week may look something like this:

Sunday, Oct. 15   4:15 p.m. Report to dressing room C, Wilson Arena

4:45 p.m. Pre-ice briefing

5–6 p.m. On ice

6:05 p.m. Post-ice briefing

We provide an example in Figure 3-5 of a weekly plan for an intermediate team that has half-hour, half-ice practices, and half-hour games each session. Leave the Notes column blank on the copies that are distributed to team personnel, parents, and players so that they can fill in their own reminders, such as which parent is picking up which player(s) at what time for transportation to a game. The coach uses the Notes column to record the focus for each practice and to list drills for that day or, if it's a game, the one or two focus points for that game.

With this weekly plan, parents, players, and assistants know exactly what their schedule is for each team event. The coach knows both the team schedule and what he or she needs to do to be prepared for the practices or games.

Weekly Schedule for __'06–'07 Bears__

Week of __February 18–24__

Date	Schedule	Notes
Sunday, Feb. 18	Off	
Monday, Feb. 19	5:15 p.m. Dressing room B, Memorial Arena 5:45 p.m. Practice briefing 6-6:25 p.m. Practice 6:25-6:30 p.m. Pre-game briefing 6:30-7 p.m. Game vs Jets 7-7:05 p.m. Post-game wrap 7:10 p.m. Departure	Focus: Offensive gone attack and shoot Drills: Give-and-go Acceleration Neutral Zone Go to Open Ice Focus: Getting shot off attack
Tuesday, Feb. 20	Off	
Wednesday, Feb. 21	Off	
Thursday, Feb. 22	Off	
Friday, Feb. 23	7:15 p.m. Dressing room 5, Wilson Arena 7:45 p.m. Practice briefing 8-8:25 p.m. Practice 8:25-8:30 Pre-game briefing 8:30-9 p.m. Game vs Fantoms 9-9:05 p.m. Post-game wrap 9:10 p.m. Departure	Focus: Protecting the net Drills: Defense 1 v 1 Zone 2 v 2 defense Focus: No free shots
Saturday, Feb. 24	Off	

Figure 3-5: Coach's copy of an advanced team's late-season hockey week.

Don't forget to finish your plan

As you may expect, the planning doesn't stop with the weekly schedule. You need a daily practice plan and a game-day plan for your own use. These plans do not need to be relayed to parents and players, but they are very important for you and your coaching assistant, if you have one. We address these plans in Chapters 4 and 5 where we discuss specific practice design and game plans.

Pick up a three-ring binder and keep all your plans and schedules in it. At the end of the year, you'll have a book that provides a complete hockey program down to the final details that you can use as a base if you agree to coach again the next year, heaven forbid. Or, you *could* pass the book on to the next coach. Be sure to jot your comments on the plans, noting what worked or didn't work so well, so that you can easily revise your mistakes and build on your strengths the next year.

Planning doesn't rule out flexibility, but remember that players and their parents have a life beyond your team, and you must show respect for their time. They'll appreciate it! Give players and their parents every opportunity to plan ahead and be organized, just like you. Doing so will make the whole season run more smoothly.

Gathering supplies and equipment

Every coach needs some standard items to run a practice, starting perhaps with a whistle and skates. You must provide some items yourself while other items may be available at the rink you use for practice. Check ahead of time so that you know whether you have to bring along items such as pucks and pylons.

The following three checklists cover most of the necessities any coach needs for games and practices:

✔ **Coach's kit bag:** Take this bag with you to every practice. A strong, medium-sized bag should be adequate to hold the following:

- Whistle

- Skates

- Socks

- Hockey gloves

- Stick

- Helmet

- Shin pads

- A sweat suit or whatever you may wear for working out

- Sense of humor

- Sense of adventure

✔ **Coach's game bag:** When you're going to a game rather than a practice, take the last two items from your kit bag and put them in a smaller game bag with these items:

- Your game plan (see Chapter 5 for details)

- Players' league registration (game) cards

- Player information sheets (see the section "Parent meeting agenda," later in this chapter, for details) — keep these with you at all team events

✔ **Team practice bag:** First, make sure you have the last two items from your kit bag plus the last item from your game bag. You'll need a strong, large bag for the remaining items that you may want to use at practice:

- Your practice plan

- Clipboard with rink diagram(s) and markers

- Rink board — a 2-foot × 3-foot dry-erase board is good, with dry-erase markers

- Stopwatch

- Hacksaw (to cut stick shafts)

- Extra tape

- Pucks (at least one per player) and pylons (if necessary)

- Fun item or drill (for example, a free fries voucher for the most improved player at practice, or a novelty relay)

- First-aid kit (see Chapter 21 for details)

- Cellular phone or handy alternative (for example, know where the nearest working phone or pay phone is located and have a couple of quarters on hand)

Determining what you need for assistants

You may have the time and willingness to assume all the team's coaching and associated duties. However, for many coaches, the demands are considerable — and you do have your day job. Having an assistant or two can offer a welcomed extra set of hands at practices. An assistant also provides the benefit of being a mutually interested sounding board. If you have to be out of town on business the night of a team practice, an assistant coach can take over your practice duties. If ice-time schedules are commonly assigned at the last minute, have a parent-manager initiate a phone chain to inform other parents and players of sudden schedule changes. When weekend tournaments are scheduled as special events, you may want to have a parent act as travel convener to organize transportation, billets, or hotels so that you don't have to do it all yourself.

Here is a checklist of team needs that you may want to consider having a designated assistant handle:

- **Co- or assistant coach:** A co-coach or assistant coach can work with you on planning and running practices, can work with you behind the bench during games, and can fill in for you in your absences from practices or games. See Chapter 22 for tips on selecting a person to fill this role. Consider someone of the opposite sex if you're coaching a mixed team.

- **Liaison:** A minor hockey coach at any level is wise to designate a communication or coach-liaison person. With very advanced teams, this person may primarily be the team's media contact. For minor hockey, this is the contact person for parents when they have hockey issues they want to discuss. For example, it is unwise for a parent who is angry about Joey's ice time to confront the coach about the issue following the game. A designated parent-coach liaison can more objectively listen to the parent and report to the coach, then back to the parent on issues that may arise. Make sure parents are informed at the outset that this is the official line of communication.

- **Practice assistants:** If you are coaching a fairly unskilled team, players benefit tremendously from one-on-one attention. If you have up to three interested moms and dads who can skate and handle a puck, you may want to use them on the ice for practices to help players during skill drills. Prior to practice, brief assistants on precisely what you want them to do so that they do not become distractions on the ice but rather provide quality instruction for the kids.

- **Team manager:** This assignment would fall to someone who can take care of administrative items, usually relating to the minor hockey association. This assistant needs to be an organized detail person, who will stay within the rules. This person may also be assigned team duties, such as logging player profiles and player medical history information, coordinating travel, and working with parents. Handling cash and book-keeping responsibilities may also be assigned to a team manager, or, if finances are a significant item in your organization, you may want a separate finance manager.

✔ **Travel convener:** This person is responsible for making a list of the people who are traveling, identifying drivers, assigning rides, booking billets or hotel rooms, informing travelers of departure times, and managing all related information.

Our advice? Consider your own preferences, the time you have available, the expectations of the minor hockey association, and the extent of parent involvement you'd like with your team, then make a list of personnel who can provide assistance to you in creating a positive experience for the kids. Contact people you know who are good candidates for the roles you need filled to see if they are willing to help. If you would like to have some roles filled but you don't know people who could fill them, take your list to the parent meeting (discussed in the next section) and ask for volunteers.

Finding other resources

Two North American hockey organizations serve as governing bodies for their respective national youth hockey programs. These organizations provide coaching certification programs and educational materials for male and female youth hockey coaches. They list and host coaches' clinics and referees' clinics, and help with certification in states and provinces across the U.S. and Canada. In addition, these organizations provide information for hockey parents that coaches may want to reference on occasion, as well as a host of other interesting hockey topics.

Both organizations provide an extensive list of books, videos, publications, and DVDs that you can purchase online. We highly recommend that you start with either or both of these organizations when looking for coaching resource materials, ideas, and clinics.

If you coach in the United States, USA Hockey's Web site (www.usahockey.com) directs you to national, state, and often regional and local information pertinent to your situation.

If you coach in Canada, Hockey Canada's Web site (www.hockeycanada.ca) directs you to regional, provincial, and in some cases local resources, including all the provincial minor hockey associations, which are listed with contact information.

Internationally, the International Ice Hockey Federation (www.iihf.com) provides contact information for the governing body for hockey in every country around the world. So if you coach in Europe, Japan, or Australia, you can use this Web site to link to what is available in your corner of the globe. The site does not typically provide hockey coaching information that you can use directly, but it does give you contact information if you want to explore the way hockey is run in various countries.

Getting Your Team Organized

After you've made all your plans for the next few months, the rest is easy — you just have to communicate those plans to the people that matter. If you're using a co-coach and/or team manager, make sure that each of you is on the same page first. Having a consistent philosophy and set of rules amongst the team leaders eliminates most problems that may arise in a hockey season. The other important steps to organizing your team are getting together with your players' parents and with your players.

You need to walk a fine line between being the person who is in charge and making everyone feel involved, as though the team is their own. This fine line is well worth walking though. Know your own mind, but also consult and delegate. When you do, you get the help you need and together you give the kids the positive experience they are looking for.

Meeting with the parents

Schedule a mandatory meeting with all parents as soon as possible after you know who you have on your team. This meeting will be your reference point through the course of the season to keep players, parents, managers, and coaches working as a team and toward team goals.

This meeting is your opportunity to tell parents how you plan to approach the season, what your coaching philosophy is, and what you expect of them and their child. This meeting is also your chance to ask for volunteers to provide the assistance you need. It's the time to collect and disseminate the necessary information, such as contact numbers, medical information, schedules, and rules. It's also the time to let parents bring forward any questions or concerns they may have regarding your coaching approach or the conduct of practices and games. Now is also the time to present procedures for dealing with issues that may arise during the season.

Be organized. Be clear. Be professional. Remember that the kids are the reason you are all there.

Purpose of the parent meeting

Generally, you want to accomplish most of the following at the parent meeting:

- ✔ Inform parents of your approach to coaching, your coaching philosophy, and your expectations of them
- ✔ Inform parents of league and team rules, regulations, and schedules, and solicit tournament interest

✔ Gather individual player information

✔ Solicit volunteer assistance

✔ Moderate potential parent concerns

Parent meeting agenda

Keep the meeting brief, to the point, and non-confrontational. Following is a guide you may want to use in setting your agenda:

✔ **Welcome and introductions:** Start off by welcoming everyone into the hockey family for the upcoming season. Then introduce yourself and the assistants you have already selected. Finally, have parents introduce themselves and maybe tell a bit about themselves, such as what part of town they live in — something that can be useful information for car-pooling, for example.

✔ **Coaching philosophy:** Briefly explain what is important to you about the players' experience, what you hope to accomplish during the season, and what you expect of the players and their parents. This is also an opportunity to let parents know that if your approach is not what they want for their child, now is the time to switch to another team with no hard feelings. Not everyone fits comfortably into the same mold. Some coaches choose to have parents sign an agreement of conduct at this point so that there will be no question of expectations and misunderstandings down the road. Such contracts are discussed in more detail in the next section.

✔ **Rules and regulations:** Have your handouts ready. Make sure that one handout covers league matters, such as equipment, rules, and safety procedures. A second handout should be your team rules, such as being on time, no arguing with the coach or officials, and supporting your teammates. Include consequences where appropriate. Discuss only the most pertinent; parents can read the remainder.

✔ **Practice and game schedule:** Provide a handout of the schedule and indicate how much time in advance you want the players to be at the rink, dressed and ready for the team briefing. Explain cancellation or last-minute-change procedures, and provide a handout with names and phone numbers of all assistants and parents to contact when necessary.

✔ **Request for volunteers:** Have a list ready, tell the parents what you need, and offer to discuss the duties with anyone who is interested after the meeting — just so the meeting doesn't run on too long. You can also ask for recommendations for people who can fill those roles at the meeting.

✔ **Player information records:** This is an extremely important package of information you need to gather from the parents. Keep it with you at all times that you are involved with the team. These records contain contact information and medical information that the coaching staff must be aware of in case of emergencies. For example, you need to know which players are on medications for things such as asthma, diabetes, or epilepsy. You must indicate that the medical information will be kept confidential if it is the parent's wish, but you must also make it clear that it is in the best interest of the child that you be aware of potential problems so that you can ensure that procedures are in place for any emergency. See Figure 3-6 for one way to record the pertinent information. Add items to the profile that may be unique to your team. For example, you may have a sponsor for jerseys and socks and may need slots for sizes.

✔ **Miscellaneous:** You may want to provide some sound advice regarding such topics as nutrition, sleep, or fitness training, depending on the age of the participants. Consider having an expert guest speak for a few minutes if your team is quite advanced, or have some simple, clear handouts prepared as tips for parents.

✔ **Questions:** This is the parents' opportunity for clarification. Be open to suggestions but do not feel obligated to make snap decisions to appease parents on the spot. It is reasonable to say, "I will make a note of your concern and discuss it with my assistants and let you know what we come up with by the first practice." Then follow up as promised.

Parents should leave the introductory meeting feeling that you need their support and commitment and that you need them to be a positive influence on all involved, not just their child.

Parent contract

Most hockey parents want to see their child have a good time and get lots of ice time. However, a few parents have been known to expect you to turn their child into the youngest-ever NHL star, or they expect you to stand aside while they do it. A parent contract signed at the initial meeting can dispel such unreasonable expectations and keep parents more on side with the team approach to hockey throughout their child's season. Some coaches have found that they can pre-empt inappropriate and abusive behavior if they present a contract at the outset for parents to agree to and sign.

The content of a parental agreement can be constructive and need not be confrontational if you include the following:

✔ Your approach to coaching this team

✔ Your goals for the kids

> ✔ Your expectations of parent behavior
>
> ✔ Consequences of not adhering to the contract terms
>
> ✔ Procedures for expressing legitimate complaints

See Figure 3-7 for some ideas on designing a parent contract.

Player Profile and Medical Information

Name_____ Date_____

Address_____ Phone_____

_____ Email_____

Family: Home Phone   Work Phone   Email

Mother_____

Father_____

Guardian_____

School_____ Teacher_____ Phone_____

Medical Information:

Family doctor_____ Phone_____

Medical conditions and medications (i.e. allergies, asthma, diabetes, epilepsy, contacts)

_____

_____

_____

_____

Figure 3-6:
Sample of
the infor-
mation you   Hockey:
need to
know about   Height_____ Weight_____ Jersey Size
your players.
              Position_____ Shot_____

Parent Contract

Team_____ Season _____

As coach of your child's hockey team, I place fun and development of each child's hockey skills at the top of my priorities. That means winning will not take priority over any player's ice time. I expect gifted players to help less gifted players elevate their play, though not at the expense of the gifted player's development. Hockey is a team game, which means the team is only as strong as its weakest player. I endorse team play, good sportsmanship, individual and team improvement in addition to respect for coaching staff and officials.

I expect parents to support my coaching approach, verbally to their children and in their behavior around the rink. Specifically, that means parents' comments at practices and games will be positive for every child or they are to make no comment at all. Parents will ignore officiating to the best of their ability and will not comment, unless positively. Parents will show respect for opposition teams whether they deserve it or not.

Parents who have issues with the coaching staff are to present their issues to the designated parent-coach liaison who will discuss your issue with the coach, and the coach or liaison will respond within 48 hours.

Parents who badmouth players, coaching staff, or officials, or otherwise exhibit poor examples of leadership and sportsmanship around the team, will be requested not to attend practices and games.

Figure 3-7: Constructive management of parent behavior.

I feel this approach creates a team attitude that provides the best chance for the players to get a positive hockey experience. Thank you for your co-operation.

I fully support this approach.   Parent Signature(s)

                                                 _____

                                                 _____

For kids, hockey is a game. Everyone associated with the team should be committed to keeping the experience fun and positive.

Your first team meeting

This meeting is for the kids and may or may not include parents. The meeting needs to be brief and lively but must set the tone for behavior and effort for the season.

The team meeting is an opportunity to meet and greet the players so that they begin to feel like a member of a team; find out some names. It's a chance to explain team rules and your expectations, such as good sportsmanship, respect for the officials and the opposition, and support for teammates. During the team meeting, you disseminate information, such as practice and game schedules, nutrition guidelines, and training plans. This may also be the best time to try on uniforms and equipment so that you don't waste practice time later. You may also want to go around the room of players and ask why they signed up or what they want to get out of the upcoming season; it may give you a sense of where they are coming from.

Keep the first players' meeting fun, firm, and informative.

Purpose of the team meeting

Here is a checklist of things you want to accomplish at your first meeting with the players:

- Get to know the players individually.
- Let the players know your style, your rules, and your expectations.
- Tell the players your plans for them over the season.
- Give players the schedule of practices and games, including dates, times, and locations.
- Ensure that players are properly outfitted for the season, including the reminder that each player is responsible for bringing a water bottle to each practice and game. The bottle must be clearly marked with the player's name and number.

Team meeting agenda

Remember that kids have a short attention span, so keep the meeting short and upbeat. You may want to include agenda items such as the following:

- **Welcome and introductions:** Introduce yourself and any staff who will be dealing with the players. Then have the players introduce themselves and say a thing or two about their hockey or other sport interests.
- **Coaching philosophy:** Keep the terms simple and on the players' level. A simple statement of what you want for them that season will do.
- **Rules:** Explain the team's rules to the players, mentioning such things as attendance, being on time, and behavior toward teammates, coaches, officials, and opponents. Be sure to include consequences for breaking rules.

- ✔ **Expectations:** Outline what you expect players to put forward regarding work ethic and attitude, including the prescribed code of conduct.

- ✔ **Season schedule:** Have a handout ready, including specifics about time and place for all scheduled team events.

- ✔ **Equipment:** Try on uniforms. Check that everyone has safe, proper-fitting equipment and that they know how to care for it. Remind them about water bottles.

- ✔ **Questions:** Give the kids a chance to be heard. It makes them feel like they belong.

- ✔ **Fun:** Plan a fun activity like a skating game or pizza party so that they can mix and laugh.

If you take all these steps in getting organized, you'll be off to a great season and face few distractions as the season progresses. This will leave you free to concentrate on your primary purpose for being there: to help kids enjoy and learn about hockey and to give them an experience that teaches them a little about what works in life.

Chapter 4

Running Great Practices

. . . .

In This Chapter

▶ Discovering the key elements that help you design great practices

▶ Getting your team ready before they hit the ice

▶ Making sure that everything is safe

▶ Starting your practices out right

▶ Working on your practice's theme

▶ Ending on a high note

. . . .

*W*hether you have 15 minutes of practice time or an hour and 15 minutes, you must make practice a great hockey experience for your players. Practice time is the best chance you have to

✔ Control the quality of the athletes' experience.

✔ Improve the players' skills.

✔ Build confidence in each and every athlete.

✔ Make sure that everyone has some fun.

Hockey games rarely offer this combination of opportunities for you or for the athletes.

Sure, most kids say they'd rather play hockey than practice. Take them at their word — they do want to play, all the time. It beats sitting on the bench. But everybody doesn't get to play all the time in real games; shifts and a team's determination to win can compromise fun. So give them what they want in practices.

How do you ensure that kids feel like they're playing all practice long? It's simple and basic:

- ✔ Keep them moving.
- ✔ Keep practice simple.
- ✔ Challenge players with something they can grasp so that you get lots of opportunity to offer praise.
- ✔ Do some things almost exclusively for fun.

In this chapter, we help you to come up with a strategy for combining all of these tasks in an effective practice to get your team game ready.

Starting with a Good Plan

Most coaches, like most players, want to improve as they progress through a hockey season. A daily practice plan is a valuable tool toward that goal for a coach. Initially, the plan serves as your guide for what you want to accomplish on ice. Later, the plan serves as a reference for what worked and what didn't, which is where you really learn.

Write down your practice plan on 8½×11 paper. You'll probably need both sides. Then put the plan on your clipboard or fold it and put it in your pocket for a handy reference during the practice.

Putting the important stuff in your plan

Every practice plan should include fun, skill-development, and confidence-building components. Kids need to have you weave these elements into the fabric of every practice. Beyond these fundamental elements, include the following list of items in your practice plan as well:

- ✔ The date and length of time you have for each practice.
- ✔ The theme(s) for that day's practice (you identify those in your master plan, which we discuss in Chapter 3).
- ✔ A clear diagram for each drill that you will use. A pen with multiple colored tips can help you make drill diagrams clear and easy to follow at a glance.
- ✔ A time slot for each drill.
- ✔ Any equipment you will need, such as pylons or balls.

> ✔ If your team is at a level where line combinations are relevant (you assign defensive pairs and forward lines), list the forward combinations and defense pairings you want to use in practice.
>
> ✔ If on-ice conditioning is relevant at your team's level, list and diagram the drill(s) for that workout.

Save each practice plan in a three-ring binder. This allows you to build a practice file for future reference. Be sure to make comments on the practice plan immediately after each practice to help you better prepare for your next practice session and to provide an excellent reference for your next season. You can post your practice plan in the dressing room prior to practice as pre-ice information for the players. Take time, however, to explain the theme for each practice along with the drills to be used before going on the ice so you don't waste valuable ice time having kids sitting and listening.

Working with a practice blueprint

A team's practice needs vary with the skill level of the team. However, hockey practices seem to have a common flow that works well. Figure 4-1 provides an example of a practice blueprint you can use for drawing up your daily practice plan — with modifications to suit your team's needs and skill level. Note the general flow from warm-up to review (for positive reinforcement) to the introduction of a new item (which involves more serious work) to fun (to finish on a high).

After you have your blueprint, decide on the drills you want to use for each segment of the practice according to your team's needs and the themes you previously established for each practice in your master plan. Then diagram the drills on the back of the plan to avoid any confusion. Remember to allocate the amount of time you want to spend on each segment so that players know what to expect and so that you get everything done in practice that you planned.

You may want to juggle the order or combine items in the plan on certain days, or permanently, according to the skill level you coach. For example, you may use one drill that serves both as a review (#2 on the sample plan in Figure 4-1) and fun (#6), or you may combine conditioning with your review drill. If you have a beginner team, your review drill may actually be an instructive theme (#4) drill. With advanced teams, you may want to indicate when some aspects of conditioning need to be done off-ice.

Another consideration, particularly for house-league hockey, is that many teams have to share ice for practices. You may have to plan for adjustments for full ice rather than half ice and 35 players instead of 18.

_____ PRACTICE LOG

Week of _____ Practice # _____ Date _____

Practice Time Available _____   <u>Allotted Time</u>

1 – Warm-up Activity	_____
2 – Skating/Puck Handling/Passing (Review) Drill(s)	_____
3 – Goalie Warm-up Drill(s)	_____
4 – Theme #1 and Drill(s)	_____
5 – Theme #2 and Drill(s)	_____
6 – Fun Drill	_____
Conditioning:	
Individual Instruction:	
Equipment:	
Comments:	

Figure 4-1:
Planning to
get the most
out of your
practices.

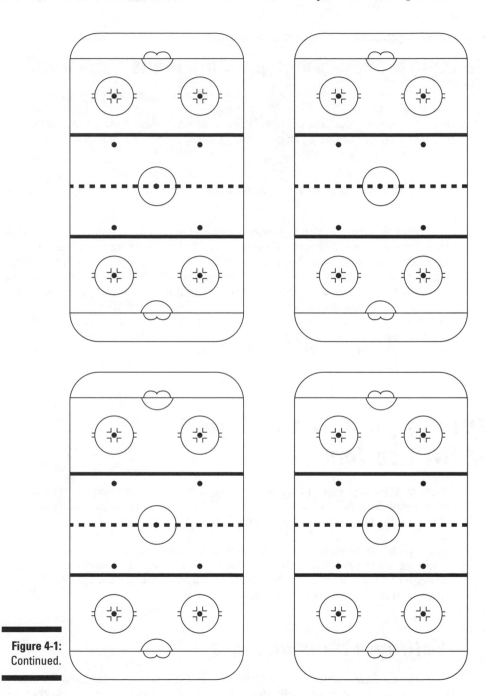

Figure 4-1:
Continued.

Planning for days when practice plans don't work

Practice plans help ensure that you actually accomplish what you set out to do. They are not, however, etched in stone. Occasionally, you may find that what you had planned is just not working — the kids are in a strange mood or players can't tie their skate laces that day.

Adjust: Play a nonsense game, set up an obstacle course, or shoot at weird targets. Always have something in your back pocket for such emergencies. Even for these type of situations, it's good to have a plan.

Note that the sample plan in Figure 4-1 has a section for indicating which athletes may need specific individual attention in keeping with the theme of the practice. You can designate an assistant before practice begins to give particular attention to those players. The sample plan also has a comments section. After each practice, make notes in this section about such things as the names of players you missed speaking to during the practice so that you can make a point to catch them during the next practice. Also, make comments about the practice for future reference: Was it a great practice? Should you have done something differently? What worked? What didn't work? Did the kids have fun and learn something? Did you?

Prepping Your Team Before You Hit the Ice

A coach typically walks into the dressing room to find the players sitting around the benches in various stages of dress. Chatter is everywhere, and the players' minds appear to be anywhere but on practice.

The coach's first job is to get players from street mode into practice mode. And you want to do that in the dressing room, not on the ice where it becomes a waste of valuable ice time. The most effective technique for making that transition is to call a mini-meeting.

Calling a mini-meeting

Designate a time, such as 15 minutes before the start of ice time, when players know you want their undivided attention in the dressing room. At that time, players should know they are expected to be fully dressed with skates laced. When you give the signal, chatter stops, parents disappear, and everyone focuses on the coach.

Never offer to pick up kids on the way to practices or games. Doing so often makes you late — in addition to being an easy habit for parents to take advantage.

During the mini-meeting, explain what the players will do on the ice for practice. You want the players to be clear about how to do the drills *before* they leave the dressing room so that they don't waste any ice time. A player's recall is best when they get to use their senses, so appeal to as many senses as possible when you explain a drill. For example, talk them through the drill so that they "hear" it, and then "show" them the drill by using your rink board diagram. Make sure that all players are seated where they can clearly see the board and check to see that they are paying attention!

Early in the season, you need to explain drills in greater detail. Be sure to ask the players if they understand the drill. Having a brief question-and-answer session is a good way to ensure that they understand the instructions. Or you can ask a player to explain the drill to his or her teammates.

Be sure to explain your practice plan in the order you want the drills done on the ice. Again, this technique facilitates recall. Be clear about each drill. Keep it simple. Be brief.

The mini-meeting is also your chance to set the tone and pace for the practice. Be upbeat and positive. Have players chomping at the bit to get out of that dressing room because they are keen, not bored!

Choosing a practice theme for the day

Select a theme for every practice and start the mini-meeting with the practice theme for that day. For example, you might say, "Today we're going to work on neutral zone play," or "Good news, team, today is a conditioning day."

You then run through the preliminary drills you have planned for practice, such as puck-handling and passing review drills. These drills may seem more general than theme-related, but you can relate them to the theme by saying something like, "You won't get through the neutral zone if you're not in control of your puck handling and passing. So we'll brush up on that first." Then move on to explain the specific theme drills.

However you describe it, you want your players to hit the ice excited and focused on the theme.

One or two themes for a practice are enough. Any more and you tend to get little accomplished.

Final Prepping As You Hit the Ice

As coach, you're responsible for making sure that the physical environment is safe for running a practice. Doors left ajar can cause injury if fallen into, and the ice may have ruts that can cause falls or twist ankles.

The rink isn't the only environment that can create risks. If a player falls and hits his head on the ice while wearing a faulty helmet, a concussion could result. Parents need to bear the burden of responsibility for seeing that their child is safely equipped, but the coach is the ultimate judge. For example, a parent may choose to let a kid play when he forgot his elbow pads, but a coach may not want to allow that.

Practicing safety first

Following is a list of safety items in the rink environment that a coach needs to check before allowing players on the ice for practice:

- ✔ Make sure the ice resurfacing machine has completely left the ice and that the maintenance door is closed and latched properly. This is a rule in most rinks, but be sure your team obeys!

- ✔ Circle the perimeter of the ice and make sure all the other doors that open to the ice are properly latched.

- ✔ Check the boards, nets, and glass for any dangerous conditions.

- ✔ Check the ice surface to see that it is in good repair. Ruts can lead to falls and injuries.

These checks soon become second nature and can be completed quickly to provide for a safe practice.

Checking up on the kids

You have one final, important check to conduct before practice begins: the kids themselves. While the players are going on the ice or warming up, observe them closely to ensure that each player is wearing the proper equipment and that the equipment is securely fastened. Don't let kids play if they appear sick. Note whether their skates are too big or their sticks too long. Some items, such as a cracked face shield, may require that the player be pulled from practice. Less serious items, such as long sticks or skates, can be remedied by the next practice.

Do all you can to ensure that the kids have a safe practice.

Starting the Practice

The first phase of practice serves two purposes: to warm-up and loosen up the players, and to set the tone for the practice. Meeting these purposes also includes some special attention for goaltenders after they've participated in the general warm-up.

Loosening up

Have players warm-up either formally or informally as they step on the ice. Make the initial activities loose, whole-body activities, such as skating and weaving with loose arm swings. Skating should include both forward and backward skating and clockwise and counterclockwise directions. Note that, for beginners, getting on the ice is normally warm-up enough, and their first theme drill may be forward or backward skating.

Conclude the warm-up with some loose stretching, especially for the shoulders, *hamstrings* (back of the thigh), *quadriceps* (front of the thigh), and *groin* (inside the thigh).

For beginners and some intermediate teams, players should then be ready for their first drill. If your team is advanced to the point of having designated goaltenders, warm them up at this point before proceeding further with practice (see "Goalie warm-ups" later in this chapter).

Setting the tone

You want to set an upbeat tone for practice from the first drill. For beginners, setting the tone is mostly psychological: Simply incorporate the elements of fun and accomplishment. For more skilled players, make the first drill a review of something they know or have already practiced so that they are not only challenged but also rewarded — even if it's only with the satisfaction of having done something right. This exercise helps to set a positive attitude as they go forward into the real work of practicing on the theme, which comes next.

Through this first phase of the practice, keep instruction simple, positive, and brief. Flow drills can form the basis for early practice drill selection once the players' skill level is sufficient to make that possible. For example, you may start a flow drill where the players skate the lines using forward and backward skating, then repeat the pattern with pucks, and then repeat the pattern a third time, ending with a shot on goal.

Use all the ice surface available for the initial practice drills and have all players moving and involved in the drills. Keep players moving with skills all players can do. This way, all players begin practice feeling competent and involved. You can add some complexity to these drills as the skill level and season progress. For example, add a passing component to skating and puck-handling drills. Have goaltenders perform all the drills to this point.

Goalie warm-ups

If you coach a team that has designated goalies, you need to have the team take some shots on goal to warm-up the goalies after the general team warm-up is completed. Always start the goalie warm-up using the longest shots your team has sufficient skill to perform with some consistency. Gradually move closer to the net as the drill progresses. Make sure players understand that their focus in these early shooting drills is on hitting the net. Coaches needn't design any more complex purpose in these drills, such as avoiding a check to get a shot away. The purpose of drills at this stage is simply for goalies to have an opportunity to make saves and handle shots.

In these early shooting drills, you can have the shooter do three to five push-ups or sit-ups immediately upon missing the net with a shot because he or she failed to make the goalie work. The kids will have fun kidding each other with this approach. Take care, though, to make sure that the exercises do not become punishment.

Running the Core Practice

The purpose of the core part of a practice is to focus on your theme(s). In working with your theme new skills are taught and new strategies are developed. Be consistent at this point; do not say one thing in the dressing room and do another on the ice.

Starting with success

Remind players of the theme and walk them through what you want so that they experience doing it right the first time. Then, if possible, use a drill the team already knows or that has some familiarity to practice the skill. For example, if the theme is 3-on-2 offense, and you covered an offensive 2-on-1 situation last practice, use that same 2-on-1 drill, modifying it to suit today's theme. The keys to core practice success are to teach clearly and build on what they know.

Everybody gets to practice

A friend was watching his 8-year-old son's practice. He heard the coach tell the 28 kids they were going to work on footwork by playing soccer on ice. Then he watched the coach throw a ball onto the ice to start the drill.

"Do you know how many kids touched that ball during that drill?" he asked us. "Three. How much footwork did the rest of the kids get to practice? How did that make them feel?"

Good questions! If you want to use a ball to work on footwork, have one ball per two to four kids and play keep-away in designated areas of the ice, such as the circles, where they are not liable to run into each other with their heads down.

Name drills after your players. It's fun and motivational. The "Charlie 2-on-1 Drill" puts Charlie at the front of the line and motivates him to lead his teammates in the drill. If you have 20 players, name a drill after each player, making sure to include everyone. This works at all ages!

Adding complexity

If you ensure the players develop a sound base over successive early-season practices, you can add elements of complexity to help players progress smoothly and rapidly. Set your themes for your core practice so that they build on the bases you have established in previous practices, rather than bouncing around from theme to unrelated theme. For example, with a beginner, a practice theme progression could go from forward starting to forward skating to forward stopping and then to forward turning. After you teach the same sequence for backward skating, you could add forward-to-backward and backward-to-forward pivots.

After skating skills are mastered, add pucks as early as possible in practice. Puck handling needs to become second nature to hockey players.

Pucks are for drill enhancement and not for individual amusement. You may want to impose a one-minute puck-and-player-to-the-bench timeout for those who misuse pucks. If you do this, don't *forget* the player on the bench!

Leaving 'em Laughing

Whenever possible, have a fun, positive activity to finish off practice. You can make the activity a scrimmage, a shoot-out competition, a skills relay race, a scoring competition, a best-play-of-the-game reenactment, or free time to practice whatever a player wants. Just make sure that everyone is involved in a positive way.

When using a scrimmage, add several pucks to maximize puck-handling time for the kids or have cross-ice scrimmages so that more kids are involved more of the time.

At the end of practice, bring the players together on the ice. Give them a quick, positive comment about the practice that leaves them high-fiving you and each other as they leave the ice.

Chapter 5

Game On!

*F*inally! You get to coach a game, to act out the picture you had in your head the day you said, "Yes, I'll coach."

As you may have noticed, 90 percent of your coaching job has already been done. The discipline, skill execution, and motivation standards you set in practices can now transfer to your games. You virtually always get back in games what you've done in practices.

So, stand back and enjoy directing the game. Let the kids enjoy playing, and make observations about what needs to be worked on at the next practice.

In approaching any game, you need to know from your hockey association ahead of time what game rules are in place, such as length of periods, amount of ice time, officiating priorities, and other topics on conduct (refer to Chapter 3 for some tips). Secondly, if you're coaching an advanced team, try to find out something about your coaching opponent: What style of offense or defense does he prefer? What are the skills of his key players? Such information helps you prepare your players for the game.

If you're coaching intermediate or beginner players for whom strategy is less of an issue, try to be aware of the other team's strongest and weakest players so that you can match skills on lines. If players can play against others of similar skill level, the game is more challenging and productive for all players. Coordinate with the other coach ahead of time if possible.

To make game coaching easy, think about the game in three phases:

✔ **Pre-game:** Includes arrival, meeting, warm-up, game plan, and parental procedures

✔ **In game:** Covers bench management, communication, motivation, emotional tone, ice time, officials, and between periods

✔ **Post-game:** Includes the on-ice handshake, dressing room talk, and departure

The extent to which you deal with these factors varies according to the skill and age level you are coaching. In the remainder of this chapter, we provide suggestions for smooth pre-game, in-game, and post-game coaching at all these levels.

Considering Age and Ability Factors

The game priorities for a coach of beginner hockey players differ remarkably from those for a coach of advanced players. Compare helping five little kids know when to go on or get off the ice versus requesting tighter backchecking (we discuss backchecking in Chapter 11). So this section starts with some general considerations to coaching a game at different age and ability levels that should be in the back of your mind through any game.

Coaching beginners' games

At the youngest age and lowest ability level, the coach can often be on the ice with the players during games. You can physically line up players for face-offs so that they begin to connect visually with correct positioning. Communication should match the players' attention span — which is short. All players at this level play the same amount, which allows you to help players on and off the ice. You open and close the doors. Sit players in units of five so that they are ready to go on the ice as a playing unit. Remember to rotate each player through the goalie position as part of the game — this is the time to provide all players with the opportunity to find out whether they have a penchant for this unique position. The expectation for all players is to have fun; the final score of the game must not be important.

Coaching intermediate players' games

As players get older, you'll see a wider range in abilities within the same age category. You still need to distribute playing time equally because the pace of learning at this stage remains dramatic. However, coaching challenges change. Ideally, the coaches of each team should work together to match players of similar skill level against each other to optimize their challenge. Communication should still be simple, consistent, and always positive.

As some players clearly start to dominate over others, you as coach have an excellent opportunity to teach team play. Have the dominant players understand the need to work with teammates for success. You want the fun expectation to remain in place, but you also want players to realize the value of team play and sportsmanship. The fun should come as much from the quality of team play and the spirit of sportsmanship as from the final score.

Coaching advanced players' games

Advanced teams are often divided into groups based on ability. If this happens, coaches still should strive to have players of similar abilities play against each other. This strategy is especially important when you coach a level where checking is allowed: Size can range considerably at the preteen age, so stress safety. Bigger players need to understand checking skills and respect their opponents. Smaller players need to know how to roll with a hit. For information about checking, refer to Chapter 15.

If your hockey association allows for the coach to assign ice time, you may begin to give more ice time to skilled offensive players by letting them play the power plays. If this is so, be sure to give other players more penalty-killing time. The most skilled players may get slightly more ice time, but never exclude any player from his or her fair share. All players at this age are still there to learn and improve and to have fun. Bench time is rarely fun.

Communication at this level can be more instructive on the bench. Still, you need to keep your communication simple, short, and positive — constructive, not destructive.

Creating Your Game Plan

The best way to ensure that you focus during the game on what is important at the age and ability level you are coaching is to do one more plan ahead of time — a game plan. (We discuss other pre-game plans for you to consider in Chapter 4.)

We strongly recommend you prepare a coach's game card for each game. You can keep it in your pocket or on a clipboard throughout the game. Have room on your game card to make notes about what you want to say at the pre-game chalk talk, during between-period talks, and at the post-game wrap-up. Also include space for future practice-planning notes. List your lines and defense pairs for the game, if appropriate. Figure 5-1 provides a sample of a coach's game card that may suit an advanced recreational team. You can modify it to suit any level. The card is designed to be two-sided (you can copy the sample back to back); fold the sheet down the middle like a book for ease of use during the game.

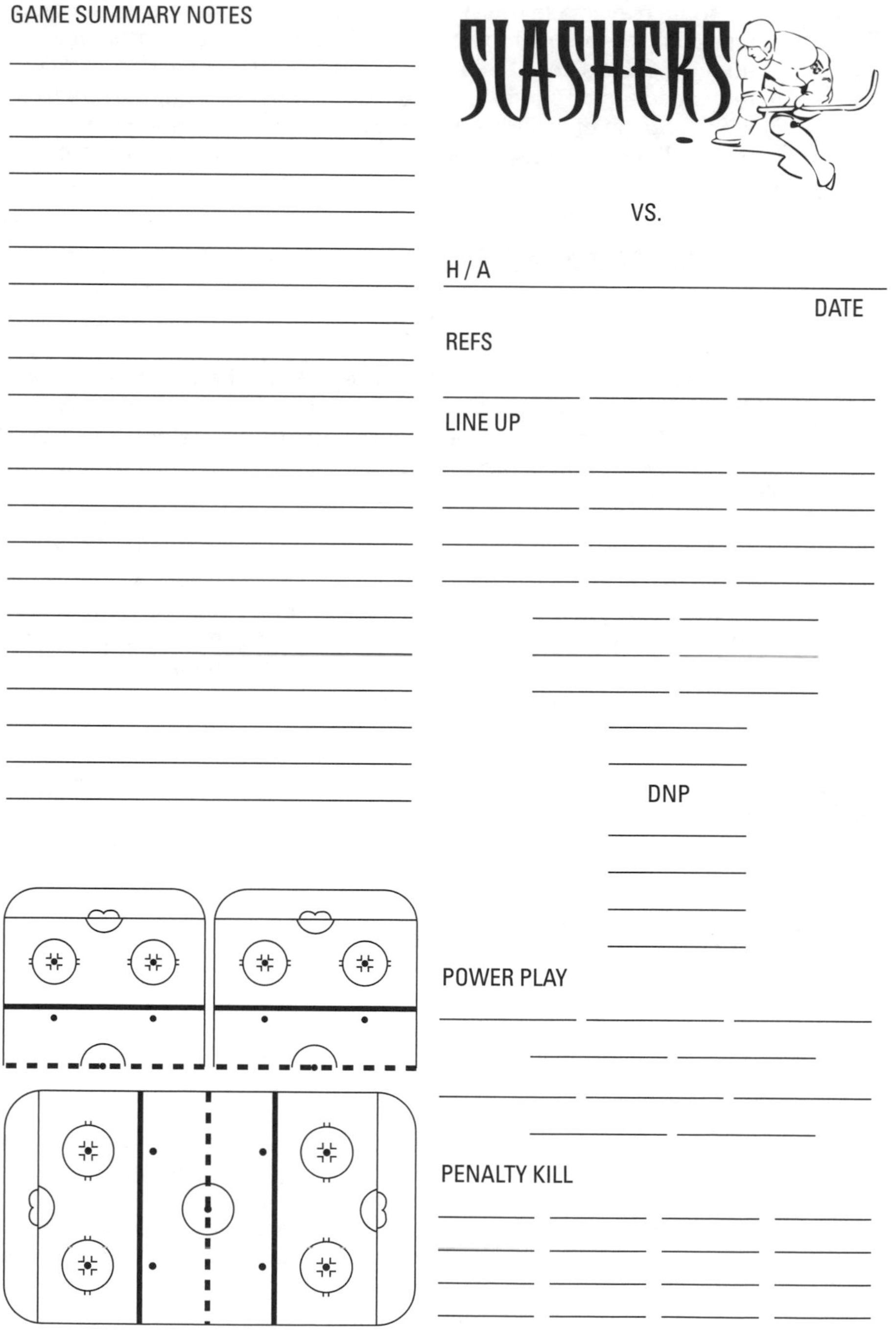

GAME SUMMARY NOTES

SLASHERS

VS.

H / A

DATE

REFS

LINE UP

DNP

POWER PLAY

PENALTY KILL

Figure 5-1:
Coach's
secret
game notes.

OPPOSITION

GAME PLAN:

1 – _____

_____

_____

2 – _____

_____

_____

3 – _____

_____

_____

LINE UP

_____ _____ _____

_____ _____ _____

_____ _____ _____

_____ _____ _____

_____ _____

_____ _____

_____ _____

_____

_____

DNP

_____ _____

_____ _____

GAME SUMMARY NOTES:

_____

_____

_____

_____

_____

_____

_____

_____

_____

_____

_____

_____

_____

_____

_____

_____

_____

_____

_____

_____

_____

1st PERIOD _____

_____

2nd PERIOD _____

_____

3rd PERIOD _____

_____

_____

SLASHERS	1	2	3	OT	Tot
SCORE	___	___	___	___	___
SHOTS	___	___	___	___	___
S. C.	___	___	___	___	___
HITS	___	___	___	___	___

OPPONENT	1	2	3	OT	Tot
SCORE	___	___	___	___	___
SHOTS	___	___	___	___	___
S. C.	___	___	___	___	___
HITS	___	___	___	___	___

Figure 5-1: H / A = Home / Away
Continued. DNP = Did not play
S. C. = Scoring chances

In principle, follow this game card design:

- ✔ **Page 1 (when folded):** Have your line-up, which for beginners may simply be your starting groups of five in order of rotation.
- ✔ **Page 2:** List one to three things you want to focus on during the game. Beneath that, leave space to note how you are meeting those objectives as the game progresses.
- ✔ **Page 3:** Include information on your opponents, which for beginners may be space to list the big players or the highly skilled kids to match with your own big or skilled player(s). Secondly, have room on the third page for any specific game information you may want to record, such as who's getting the shots and from where, or how the third period was played.
- ✔ **Page 4:** Keep post-game notes, such as future practice suggestions or some weakness you noticed in an individual player that needs work.

The rink diagrams are for individual or line instructional purposes, such as showing a player where she moved on the last play versus where she would have been better to move in her defensive positioning.

Walking the Pre-game Chalk Talk

Before a game, you need a few minutes of the players' time and undivided attention to get them focused on what you want during the game. To protect that time from interruption, decide on an arrival time for games that works for you and your preparation needs. For example, you may want ten minutes to talk prior to game time. Determine your dressing room procedures accordingly and inform the parents of your policy.

Have players wear something special to games, such as a jacket with a team logo or a team hat. This helps to make the game special to your players and that may help you get them focused more easily for your chalk talk.

Establishing dressing room procedures

Young players mainly need to get their equipment on and get on the ice for warm-up; they don't need much of a talk. However, you need to set a pre-game arrival time so that you have no last-minute panic to get on the ice. If you need parents to help players with their equipment, set the arrival time that gets the job done a few minutes before game time.

For players who are able to get themselves ready for games, you may determine that they arrive at the dressing room 45 minutes prior to game time, so they have time to get dressed and be ready by the 10-minute chalk-talk time.

Sadly, in this day and age, we must advise coaches that you never want to find yourself alone with any player in the dressing room. Always have an assistant or parent nearby.

For any age, have a strategy for parents. Parents must be clear about dressing room procedures — when it's okay to be in the room and when they need to leave.

Let parents know in advance that, if they want to talk with you about something, they need to do so outside the half-hour before and after practices and games. Inside this time period is for kids.

Practicing the KISS approach

KISS is an acronym for "keep it simple, stupid," and that is the rule for pre-game chalk talks. Keep the meeting short. Present your game plan making no more than three points. One point can relate to offense, one to defense, and one to a topic such as team play, motivation, discipline, or fair play. Then, with a cheer, send the players out for warm-up, assuming they have one.

Make the warm-up simple: skating, with a minimum of passing and shooting. Then it's back to the bench for a reminder of the game plan focus in three words or less, and on with the game.

Plan a basic warm-up that you can use every game. Make sure to rehearse the warm-up in practice sessions so that players always know what to do, rather than having to think it through and risk getting distracted from the game focus.

Setting Up the Bench

Good bench management makes for smooth shift changes, which makes a team more effective on the ice. It also results in fewer too-many-men-on-the-ice penalties. Two factors that influence smooth bench activity are where players sit and how they switch on and off the ice.

Handing out seating assignments

Beginners and some intermediate players should play every position. Have these players slide along the bench, staying in order, moving toward the offensive-end door until their turn comes to go on the ice. As coach, you need to assign positions to the next five players sitting on the bench while they're waiting their turn to go on. When the whistle blows for a player change, all players will know their new position before going on the ice.

As players get bigger and stronger, they'll start playing specific positions. At this stage, have defensemen sit near the door closest to the net they are defending. Forwards should sit with their line mates at the end of the bench nearest the opponent's net.

Switching strategy

Young players should come off the ice through the door closest to their own goal and go on the ice through the door nearest the opponent's goal so that they can be in the best position to join the attack. When players sit on the bench according to position, have defensemen use the defensive-end door for changing, and have forwards use the door nearest the opponent's net. When players are physically able to do so, have them come off the ice using the doors at their respective ends of the bench and have the players going on the ice go over the boards.

You'll find that having the defensemen and forwards who are going on the ice over the boards toward the middle of the bench is usually easier. This allows players coming off the ice to have more room to get on the bench.

The coach calls out the names of the players who are next to go on the ice while they are waiting on the bench. Then as the line change begins, the players call out the names of the players they will replace. This helps the players stay focused and helps to avoid too-many-men penalties against your team.

These switching strategies keep players going in one direction only in any one bench area and minimize confusion and potential collisions between players.

Include a drill during practice sessions that helps each player be aware of when a line change is occurring and be able to execute the change smoothly. Simply have a five-player unit involved in a drill on ice. Then blow the whistle and have these five go to the bench and five new players come on the ice. Clear up any confusion.

Communicating on the Bench

Keep open two lines of communication on the bench. First and foremost, communication needs to go from the coach to the players with very little in the reverse direction (upon request only). Some of this communication occurs during the game and some during breaks in the game, but the operative feature is that the communication is done on the bench.

Trying to communicate with players on the ice by yelling out instructions really is a waste of time. Save your breath! Talk to your players when they get back to the bench.

The second line of communication goes from officials to coaches. Again, very little of this communication should go in the reverse direction (for rules clarification only). If a big issue does arise, wait until after the game to make your point.

Apply the same rules to all personnel on your bench, including assistants, trainers, and players. Remember that, as the coach, you set the standard. Rules need to include such things as no yelling at the officials, positive talk only amongst teammates, and no criticism of others.

Talking to players

Always make in-game communication positive. You add motivation to the players to whom you give the positive comments as well as to players on the bench who overhear the comments. Even if your personality is rather laid-back, you can be upbeat and a bit of a cheerleader on the bench by being positive.

Coaches impress kids with their actions too

A friend's 9-year-old son was having a great hockey game; his team was leading 4-1 and everyone was playing and having fun. Then, with two minutes left to play, his coach pulled their goalie — the ultimate insult when a team is already well ahead in the game. One of his teammates scored, making it 5-1. The coach put their goalie back in, and his team scored again, easily on the demoralized young opponents. The game ended with a 6-1 score.

What was that coach thinking? More importantly, what lesson did he teach his own players: whack 'em when they're down? What did those kids learn about sportsmanship and respect? He showed them, loud and clear.

At the same time, always keep your emotional level under control. If you get out of control on the bench, you can be sure your players will get out of control emotionally too. Remember the old adage that actions speak louder than words. You tip the kids off to your psychological state if you whack a stick against the boards. Similarly, you show contempt for sportsmanship if you play your top players all the time.

Communicating between periods

The first priority of the break between periods is for players to rest and re-group. Leave the players alone for a few minutes. Even if teams simply change ends, relax first and then re-group. With young players, you may simply repeat your focus phrase or the theme for the day: "Remember, keep your head up and your stick down."

With more competitive teams who get a break in the dressing room, you can institute some minor playing adjustments if needed. For example, "They're beating us on the left side. Right defense, play up tighter; centers, pinch in a bit to cover their backs." Again, slip a positive comment in somewhere: "You *can* stop them," or "You're doing great on offense. Keep it up." Keep any comments about the changes the players need to make brief. Less is better.

Communicating with officials

Referees often mirror the performance of young teams and players: They make good calls and not-so-good calls. Make the role of referee one that demands respect from your players and from your staff. You are the only team member who should be permitted to challenge officials. Any challenge needs to be made in a mature way. If not, don't make a challenge. An even better policy is to hold any rules challenges until after the game. Then ask genuine questions of the officials in a post-game meeting.

Wrapping Up after the Game

After the game, players are physically and emotionally tired. Their energy levels may be high or low, depending on the outcome of the game. This is a good time to instill some team traditions. Win or lose, all players could, for example, rally around the goalie for a quick team cheer before any ritual handshake with opponents. If a handshake does take place, make sure it is done with a spirit of sportsmanship.

In the dressing room, be sure to maintain a light atmosphere. This is not the NHL. Win or lose, young players should feel at least some sense of accomplishment and satisfaction with their effort and with their teamwork as they gather in the dressing room with teammates. Sometimes when you lose, the other team was just better or luckier that day. Focus on what the team did right.

You may want to consider having a granola bar award for the most improved player in a specific skill that you've been working on all week.

Parents need to know what you want them to do post-game, such as meeting their child in the lobby at a specific time. You do *not* want parents in the dressing room criticizing team or individual play, not even their own child's.

Make the departure from the dressing room full of positives: "Nice effort." "Thanks guys." "See you at practice." Even, "We'll get 'em next time," if need be.

Also send players away with the necessary information for the next event(s), such as the next scheduled practice, game, or off-ice workout. Make sure the players check for all their belongings before departing.

Game Time in a Nutshell

After the game is on, you don't have much time to think; you just have time to react. To predispose your actions toward something approaching "positive," run down this list before each game begins:

- ✔ **Show respect.** Be respectful toward the opposition, the referees, and the team's game plan.
- ✔ **Set your focus.** Look to your team's strengths and the opponent's weaknesses.
- ✔ **Keep it simple.** Have a game plan that focuses on no more than three clear points.
- ✔ **Explain bench management.** Decide how you want to run the bench, then let all players and team personnel know how the bench will work.
- ✔ **Check player motivation.** Players can range from fired up to focused to flat. Give them specific targets or goals for their game so they can focus. Ideally, you want them relaxed yet upbeat.
- ✔ **Give players confidence.** Let each player know that they can get the job done, just like they did in practice or a previous game.

✔ **Reinforce honest effort.** Players should know the importance of working hard every shift. That means that to try and fail is better than failing to try.

✔ **Establish discipline.** Remind players to stay with the team game plan and play by the team rules of sportsmanship, team play, and respect.

✔ **Constructive communication.** At this stage, players are there to learn from experience; they won't play perfect hockey games. Be constructive with all communication and conclude with a positive comment.

✔ **Go home.** Do not give any long, post-game review. The kids came to the game for a good time. Make notes of what you need to do next practice, find something positive to say to the kids, then close the door behind you.

Part II
Coaching Beginners

The 5th Wave   By Rich Tennant

"We covered the basics today—skating backwards, handling the puck, and why I have hair growing out my nose."

In this part . . .

This part outlines the skills beginner hockey players need to learn to get started. We give you techniques and step-by-step progressions to use to teach these skills effectively. We also provide specific drills that you can use to help players practice these skills. We conclude this part with some suggestions for focusing your coaching approach at this level.

Chapter 6

Teaching Fundamental Skills

· ·

In This Chapter

▶ Teaching beginners how to skate forward and backward

▶ Showing players how to control the puck with their stick

▶ Instructing beginning players on how to pass and receive passes

· ·

A great teacher and hockey expert, John "Doc" Meagher, once wrote, "Excellent hockey performance results from a mastery of the fundamental skills of skating, puck handling, passing, shooting, and checking." Doc Meagher's statement is as true, and perhaps more profound, today as it was when he wrote it in *Coaching Hockey* in 1972. We suggest that you take the Doc's advice and teach beginners to do the simplest of hockey skills very well.

The best place to start for beginners is with basic skating and puck skills. These fundamentals of hockey are developed easily if taught in sequence, such as the one presented in this chapter. The sequence is continued later in Part III for intermediate players and in Part IV for advanced players so that you can refine their skills as the players grow through each level of the sport.

Coaches must start at the most basic levels and should refuse to move on to more advanced levels until the basics are solidly in place. Otherwise, development at the higher levels is seriously compromised. With endless drills available to teach fundamentals, it is neither difficult nor boring to make abundantly sure your players are comfortably efficient with a skill level before moving on to a more advanced level. Make learning the basics fun for your players by including game drills and contests. At the same time, keep drills within the skill level of your players for optimum progress.

Include a fun drill in every practice plan. Almost any game that you can play on land can be played on ice and will provide a teaching component for some hockey skill. An example is the children's game of frozen tag; it's fun on ice and works on skating skills.

In Chapter 7, you can find drills for practicing the skills we discuss in this chapter.

Teaching Skating Skills

The only place to start hockey instruction is with skating fundamentals. Even after players learn to skate, their practices should include drills that improve some aspect of their skating.

Good skating features many diverse elements, such as an ability to move forward and backward, and to turn and switch from forward to backward and back again. As with most skills, these pieces are best taught in sequence. For beginners, start with focusing on the skills associated with forward and backward skating. This includes teaching the basic body postures to assume, how to start, how to get a good stride, and how to stop. After players become competent at these skills, you can work on pivots, turns, and lateral movement, all of which we cover in Part III of this book. However, you may have players who progress quickly through the forward and backward skating skills, so keep moving. The intermediate level is generally the progression you hope for toward the end of a beginner's season.

The upcoming sections provide an effective sequence for instructing forward and backward skating to beginners. Note that we don't recommend introducing pucks just yet. Pucks cause focus overload if included too early in instruction and inhibit players' skating progress. Refer to the section "Teaching Stick and Puck Skills," later in this chapter, to discover how and when to introduce pucks.

Some teams hire a professional skating instructor to teach good skating technique in a practice. Discuss sharing the cost with other teams who would like to join in the opportunity.

Forward skating

If you watch 20 hockey players skate the length of the ice, you'll probably see 20 different forward-skating styles ranging from easy and fluid to short and choppy. So, teaching young players how to skate well is well worth the time. Here are the pieces you need to put together to help players achieve strong, fluid forward skating.

Ready position

Forward skating begins with having players assume a proper starting stance. This stance provides the basis for both stability and mobility. Here are the steps for the players:

1. Stand with your skates shoulder-width apart and your skate blades turned slightly out.

2. Bend slightly forward at the waist and put a bend at the knees that places your knees out over your skates.

3. Place two hands on the stick, keeping the blade of the stick on the ice. Place the top hand at the top of the stick shaft with the top edge of the glove flush with the end of the stick. Bend that elbow so that your hand is level with the hollow at the waist and in front of the body.

4. Reach the lower hand approximately a forearm length down the shaft and grip the shaft so that your arm is straight through the elbow and isn't locked. The lower hand will be adjusted up and down the shaft for certain shots and passes that come later, but for beginners, keep the placement consistent.

5. Keep your head up.

See Figure 6-1 for an example of a good ready position.

Stick length is very important. If the blade of the stick isn't flat on the ice when the player is in the ready position, then the stick length is wrong. If the toe of the blade is off the ice, the stick is too long. If the heel is off the ice, the stick is too short. To determine proper stick length, have each player stand erect on their skates, holding their hockey stick vertically with the tip of the blade on the ice between their feet and with the butt end near their face. The stick's butt end should be between the player's chin and nose. Cut off any excess. Get a new stick if the shaft is too short.

Forward starting

From the ready position, while players remain in place, have the players slide their skates slightly back to bring their heels together as they turn the toes of their skates out to create approximately a 45-degree angle.

Check to see that players keep their knees bent and maintain the slight forward bend at the waist described in the preceding "Ready position" section.

Players can use a chair or the boards for support while practicing this heel action. If a player is struggling, you can support him by holding the stick parallel to the ice while he holds on to the stick for balance.

Figure 6-1:
Ready,
set . . . from
the front
and side.

When players are comfortable with the heel action, add additional forward lean from the waist. This forward lean should automatically start the player actually moving forward. See Figure 6-2 for the appropriate body position. Players are forced, at this point, to take a step, usually with their dominant leg, to retain balance. That step is their forward start.

Initially, have players keep both hands on the stick and check to see that they keep their heads up. As they gain balance and confidence, you can have them release the lower hand off the stick.

Forward striding

After players achieve forward movement, add the forward skating stride. As the dominant foot steps forward, have players turn the nondominant knee and skate out to a 70- to 90-degree angle. Then have the players push off by fully extending the nondominant leg until it can push no further. See Figure 6-3 for this full stride position. Then have players return the skate to the start position, keeping it close to the ice all the way back until it touches down beside the dominant foot. They may need to glide momentarily to retain balance, in which case their blades can point straight forward at the end of the stride recovery.

Figure 6-2:
. . . Go!
Forward.

Figure 6-3:
Push all
the way.

In preparation for the next stride, check to see that players' knees are bent and angled out over their skates at about 45 degrees. Then have the players lean forward to initiate a step out with the nondominant foot. This time, the dominant leg must turn out 70 to 90 degrees and push off to full extension. Once again, have the players follow the extension with a low return to the ready position.

As players maintain balance and get full extension on the strides, you can begin to speed up the transition from dominant to nondominant legs until their strides alternate smoothly. If they are having trouble getting the full stride, have the players push off and return the same leg four to six times in a row, and then switch to the other leg. This drill is also useful for strengthening a weak stride.

The next step is to coordinate leg and arm action. When striding with the left leg extended back, the right arm should reach forward and vise versa. On the back swing, elbows should go no higher than the shoulders while keeping the stick blade on the ice, whether using one hand or both hands on the stick.

Younger skaters have a tendency to use cross-body action with their arms. Balance improves if you encourage a forward-backward motion and eliminate any cross-body motion.

Edges

Encourage players at this stage to explore their skate edges. Each skate has two edges, an inside and an outside edge. When skating forward, players use the inside edge to push off against the ice to gain forward momentum. Other skating skills discussed in this chapter use inside and outside edges.

Introduce edges by having players do some fun skating, such as slalom skating in which they keep their feet parallel while they weave left and right like slalom skiers going down a hill. Or you can use hourglass skating in which players start with their feet together, then press them out, away from each other, then draw them back together, making an hourglass shape on the ice. One way to practice these movements is to have players skate forward at half speed to the blue line, then skate slalom or hourglass to the next blue line, then forward skate to the end of the rink.

Forward stopping

The forward stop is typically a challenge for young players. They often begin stopping by using the snowplow technique similar to what is seen in skiing. In it, players toe in and press the outside edges of their skates against the ice. Ultimately, this is not a useful hockey stop. We recommend you teach the one-foot drag as a better stepping stone.

To use the one-foot drag, have players put their weight on one skate and place the other skate perpendicular to and behind the supporting skate. The player then drags the perpendicular blade against the ice, pressing down until he comes to a stop. See Figure 6-4 for the proper foot position. Have players practice this technique using both the left and right foot as the support leg, which gives them a base for eventually learning the two-foot stop to either the left or right.

Figure 6-4:
When all else fails, drag a skate.

To teach the proper two-foot hockey stop from the one-foot drag, instruct players to

1. Place two hands on the stick and have the stick blade on the ice.

2. Push off for one forward stride.

3. Place the skate that pushed off at a 'T' position behind the heel of their front skate and drag their back skate on the ice to slow their progress.

4. Shift their weight to the dragged skate as they simultaneously lift the front skate and place it parallel to the dragged skate.

5. Press against the ice using the outside edge of the dragged skate and the inside edge of the previously supporting skate, keeping their weight on both blades, slightly toward the toes.

6. Assume the ready position as soon as they have stopped.

When players can drag-stop into a parallel stop, they are ready for the final phase of learning the two-foot stop. Have them start by doing some two-foot jumps in place keeping feet shoulder-width apart. Next, add a quarter turn to the jump, still having them land in place. Do this to the right and to the left. To succeed at the quarter turns, players have to lead into the turn by turning first their shoulders and then their hips in the direction of the quarter turn. That same action is required going into the proper hockey stop, so this exercise is a good way to develop the habit. Once you see players using the shoulder and hip lead, they are ready to return to instruction on completing the forward hockey stop.

Gradually build up to having the players turning both skates as soon as they initiate the drag, using the shoulder and hip turn, then pressing the blades against the ice as explained earlier in the section. See Figure 6-5 for the correct body position in a proper two-foot hockey stop. Slowly build up speed leading up to the stop. These steps will increase the chances of players successfully developing this stopping technique.

Figure 6-5:
Stopping
like a pro.

Throughout your instruction, make sure players bend their knees so that the legs can act as shock absorbers. This technique will ultimately allow them to perform the stop at any speed.

A great way to practice stops once players can perform this skill while skating with some forward speed is to line them up on the goal line. On the whistle, have the players take two or three strides and then stop, facing the boards. (Use the players' bench boards to be consistent.) Repeat this, covering the length of the ice. Coming back down the ice from the opposite end, have players face the same side of the ice (players' bench). This results in having the players practice stopping on both the left and right sides. Use the bench as the side to face in all skating drills involving turns, stops, or starts so that players always get to practice the action to both the left and right sides.

Backward skating

Just when players feel like they're getting somewhere, you'll go and introduce backward skating! You may have to remind them that skating forward to score goals is only half of the game of hockey; they also have to do some fancy stuff backwards to stop the other team from scoring.

To progress quickly through the backward skating skills, use a similar sequence to what we recommend for forward skating: ready position, starting, striding, and stopping.

Ready position

Backward skating begins with a stable yet versatile ready position that differs slightly from the forward ready position. This time, players take their lower hand off the stick so that they can bring their upper body more upright from the waist. This should put their shoulders over their hips. They also need to bend their knees more deeply so that they look like they are about to sit. Make sure they keep their heads up. See Figure 6-6 for the proper body position.

Check that players keep their sticks on the ice with the lower arm straight and the blade of the stick toeing inward. Check also that players' skates are shoulder-width apart and slightly toed in.

Backward starting

To prepare players to start going backwards, have them in the ready position with the heel of the dominant foot turned out to approximately a 45-degree angle. Make sure they keep their weight over both skates. They then put pressure on the inside edge of the turned-out skate. See Figure 6-7 for the correct body position and foot placement.

Figure 6-6:
Skating
backwards.
Ready,
set, . . .

Figure 6-7:
Go!
Backwards.

COACHING CUE

Check to see that players' backs and heads are upright, not bent forward looking at their feet.

Backward striding

From the backward start, have players start to cut a big c (inverse c with the right leg) in the ice as they push with the inside edge of the blade. This action forces the players to push from the hip, rather than just from the ankles or knees. A hip drive provides a much stronger stride. See Figure 6-8 for an example of a good backward skating stride. Toward the end of the c, players should return the pushing skate to the starting position beside the supporting skate.

Figure 6-8:
Push from
the hip.

In the early learning stages, when players return the pushing skate, you can have them glide with skates parallel and shoulder width apart. This gives them a chance to feel for the correct posture and balance. As they master their balance, they'll return the pushing skate to the toe of the supporting skate with the heel turned out so that they are immediately ready to transfer their weight and begin a stride with the other leg.

During the recovery phase when players need to use a glide, have them think of cutting a question mark in the ice with the inside edge of the blade, then flattening out for the stem of the question mark.

As players begin to alternate left and right backward strides down the ice, check to see that they are maintaining a good backward skating posture with their shoulders over their hips, their heads up, and their stick blades on the ice. Also check that they are pushing with their whole leg from the hip, and not just from the knee down.

Arm action, when skating backwards, is initiated at the elbow and moves in a forward to backward motion. Players should drive backward with the opposite elbow to the pushing leg, to a maximum of shoulder height. Arm action is more controlled in backward rather than forward skating.

Backward stopping

The backward stop begins with players placing both hands on the stick while keeping the blade on the ice. Have players bring both heels together while the knees bend out over their skates. Players will have to lean slightly forward from the waist to maintain balance. Have them press the insides of their skate blades against the ice until they stop. When players stop this way, they end up in the forward ready position. See Figure 6-9 for the body alignment and foot position in a backward stop.

Figure 6-9:
Whoa there — backward stopping.

Make sure players keep their heads up and their sticks on the ice throughout the stop. Also emphasize the knee bend to control balance and pressure against the ice.

Use slow speeds when first teaching the backward stop. One or two strides are all that is needed for adequate speed. At the same time, keep players away from the boards as they practice to avoid having them fall into the boards and risk injury.

One way to practice initial backward skating and stopping is to have the kids skate backwards around the perimeter of the ice. When you blow the whistle, they all stop. On two blasts, they resume backward skating. Be sure to change direction halfway through the drill so that both legs get to be the outside pusher on corners. Vary the length of time between whistles, sometimes making it very short, for fun.

Teaching Stick and Puck Skills

The statement, "He who handles the puck least handles it best" holds a lot of truth. Generally though, players love to have the puck on their stick. So you may as well make sure they get good at it.

Concentrate on these four areas of instruction while helping beginning players develop their puck skills:

- ✔ Stationary puck handling
- ✔ Forward skating with the puck (using two hands and one hand)
- ✔ Skating backward with the puck
- ✔ Stopping with the puck

You can teach each skill using a progression like the one explained in the next section. Then turn to Chapter 7 for drills that you can use to practice these skills.

Puck handling

If players can't handle the puck well, they'll never play the game of hockey well. Control and accuracy are the end points players must reach to master puck skills. They can get there if you start at the most simple level and gradually work up to the more complex versions of the skills. That sequence starts here.

Stationary puck handling

Start working on puck handling with players in the ready position.

Players need to have both hands on the stick, as described in the "Ready position" section earlier in this chapter, with their sticks in front of their bodies and the pucks in the middle of their stick blades. Players then move the puck to the left and right, going only as wide as their skates. Check to see that they maintain the proper *ready stance* while moving the puck back and forth, with their skates shoulder-width apart, their knees bent, their trunks leaning forward from the waist, and their heads up.

As they push and catch the puck from left to right, tell players to cradle the puck at each end of the puck-handling movement. That means the stick blade should lean over the puck, both when pushing or catching, yet still be in contact with the ice surface. See Figure 6-10 for the correct stick and body position.

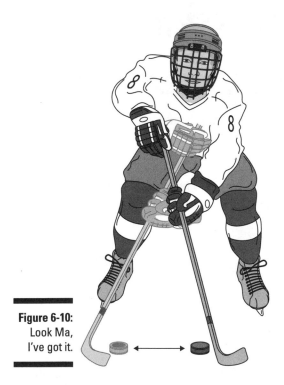

Figure 6-10:
Look Ma,
I've got it.

Check to see that players roll their wrists to allow the blade of the stick to cradle the puck, rather than using a stiff-arm action. Listen for players who slap or bat the puck rather than push or slide it. Sliding gives greater control. Be sure that players shift their weight to the left and right as they catch the puck so that they have weight (provides power) behind their next slide.

Initially you can allow players to look down toward the puck to see what they are doing. But as soon as possible, encourage them to "feel" the puck on their stick rather than look at it. Ultimately, you want players to keep their heads up all the time they are puck handling.

Have players use a comfortable grip on the stick for best control. Squeezing the stick tightly only makes puck handling more difficult. Relaxed muscles in the forearms allow for the best puck handling.

After players become competent at handling the puck in front of their body, you can begin to work on having them handle the puck outside their skates. Start by extending the width of the puck handling to slightly wider than the skates. Have them bring the puck back to the middle with each left or right slide and catch.

The next step is to have them slide the puck so that they have to lean totally outside the skate to catch the puck and bring it back to the middle. Have them do the same action to the outside of both the right and left skates going back to the middle each time.

When players get comfortable with these basic puck-handling moves, you can add drills that include other movements while still stationary, such as the figure eight drill in Chapter 7. Check to see that players always slide and cradle the puck, rather than slap and bang the puck.

Forward-skating puck handling

Skating forward with the puck requires a few minor adjustments to stationary puck-handling skills. First have players skate forward without the puck, keeping their normal skating stance, with a bend at the waist, head up, and full skating stride. Instruct them to keep two hands on the stick and to turn the toe of the stick slightly out while bringing the heel of the stick in. This allows better control of the puck as they move forward because the puck now needs to be propelled forward at an angle so that it stays ahead of the skater. Have them practice sliding an imaginary puck side to side, angling forward as they skate the length of the ice while you check the angle of their stick blade as they move it back and forth. Also check that placement of the blade stays far enough in front of their body that they would be able to see the puck without looking down, yet not so far in front that the puck would be difficult to control.

Next, add pucks as players skate the length of the ice. See Figure 6-11 for an example of good puck and body position while skating forward. Note that when the puck is in contact with the stick blade, the puck should rest between the heel and the midline of the blade. Encourage players to keep puck movement inside their skating stride width for best control.

Figure 6-11:
Now you're getting somewhere.

Check that players angle the puck forward, that they can see the puck with their heads up, and that they push and cradle the puck as they send it forward.

Sometimes in hockey, a player will want to have only one hand on the stick. To switch to one hand, the player removes the lower hand from the stick and adjusts the position of the stick so that the top hand moves outside the player's body. This brings the blade of the stick parallel to the hips with the heel of the blade roughly in front of the shoulder of the gripping hand. The player then keeps the puck in the middle of the blade and directs it forward smoothly against the bottom edge of the blade. A player does not push the puck from side to side as in two-handed skating with the puck. See Figure 6-12 for positioning for one-handed puck handling.

To return to two-handed control, the player simply keeps skating, places the lower hand on the stick again, and returns to angled slide-and-catch forward action.

After you've taught these skills, have the players practice by skating the perimeter of the ice. On one whistle, have them switch from two hands to one hand on the stick. On the next whistle, have them return to two hands. Remember to have players skate in reverse direction halfway through the drill.

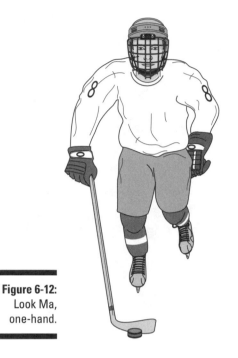

Figure 6-12:
Look Ma,
one-hand.

Backward skating with the puck

Players are to keep two hands on the stick as they skate backwards with the puck. They then turn the heel of the stick blade slightly out, bringing the toe of the stick in, as they skate backward down the ice. Players control the puck by using a wrist roll action to alternately cup the blade over the puck to the right and left while keeping the puck consistently in front of their bodies. See Figure 6-13 for good puck and body position.

Check to see that players maintain the correct body position with their shoulders over their hips, their knees bent to simulate an almost sitting position, and their heads up.

Stopping with the puck

Players need to be able to control the puck when they come to a full stop and also to protect the puck from being stolen. They need this skill when skating both forward and backward. The techniques for stopping with the puck build on the skills developed to this point.

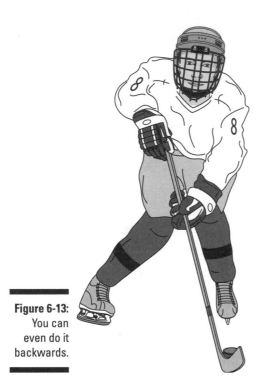

Figure 6-13:
You can
even do it
backwards.

Forward stopping with the puck

Players use the same technique they learned when stopping without the puck, which includes bending the knees, bringing the skates parallel, keeping the head up, and having two hands on the stick. To control the puck, have them add a roll of the wrists to close the blade of the stick over the puck against the direction the puck is sliding. See Figure 6-14 for an illustration of the technique.

After stopping, have players immediately resume the ready position with the puck on the blade of their sticks and their heads up, looking for possibilities. Also practice with the player being checked by another player. The stop in this case is then made so that the player with the puck keeps her body between the checking player and the puck.

Backward stopping with the puck

When skating backward with the puck, players should stop as taught without the puck by turning the knees and skate blades out and pressing the inside edges of the skate blades against the ice. As they do so, have the players roll the wrists to lay the stick blade forward over the puck to cushion the stop. See Figure 6-15 for the correct action.

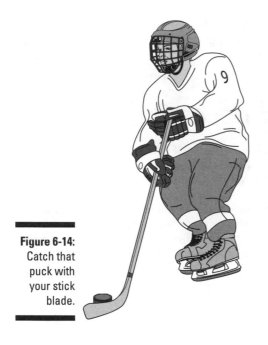

Figure 6-14:
Catch that
puck with
your stick
blade.

Figure 6-15:
Keep it out
of your feet.

Players should resume the ready position as soon as they are stopped, with the puck on the stick blade and their heads up looking for opportunities. If the player is being checked, she must place her body between the checker and the puck as she stops and assumes the ready position.

To practice forward or backward skating and stopping with the puck, have players skate the perimeter of the ice, stopping on one whistle and resuming skating on two blasts. Be sure to reverse direction halfway through the drill.

Teaching Passing and Receiving

Passing and receiving can make or break a team. If these skills are done well, a team can mount an attack and can avoid checking opponents effectively. If done poorly, the team is never in control of the puck for long.

Start beginners off with the basic forehand and backhand passing-and-receiving techniques, performing them in a stationary position. After the players master these techniques, you can add skating to the drills. At an intermediate level, you can go beyond the basic passes, to such skills as the flip and snap passes, which we discuss in Chapter 9.

Forehand passing

To begin teaching the forehand pass, have players in the ready stance with a puck placed behind and out from their back skate. The blade of the stick needs to lean over, or cradle, the puck while staying in contact with the ice with the puck sitting slightly to the heel end of the blade. See Figure 6-16a for the correct position.

Players then make one smooth forward motion, as they shift their weight from the back to the front skate and drag the puck across the front of their body, maintaining contact with the puck all the way. As the stick approaches the front skate, players push or slide the puck in the desired direction. See Figure 6-16b for the described action. Reinforce the notion that this is a push or slide action, not a slap.

Keep the follow-through with the stick low and close to the ice while the blade of the stick goes from being nearly perpendicular to the ice on release to being *closed* (blade over the puck) again as the blade completes the follow-through. See Figure 6-16c for the follow-through position.

Remind players to keep their eyes on the target (that is, their teammate's stick blade) and not on the puck as they release it. Check also that players keep their hands out from their bodies where they have more freedom to move than if they keep them in close.

a

b

Figure 6-16:
Ready. Let
her rip. Then
finish your
pass.

Figure 6-16:
Continued.

c

Don't worry about accuracy at first with the pass. Have players concentrate on keeping their knees bent so that they can transfer their weight from the back skate to the front skate as they drag the puck forward. Also be sure they roll their wrists to allow for proper angling (closed in Figure 6-16a, open in b, closed in c) of the stick blade.

After a player gets the idea of generating the pass from the back start position, place the puck in front of her body so that she has to sweep the puck back to the behind-the-back-foot start position first to learn to place the puck in the best position for a pass.

You can teach the pass with players just aiming at the side boards so that everyone has a puck and gets to practice the mechanics without worrying too much about accuracy. Then have players practice passing in pairs, only a few feet apart at first so they don't try to power the puck. After they get the mechanics and some aim, you can gradually move the players farther apart.

Backhand passing

Place the puck on the player's backhand side just behind the back skate. As the player places the backhand side of the stick blade on the puck, he wants to have the top hand on the stick in front of and away from the body for optimal freedom of movement. As in the forehand pass, players need their weight on the back skate with the stick closed over the puck. See Figure 6-17a to confirm positions.

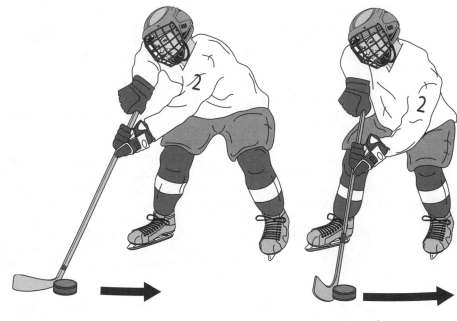

Figure 6-17:
Ready. Let her go. Then finish your backhand.

a

b

c

Have players simultaneously shift their weight to the front skate as they sweep the puck forward and slide the pass in the desired direction. The puck will leave the stick sooner than in the forehand pass, usually before it passes the front skate. See Figure 6-17b for the timing of the release.

The follow-through should continue until the arms are as fully extended as possible, with the blade remaining low to the ice. Players should continue to keep the blade low as it is returned to the ready position. See Figure 6-17c for the follow-through action.

Check that players keep their heads up with their eyes on the target throughout the pass. Reinforce the notion of pushing or sliding, not slapping, passes. Players who slide their passes use their wrists rather than just their arms, thereby gaining greater control and accuracy.

Eventually, have players practice the pass by placing the puck in the center of their bodies so that they have to pull the puck into the correct starting position behind the back foot before initiating the pass. Weak passes can result when passes start in front of the body.

As in the forehand pass, you can teach the backhand pass using the boards so accuracy isn't an issue. Then have players practice in pairs, initially using very short passes.

Forehand pass receiving

Beginner players typically have passes bounce out of control off their sticks when they try to receive a pass. Begin pass receiving with both hands on the stick and the stick held out from the body with the blade on the forehand side where they expect to receive a pass. The blade should be on the ice at an angle that presents a perpendicular wall as a target for the passer. As the puck approaches the stick, have players move the blade toward the approaching puck to line up for contact. See Figure 6-18a for anticipating contact.

Next, have players pull the blade back as puck contact is made and cushion the incoming puck until the blade closes over the puck. See Figure 6-18b for the cushioning action.

Completion of the cushioning action should put the player immediately in position to make a pass or carry the puck.

Figure 6-18:
Anticipate
and cushion
the puck as
you catch it.

a   b

Check that players present a target to the passer, that they watch the puck come onto their stick, and that they make cushioned contact. Remind players that their eyes should leave the puck as contact occurs and go back up to look for the next opportunity, such as an immediate pass to a teammate or a shot on goal.

Practice receiving alone initially, then add a subsequent pass to the combination. After players master the pass-receiving techniques, you can add slow skating to the sequence.

To practice forehand pass receiving, first have players work in pairs staying in place. Then have them practice while slowly skating the length of the ice.

Backhand pass receiving

When receiving a pass on the backhand, players must start with the blade of the stick on the ice perpendicular to where the pass is coming from. To get the blade perpendicular to the incoming puck, have players move the top (upper) hand on the stick across the front of their body and place it under the elbow of their lower hand. See Figure 6-19a for the correct position.

Figure 6-19:
Meeting and cushioning the incoming puck.

a   b

Players should then watch the puck approach the stick blade, as in forehand pass receiving, and give with the puck as it comes in contact with the blade. They cushion the puck as it slides across their body until the blade closes over the puck. See Figure 6-19b for the cushioning action.

Once cushioned, players should be in a position to immediately release a backhand pass, shoot, or draw the puck to the ready position for a forehand release.

Check that players watch the puck arrive on their stick blade, then immediately look up to see what can come next as they cushion the puck.

Initially, practice receiving only. When that skill becomes consistent, add slow skating to the sequence, and then a subsequent pass.

As with forehand pass receiving, have players work in pairs, staying stationary initially, then skating the length of the ice.

Unusual pass receiving

Occasionally a player may need to receive a pass with a skate or hand. Teach players that when the puck is coming toward their skate, to angle the toe of the skate blade so that it directs the puck forward toward their stick blade. See Figure 6-20 for the skate pass-receipt action.

Figure 6-20:
Catching a pass with your skate.

As in all pass receiving, players must provide some give when the skate blade contacts the puck so that the puck slows down and the bounce can be controlled and directed. Check that players maintain proper skating posture as much as possible while they do this.

If the puck is coming toward a player in the air, the quickest way for a player to get control may be to use her hand to receive the puck. In this case, have the player remove her lower hand from the stick, open her glove hand, and watch the puck come into her glove. Again, the player must cushion the puck by giving with its direction until she can direct the puck toward her stick blade. See Figure 6-21 for hand action in pass receiving.

Figure 6-21:
Almost like
a ball
catcher.

Remind players that they cannot carry the puck in their glove or close their hand over it; they can only direct the puck to their stick or direct it to a teammate who is parallel to or away from their offensive direction.

Chapter 7

Drills for Beginners

• •

In This Chapter

▶ Using drills effectively

▶ Working on skating, balance, and mobility drills

▶ Handling puck-control drills

▶ Running drills for effective positioning

• •

*T*housands of drills are available for teaching and practicing hockey skills. Some drills are certainly more effective than others. However, the important thing is that the coach's approach can render a good drill lousy or excellent.

This chapter focuses on running drills that will help beginner players develop their skating, puck-control, and passing and receiving skills. You also get tips on making your drills excellent.

Prepping for Excellent Drills

To aim for conducting excellent drills, start by having your rink diagram board available in a highly visible location. Be consistent with the location so that players know exactly where to go for their pre-practice or on-ice instruction.

Secondly, when you call players to the rink diagram board on the ice, have them kneel on one knee in a semicircle so that they can clearly see and hear your instructions.

Finally, decide on whistle commands and convey them to the players ahead of time. Common signals include one long blast, which means stop activity and go straight to the coach; and, while skating a drill, one short blast means speed up, a second short blast means slow down, and two quick blasts mean stop and go the other direction.

Be sure you have no distractions behind the boards, such as flashing signs, children playing, or parents distracting players' attention when you are giving drill instructions.

After you have these organizational items in place, these time-tested principles for conducting drills will maximize their effectiveness:

- ✔ Give clear, quality instruction and constructive feedback.
- ✔ Keep instructions and demonstrations short.
- ✔ Keep players as active as possible when doing drills; avoid having players standing around.
- ✔ Let players work on a skill after you have given instructions, then return and give them feedback.
- ✔ Be positive and enthusiastic.
- ✔ Make everything as much fun as possible.
- ✔ Be patient, constructive, and consistent.
- ✔ Be a little demanding — is a good thing.
- ✔ Keep the drills simple and safe (for example, avoid having players cross each other's skating paths).

When doing skating drills, lines formed on the goal line are excellent as a starting point for instruction or demonstrations.

We have designed the drills in this chapter to run either full ice, half ice, in a single zone, or across ice. The size of the group may require some drill modification, but rarely will it stop the drill from being done effectively.

Typically, forward-skating drills are used for backward-skating practice and backward-skating drills are performed forward, once skill levels allow. Refer to the Cheat Sheet at the front of this book for a legend of symbols used in the drill illustrations.

Repetition of a skill done correctly is your greatest teaching tool as a coach. Players will be excited each time they accomplish a level of proficiency in a skill. Build on that. But don't be in a rush to go on to the next step. Positively, but firmly, insist on correct execution of skills.

Drilling to Improve Skating Skill

The following drills are for use with beginner-level hockey players after you have provided basic instruction on skating and after they have had a chance to try doing what you have explained. The drills help beginners practice the skills of forward and backward skating, using edges, starting, stopping, puck handling, and passing and receiving. The drills progress from elementary, with the primary goal of developing balance and maintaining skating posture, to more difficult, for developing mobility.

Stress proper technique throughout all drills, especially at the beginner level. You're better off reinforcing a good pattern now than undoing a limiting pattern and re-teaching the correct skill pattern later.

Step-overs

The initial purpose of this drill is to improve balance, but eventually it will help players feel comfortable when they are on one skate. The drill relates to a game situation when a player may have to step over an object on the ice such as a dropped stick or glove.

How it works: Initially, have players stand erect with one hand on the stick and the stick on the ice. Then lift one foot and put it back down. Repeat for the other foot. Alternate slowly until players can keep their balance. Next, have the players lift their knees higher and march in place more quickly. Then have players step forward, alternating feet.

Coaching pointers: Stress that players keep their posture, with the head always up and the stick on the ice. Remind players to bend their knees to help with balance.

Stationary jumps

This drill helps players balance on skates. It also reinforces the need for players to extend through the hips and knees for power and to cushion the landing by bending at the knees.

How it works: Have players stand with their arms at their sides. Tell them to jump up, pushing off from the toes, and land with bent knees. Start with small jumps and progress to as high as possible. Mix three small jumps and one big jump for fun.

Coaching pointers: During small jumps, remind players to keep their heads up. As the jumps get higher, focus on having players keep their knees bent to cushion the landing to improve balance.

Push and glide

Players need to use full extension with each stride in skating. This drill emphasizes the stride portion of forward skating by using an exaggerated glide between each stride.

How it works: Have players start on the goal line in the ready position. On your "go" signal, have the players point the right skate forward and push off with the left skate using full extension and then recover to glide for a count of two or three in the ready position. Have them then point forward with the left skate, push off with the right skate, and then glide. Use this alternating pattern the length of the ice. See Figure 7-1 for the drill pattern.

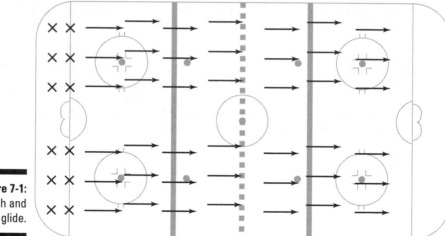

Figure 7-1:
Push and glide.

Coaching pointers: Stress pushing from the hip, then fully extending the leg on the stride. Have players point their skate backward by extending at the ankle. Check that they keep the nongliding skate under control and that they maintain proper skating posture. Eliminate any up-and-down motion in the upper body.

One leg stride and glide

This drill is a progression from the preceding drill ("Push and glide") so that players get the feel of the power they can add to each stride by using full extension of the leg.

How it works: Have players stride with their left leg while the right skate points to the opposite end of the ice. Emphasize full extension of the left leg as they glide for a count of two or three. Then have them recover to the start position and repeat using the same leg so that they go the full length of the ice striding only with the left leg. On the return up the ice, they stride only with the right leg. The drill pattern is the same as in Figure 7-1.

Coaching pointers: This drill is similar to the preceding drill in which full extension and posture are the coaching points. Get players to feel the extra power in each stride as they use full extension and proper posture.

Skate and glide

The idea behind this drill is to have players feel comfortable with speed in their stride. The drill also helps players keep their speed from getting out of control by allowing them to rebalance on the glide.

How it works: Starting on the goal line, have players skate as strongly as possible to the top of the face-off circles. Then have them glide in the ready position to the center line. They then skate from the center line to the top of the next face-off circles and glide to the far goal line. See Figure 7-2 for the skating pattern.

Coaching pointers: Emphasize skating posture. The player's head should always be up. Players should have forward lean at the waist and keep their knees bent. Look to eliminate any up-and-down motion of the upper body.

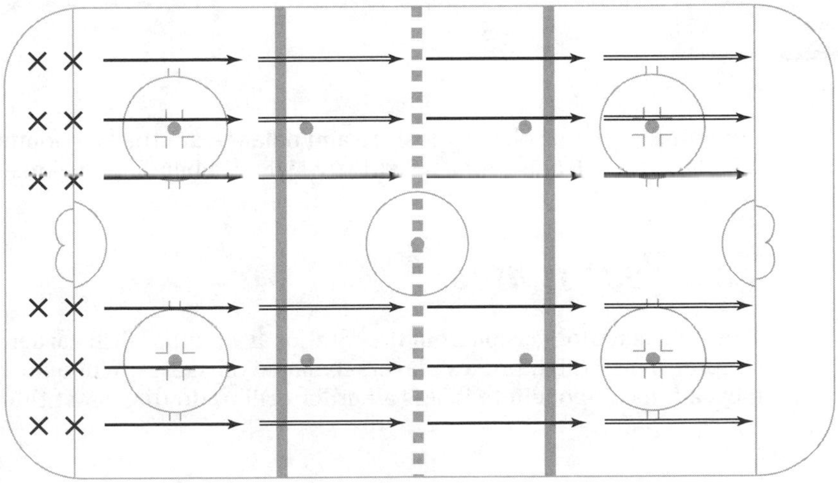

Figure 7-2:
Skate and glide.

Moving step-overs

In the first drill in this chapter ("Step-overs"), we recommend step-overs while stationary to help players get comfortable on their skates. This drill is a progression from that first drill, adding forward skating to the step-overs. The degree of difficulty increases, requiring greater coordination.

How it works: Start players on the goal line. Have them skate toward the blue line at half speed and step over each blue line and the center line as they come to it. Step with the right foot going down the ice and with the left foot coming back. See Figure 7-3 for the skating pattern. When players can do this drill without falling, ignore the lines and have the players pass their stick under their leg every third stride as they skate the length of the ice.

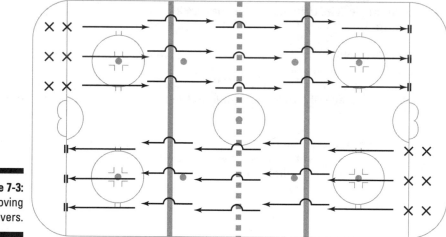

Figure 7-3:
Moving
step-overs.

Coaching pointers: Skating posture and balance are the key points — heads up all the time, leaning forward at the waist, and bending the knees.

Two-foot jumps

This drill is a progression from the "Stationary jumps" drill earlier in this chapter. This drill improves players' balance on skates. While the drill does have a fun component to it, it is a harder drill to do than most think.

How it works: Start players on the goal line. Have them skate toward the blue line. As they reach the blue lines and center line, have them do a two-foot jump over each line. Emphasize good bend at the knees and good skating posture. Start with small jumps and progress to bigger ones. See Figure 7-4 for the skating pattern.

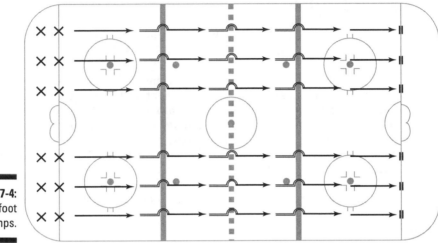

Figure 7-4:
Two-foot
jumps.

Coaching pointers: Proper skating posture is necessary for players to maintain their balance as they do this drill. Repeat the skating posture mantra of head up, forward lean with the upper body, and bend in the knees. Even exaggerate with a near-crouch before and after the jump so that players learn to cushion the landing.

Line touches

This drill takes players out of their normal erect skating posture. The drill challenges players to maintain their balance as they lower their bodies closer to the ice surface, make contact with the ice, and then return to their original posture.

How it works: Have players skate the length of the ice touching each line on the ice with an alternate glove as they skate by. Emphasize knee bend and regaining skating posture.

Coaching pointers: Have players start by slowly going down to touch each line and slowly returning to the start position. Heads should be up all the time. Have players keep the blades of their skates flat and under control, not using inside or outside edges.

Mixed-up drill

This fun drill mixes in different skills requiring balance, posture, and skating footwork. Its mix begins to simulate the mix of skills used in a game.

How it works: Have players skate the perimeter of the ice. As they come to the lines, have them step over (with the right foot) the first blue line, touch (using the right hand) the center line, jump the next blue line, and stop and walk the goal line as though it was a tightrope. Going down the other side of the ice, players step with the left foot and touch with the left hand. When they come to the goal line, they stop, skate backwards, and then stop where they began. Repeat the circuit a couple of times.

Coaching pointers: Keep checking for correct skating posture. Keep stressing heads up all the time.

Edges

To be a good skater, players have to be able to control both outside and inside edges of their skate blades. This drill introduces edge control, where players will be on the edges of their skates as they weave around dots and pylons.

How it works: Have players skate the perimeter of the ice, weaving alternately left and right as they go around the dots or through pylons. Start weaving with both feet, progressing to one-foot skating the weave. See Figure 7-5 for a weaving pattern.

Coaching pointers: Have players keep their sticks on the ice, maintain proper skating posture, and keep heads up. When weaving on both feet, accent knee action as the body weight switches from right to left on the weaves. On one foot, have players keep the raised skate close to the other skate to help with balance.

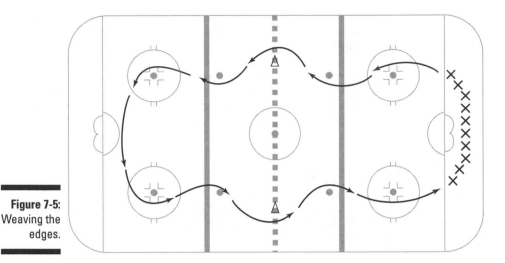

Figure 7-5:
Weaving the
edges.

Bobbing

This drill works on balance and body position when backward skating. This is another of those drills that looks a lot easier than it really is.

How it works: Have players start on the goal line and skate backwards the length of the ice. Between the blue lines, have them go from proper backward-skating posture to straight legs to as low as possible in a continuous bobbing action until they pass the second blue line. Then have them return to proper backward skating and stop at the far goal line.

Coaching pointers: Backward skating requires that players have their shoulders over the hips. Have players skate with their upper body erect, head up, and stick on the ice. Start slowly with the bobbing action and gradually speed up as players become comfortable with the drill.

Leg-overs

This drill helps develop backward balance on one foot. The drill also helps with coordination.

How it works: Have players leave the goal line skating backwards. While going slowly and keeping the stick on the ice, have them lift the right foot slightly off the ice. With their left hand on the stick, pass the stick under the right leg to the right hand. Return the right skate to the ice. Repeat with the left leg. Be sure players can do this drill while skating forward before they try it with backward skating.

Coaching pointers: Be sure the players keep sticks in contact with the ice all the time. Some players have a tendency to lift the stick in an attempt to make the drill easier. Remind players of proper backward-skating posture with the shoulders back and over the hips, stick on the ice, and the head always up.

Starts 'n' stops

Players need to be proficient at starting and stopping, whether skating forward or backward. They start and stop a great deal over the course of a game. This drill lets them practice both.

How it works: Line players up along the blue line with their backs to the center line. Have them skate backwards to the other blue line, stop, skate forward to the first blue line, and stop again. Repeat this sequence. See Figure 7-6 for the pattern. To add a fun element, place pucks across the ice at the top of the circles and on the third repetition, and have players continue skating forward over the blue line, pick up a puck, and go in for a shot on net. Then repeat the drill.

Coaching pointers: Your emphasis on the stops is on maintaining good skating posture. Have players keep two hands on the stick while starting and stopping. Each stop should end with players in the proper starting stance. On the starts, emphasize quick and firm pressure against the ice, which comes from retaining bent knees, a proper lean, and a head-up skating posture.

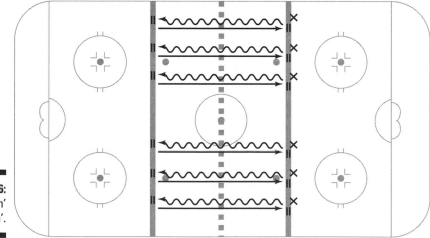

Figure 7-6:
Startin' 'n'
stoppin'.

Drilling to Improve Stick- and Puck-Handling Skills

The following drills start at very basic levels to help develop puck control while carrying, passing, receiving, and stopping with the puck. You can add complexity to the drills as players become more competent.

Figure eight around the gloves

The purpose of this drill is to get players comfortable using both sides of the stick blade while handling the puck. Using a stationary drill allows players to concentrate on handling the puck when they don't have to be concerned with skating or other skills.

How it works: Place gloves on the ice (just over stick-blade length) in front of each player's feet and shoulder-width apart. Starting with a puck between the gloves, the player stickhandles the puck in a figure-eight design, up between the gloves, around to the left, up between the gloves again, and around to the right. Repeat. The only skate movement is a slight slide forward as the puck moves away from the player and back as the puck moves toward the player. Players' wrists should do most of the work.

Coaching pointers: Success in puck handling comes from proper wrist action. The wrists and forearms should be relaxed to allow the blade of the stick to protect the puck. Talk to the players about rolling the wrists, that is, flexing, extending, and angling the wrists to get proper blade action. Stress heads up all the time while puck handling.

Puck carrying

After getting the hang of stationary puck handling, this drill, a progression from the preceding drill ("Figure eight around the gloves"), allows players to work on moving about the ice while still maintaining control of the puck.

How it works: Use pylons to mark a pattern on the ice for players to skate around while they control the puck. Start with a very simple pattern, such as the one illustrated by the arrows in Figure 7-7. As puck handling improves, make a more complex circuit with a greater degree of difficulty. Remember though, at this point, that the players are not yet ready for tight turns.

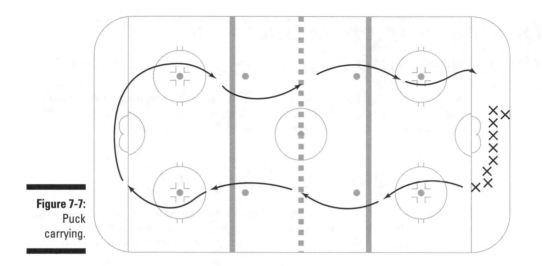

Figure 7-7:
Puck
carrying.

Coaching pointers: When skating forward with the puck, the head is always up and the puck is kept on the stick in front of the body with two hands on the stick. Look for proper forward-skating posture. Check that players keep lateral puck movement within shoulders' width.

Start 'n' stop puck control

You want your players to develop the ability to control the puck while they perform various skating skills. This drill helps players practice keeping the puck under control as they start, skate, and stop forward and backwards.

How it works: Use the same stop-start sequence explained in the "Starts 'n' stops" drill earlier in this chapter, but have players do the entire drill with pucks. Emphasize puck control.

Coaching pointers: Keep a close eye on skating posture. Players tend to straighten their legs while starting and stopping. Remind them to maintain the bend in the knees while starting and stopping. Head up all the time — no peeking at the puck! Also make sure they cushion the puck while stopping.

Passing and receiving

This drill helps players add passing to the puck-handling and skating skills they are developing.

How it works: Have players skate the perimeter of the ice in pairs. Instruct them to take three strides, and then pass the puck to their partner. The partner does the same. See Figure 7-8 for the passing pattern. After two or three laps, stop and reverse direction. Then repeat the whole drill after the partners switch from inside to outside positions to allow both players to practice forehand and backhand passes.

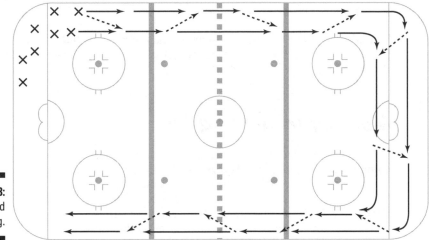

Figure 7-8:
Passing and
receiving.

Coaching pointers: Both players should keep their sticks on the ice all the time. Encourage a sliding motion with the stick and eliminate any slapping at the puck. Be sure the player receiving the puck presents his stick blade as a target for the passer. The passer should aim slightly in front of the target to allow for the forward-skating motion of the players.

Drilling to Improve Hockey Sense

Hockey sense drills are mini-games that players can have fun with while they subtly learn how to get into the best position, what clues to look for in anticipation of what to do, and how to maneuver effectively. In these games, experience is the best teacher.

Frozen tag

Frozen tag, on ice, works on agility and mobility in players' skating skills. They will experience stops, starts, acceleration, and laughter.

How it works: Have players leave their sticks on or in the net. One or two players are selected to be "it" and try to tag other players. When a player is tagged, he remains frozen in place until everyone is tagged. Start over with new players who are "it." To make the game more competitive, identify small teams of "it" (two or three players) and time how long it takes each team to freeze all the opponents. To keep more people more active, let nonfrozen players unfreeze frozen players by retagging them. Limit the area for the game according to the skill level of the players; the whole ice surface may be too much for beginner skaters.

Coaching pointers: All players need to play heads up all the time in this game. Often the best skaters are the last to get tagged, so be sure to mix weak and strong skaters together on the "it" team.

Monkey in the middle

This drill helps players learn to take away passing lanes and to find the passing holes against a defender. Players also learn to get into position and to move the puck quickly to help ensure a successful pass.

How it works: Have players work in groups of three or four with each group at a circle. One player, the "monkey," goes in the middle with the other players opposite each other (if two players) or in a triangle formation (if three players) around the circle. These players pass the puck across the circle to each other, trying to avoid having it tipped or stopped by the monkey. See Figure 7-9 for the drill formation. When the player in the middle intercepts a pass, the player who sent the pass switches position and becomes the monkey in the middle. All players can shift as much as half of the circle to improve their passing chances.

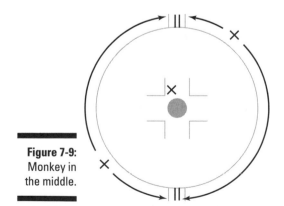

Figure 7-9:
Monkey in
the middle.

Coaching pointers: Have players on the outside of the circle keep their sticks on the ice. Encourage players to keep the puck moving all the time. Have the monkey be aggressive and move facing the puck at all times. Check that all players move their feet to get into position as opposed to reaching or leaning.

Three-on-three scrimmage

Players need to develop the ability to work together. This game helps players learn to read off each other, anticipating what a teammate is likely to do. It also helps develop passing, skating, puck handling, and heads-up team play while under pressure. The element of competition in the game is a good motivator for players to work hard.

How it works: Set up quarter-ice game surfaces as illustrated in Figure 7-10. Designate the goal lines and blue lines as "goal" lines for scoring points. Have three-player teams play against each other with the objective being to skate with the puck across the "goal" line to get a point for their team. Restart after each point by giving the team scored against the puck on their goal line.

Coaching pointers: Encourage players to get to open ice where they can be a passing option when a teammate has the puck. When the other team has the puck, have players move to take away passing options by putting their sticks in passing lanes.

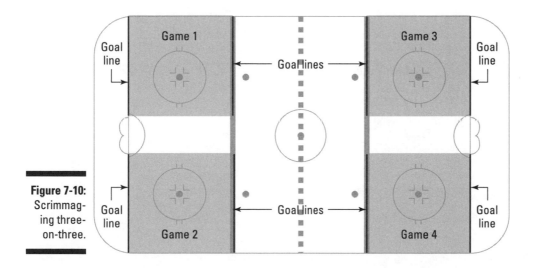

Figure 7-10: Scrimmaging three-on-three.

Chapter 8

Basic Coaching Strategies

· ·

· ·

*T*his is the moment you've been waiting for as a coach — your chance to shine as a great hockey strategist. The game is about to begin. Your beginners are stepping onto the ice. Some lose their balance and fall. What strategies do you need to employ to have a successful game?

First, forget trying to win the game. The kids have more important things to do, like getting to play a lot and having fun.

When you coach beginning hockey players, remember these three major coaching strategies, which lead to having a successful game:

- ✔ Maximize the opportunity for players to develop their basic skills, primarily skating.

- ✔ Ensure that all team members have fun.

- ✔ Begin to help the kids learn a bit about the game.

The means to employing these three strategies are quite simple. First, give every player equal ice time. That lets everyone play as much as possible, so they all get time to develop their skating. Secondly, rotate all players through all positions. This gives each player a feel for the game from different perspectives. It also allows different skills to evolve, so they'll eventually find out what they're good at doing and what position they like most.

You will likely need to provide simple game instruction to help beginners start to develop some game sense. For example, typically, beginners all converge on the puck. Instruct them that the nearest player to the puck is to go after it; the others should spread out not too far away, heading toward the goal they want to score in. This will put them in a position to receive a pass or go for a loose puck.

Beginners typically try to carry the puck rather than look for pass opportunities, or they simply send the puck in any direction. So some instruction, such as "find a teammate to pass to," may be useful.

Sometimes you get a beginner who's simply lost out there, so he just stands around watching or looking for his parents in the stands. Instruct players to always be skating in the direction the puck is going, so they have a focus and at least get some skating practice. This will also increase their odds of accidentally getting involved in the play, which will give them a bit of experience and, hopefully, satisfaction.

This game strategy is about all you need at the beginner hockey level. However, beyond the game, we suggest a few other coaching strategies that you may want to consider further, such as keeping everybody happy, helping everyone accomplish something, and stopping periodically to take an objective look at how you are doing as a coach.

Keeping Everybody Happy

First of all, don't feel bad if you discover that there's just no way you can keep everybody happy! The dynamics of a team often don't allow for peace and harmony all the time. But you can use certain strategies to help you avoid the common pitfall of trying to keep everyone happy.

Be clear in your own mind about the goals you set prior to the season. Then be sure all goals are clearly defined, understood, and accepted by your staff, players, and parents. Thereafter, when someone is unhappy about an issue, you can point to the appropriate goal(s) to help keep individuals focused and help them understand your position on the issue.

Then, be consistent. You'll have times when it may seem easier to give in to a player or parent and deviate from your predetermined goals and strategies just to make someone happy. This usually results in a short-term happy for one person and a long-term unhappy for the rest of the team — and for you. If you remain consistent, everyone will know what to expect, and they'll pressure you less to make exceptions.

Generally, players want to play and parents want to see their kid(s) play. Keep that in mind as an overall strategy, and you'll keep most people happy most of the time.

Another way to keep people happy is to solicit feedback. This is particularly useful during the season if you don't feel you have a good read on participant satisfaction. Your hockey staff or parent assistants should be your first source of feedback. They should feel comfortable offering feedback any time, without you having to solicit it.

With young players, a casual mid-season team meeting following a practice or during a holiday pizza party may provide sufficient feedback. Informally ask questions: How's the season going for you? What do you like about what we're doing? What don't you like? Most players will be happy you cared to speak with them.

If you feel the need, a mid-season parent meeting could be useful. Take the approach that this should be more an information session than a parent gripe session. Control the agenda: Give parents an update on the team, report on how the team strategies are working, and lay out any changes you feel need to be made. Have at least one assistant present at these meetings so that you present a common team front. Never let discussions get personal. Issues are about the team. The kids' goals are the priority.

Helping Everyone Accomplish Something

Both players and parents can be kept reasonably happy if you provide opportunities to experience a sense of accomplishment through games and practices. One way to do this is to set attainable goals for each practice session and to help all players reach the goals. Players will leave the rink feeling good about what was accomplished.

List these goals in your plan at the first of the year. An example for the practice following backward skating instruction is to have all players be able to skate the length of the ice backwards without falling by the end of practice. These accomplishment goals can be simple. The important thing is that they are doable, which gives the players a sense of satisfaction. It also gives the coach something — an objective measure of progress.

Another way to see accomplishment is to use simple tests to check progress. This, in turn, provides positive feedback for players. These tests can be as basic as timing players as they skate one lap of the ice. Be sure to record the results of any test you use. As skating improves, retest and show players how much faster they are. The results will help you show players what gains they are making, and you can all see what you are accomplishing as the season progresses.

Insight into a coach's impact

A huge Italian family gathered to celebrate Tony's 70th birthday. They invited all his friends they'd been able to contact. That group included the minor hockey team Tony played on while growing up in small-town Canada. More amazingly, the coach was also in attendance, still sporting a sparkle in his eye for life at nearly 90 years of age.

The team had come together in the 1940s when the town fathers of a hard-working, largely Italian-immigrant community decided they needed a rink to keep young boys off the streets and out of trouble. As soon as a rink was built, Coach Carducci corralled most of the 10 to 12 year olds in town and convinced them to give hockey a try. Before long, signs of talent emerged and their increasingly famous "Spaghetti Line" began overwhelming the opposition. Tony centered that line.

One of Tony's wingers on the "Spaghetti Line" stood to speak at his birthday party. "I know we're all here to honor Tony for making it to 70. But first, I know he'd want me to say how honored we all are to see Coach Carducci here. If it weren't for him taking this bunch of trouble-makers off the streets 55 years ago, and teaching us discipline and commitment for starters, most of us wouldn't be standing in front of you today. If we were still standing, we wouldn't be the successful business, professional, and family men we are. Coach made us what we are today. I just want to say thank you, from all of us."

Tony and his buddies still play hockey once a week. Coach Carducci is still coaching them in spirit.

Keep individual test results between you and the player or compare players to themselves, not to others on the team. Having a player suffer the embarrassment of being last on a particular test serves no purpose. However, positive pieces of information can be motivational for the team, such as stating, "The player to catch this month is Mary. She had a 21-second lap."

Keep tests simple. You can use a drill that is familiar to the players as a test. For example, you could count the number of completed passes made by a group of players over a 30-second time period. In this test, players are stationary around the outside of a face-off circle and are working in specific groups.

Positive reinforcement helps to create the environment needed for accomplishing goals. Always make tests, drills, and practices overflow with positive reinforcement. Verbal and visual encouragement, such as a high five, glove tap, or pat on the helmet, can work wonders in the development and sense of accomplishment of young players.

How Am I Doing So Far?

So, where do you get your sense of accomplishment, coach?

It's nice to know what kind of job you are doing as you go along. It also gives you a chance to catch and modify any weaknesses in your approach. Where do you turn?

Usually, a formal evaluation process is part of your minor hockey association. These evaluations can be useful and should be treated with respect. The association must stay abreast of the quality of product it provides to those involved.

However, you might like to know, as the season goes along, if you could change some things to improve the quality of your coaching.

Start by checking what you're doing against the goals and strategies that you laid out prior to the season, because these are what you've based your coaching on. All your actions should connect positively with your goals. If an action doesn't gel — adjust it!

You can also have others give an evaluation. Be selective here — the "others" need to be knowledgeable about coaching and also about your individual coaching circumstances. Some associations have mentor coaches. Make use of a mentor coach, if available, even if you have to find your own.

Compare apples to apples. Just because you saw a coach at a higher level do something you liked, that doesn't necessarily make it something you should do. Often coaches in minor hockey try to emulate NHL or other high-profile coaches. It is rarely the right thing to do.

Another option for seeing how you're doing is to evaluate your team's performance. Do this in a general way. For example, make a list of questions to ask: Are my players comparable or competitive with other players the same age? Is discipline an issue on our team? Do we have good effort as a team? Am I seeing improvement in the skill levels of all players? Do all the players seem enthusiastic?

Remember that a team's record doesn't necessarily reflect the quality of its coach. Teams can build a good record in spite of poor coaching. A poor record may not reflect team progress. Go for the progress.

Finally, look at the players' faces as they participate in practices and games, as they leave the ice, and as they leave the rink. If you see lots of smiles and grins, it is a good indication that you are getting high marks on the players' evaluation of your coaching.

Part III
Coaching Intermediate Players

The 5th Wave   By Rich Tennant

I would say your stickhandling needs a little work.

In this part . . .

This part presents the skills players need to progress beyond a beginner level in hockey. We include techniques and step-by-step sequences for you to teach these skills well. We introduce goaltending skills at this level. We also provide drills for reinforcing the skills in practices, as well as more advanced coaching techniques to help you develop along with your players.

Chapter 9

Teaching the Finer Skills

· ·

In This Chapter

▶ Introducing change of direction

▶ Instructing shooting and scoring, and ways to stop opponents

▶ Improving face-off techniques

· ·

*W*hen players can perform basic skating and puck-handling skills, they are ready to tackle more complex skills. However, you must continue to reinforce those basic skills in practice sessions because it takes considerable time and experience to master basic skills. In addition, if players have come to your team from a previous coach, you cannot assume that an earlier coach used *Coaching Hockey For Dummies* and gave those players the same top-quality skills instruction and practices that you do. You may have to start by giving your intermediate players a thorough skills review.

After you've determined that your players are reasonably competent at performing the basic hockey skills of skating, passing, and receiving, you can proceed to instruct them in the skating skills of lateral movement, pivoting, and turning. The stick and puck skills they should learn next include performing more complex passes, shooting and scoring, stickchecking, stealing and protecting the puck, and taking face-offs.

As you teach these finer skills to intermediate-level players, keep these overall coaching points in mind:

- ✓ Continue to reinforce the basic skills.

- ✓ Skating posture is still very important: head up, knees bent, stick on the ice.

- ✓ You can be more demanding at this level, but in a positive way.

- ✓ Mental aspects, such as expectations and achievement, become more prevalent.

- ✓ Fun components are always required!

Adding to Basic Skating Skills

At the intermediate level, you want to focus on improving agility and mobility in players' skating. This involves teaching players how to move laterally and how to pivot and turn. When you teach these skills, be sure to provide instruction and practice at turning both to the right and to the left, as well as when skating forward and backward.

Mastering lateral movement

In a hockey game, players may be required to shift quickly from going forward or backward to going to their left or right. The crossover is the technique used when a player wants this quick, sideways movement. Good edge control is required to perform crossovers, so make sure you have done some edges instruction as a review before you begin to teach crossovers (refer to Chapter 6 for more information about coaching edge control).

Forward crossovers

Start by having players stand in place and simply step the left skate over the right and bring the right skate around to place it beside the left skate. Repeat this action starting with the right skate stepping over the left skate. Players should have their sticks on the ice with one hand on the stick. They should keep a slight bend at the waist and a more exaggerated bend in the knees. See Figure 9-1 for the correct crossover body position.

When players can step over each skate and maintain balance, add slow forward motion allowing some glide while their skates are parallel. As they step over with forward momentum, players must press against the ice with the outside edge of the foot being crossed and push from the inside edge of the foot crossing over. Next, have players do a slightly wider crossover step as they skate the length of the ice. Then have them alternate three strides of skating forward and then a crossover so that they alternately cross over to the left and to the right.

As players get more comfortable with the crossover, have them skate forward, then do three or more crossovers in a row to the left, then skate a few strides and do the same to the right. Progress from doing slow crossovers to quicker stepping. Also have the players gradually widen the crossover until it becomes an exaggerated step. More knee bend will be required to achieve a quick, wide succession of crossovers.

Backward crossovers

Use backward skating to teach crossovers. The technique for backward crossovers is similar. But first, review the backward skating posture. Players should have their shoulders over their hips (avoid forward lean) and an exaggerated knee bend. Make sure they keep their heads up. Players will have a tendency to look down at their feet, which makes balance more difficult. See Figure 9-2 for the backward skating crossover position.

Figure 9-1: Moving sideways.

Figure 9-2: Going sideways while going backwards.

Start by having players skate backward slowly, then step left over right and bring the right skate parallel to the left skate to retain balance. Do the same steps starting with the right skate. As balance improves, have the players skate a few strides backward, then do a single crossover and eventually multiple crossovers to the left, then a few more strides, then repeat to the right. Gradually increase stepping pace and width.

Pivoting and turning

The other skating skills that players use to change direction in hockey are pivoting and turning. A turn is a change in direction that requires the player to skate in the opposite direction. A pivot is a switch from skating backward to forward or the reverse while the player continues on in the same direction.

Skating turns

Young players have a tendency to glide around turns; instead, they need to learn to skate turns. When they learn to stride through turns, they maintain better speed and control.

Have players skate forward and begin the turn by crossing the outside skate over the inside skate. At the same time, they must shift their hips toward the inside of the turn. The head and shoulders must stay over the feet, not lean into the turn. Players then push with the outside edge of the inside skate to full leg extension. After full extension, have players return their inside skate, keeping it low to the ice, to a position under the inside shoulder, while the outside leg pushes against the inside skate blade edge to full extension. See Figure 9-3 for the correct body position while skating a forward turn.

Throughout turns, keep the stick blade on the ice to the inside of the turn. This helps with balance and overall execution of the turn.

A left-handed shooter will have two hands on the stick while turning to the right and one hand while turning to the left. In both cases, the stick is to the inside of the turn. The reverse is true for right-handed shooters.

Make sure that steps in turns are not too large, or balance will be compromised. Have players skate the circles on the ice using slow, deliberate steps with full extension. Gradually increase stepping pace so that it becomes almost like a run, but also make sure the knees stay well bent so that players can achieve power from full leg extension. Also ensure that players always keep the returning skate close to the ice. Have players skate the circles in both directions so that they learn to skate turns to both the left and the right.

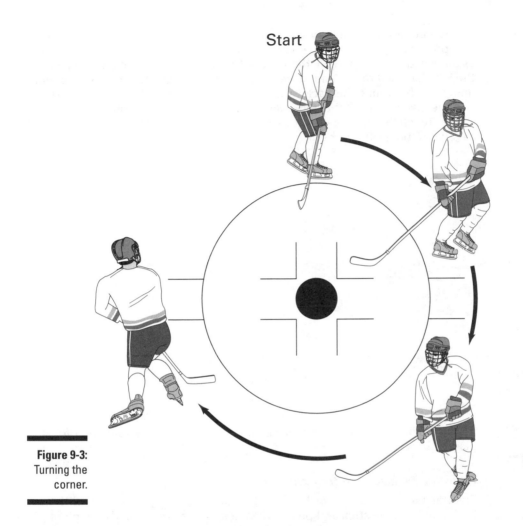

Figure 9-3:
Turning the
corner.

Next, instruct and have players practice skating backward turns using the same progression as in the forward turns. The technique is the same, but check to see that they use the basic backward skating body position, especially as they shift their weight at the hips toward the inside of the turn.

Pivoting forward to backward

When pivoting from forward to backward, players start with both hands on the stick and pull the hands in close to the body. This improves balance and ensures that the stick is under control during the pivot. To pivot to the right side, instruct players while skating forward to keep their left skate on the ice pointed in the direction they are going and pick the right skate up and rotate it approximately 180 degrees so that right and left skate heels almost touch, as shown in Figure 9-4. Have them place the right skate on the ice and pick up the left skate and rotate and place it parallel to the right skate. Players should immediately assume the backward skating position with their stick on the ice and the lower hand off the stick, and then push off with a normal backward stride. Teach this same sequence with the right foot leading so players learn to pivot to both left and right.

Figure 9-4:
Turning
on a dime.

Stress the heel-to-heel position during pivots. It is an easy visual point for players to relate to.

Pivoting backward to forward

Pivoting backward to forward starts with players skating backwards with both hands on the stick and pulling the stick in close to the body. To pivot to the left, players must pick up the left skate and rotate it approximately 180 degrees in the direction of the turn until in a heel-to-heel position. They then shift their weight onto the left skate as the heel of the right skate shifts so they can push off with the inside edge of the right skate. The lower hand drops off the stick and players assume the normal forward skating posture. See Figure 9-5 for positioning for the push-off. Practice the same instruction sequence leading with the right skate so that players learn to pivot to both the left and right.

Watch for up-and-down motion with the shoulders and upper body. It takes momentum away from the direction the player wants to go. Stress knee bend to eliminate this negative motion and to increase the efficiency of pivots by making it easier for players to shift their weight and exert power on the push.

Figure 9-5:
Backward
turning on
a dime.

After giving players time to learn and practice pivots and turns, set up a slalom course on the ice that includes left and right turns and pivots from forward and backward skating.

Teaching More Advanced Stick and Puck Skills

Intermediate-level players are ready to move on to more challenging passing, shooting, and checking in their stick and puck-handling skills. Coaches should stress that players keep their sticks on the ice to be ready to execute any puck-handling skill. After you've instructed the players in the skills and given them the time to practice, you can begin to emphasize quickness with proper execution of skills. Be cautious about progressing too quickly; players may compromise the fundamental techniques that they've learned earlier to try to keep up, which will haunt them later.

Practicing more difficult passes

As players progress through various hockey levels, they'll recognize opportunities in a game when the usual forehand or backhand passes are at risk of being intercepted. The flip pass and snap pass can both help reduce that risk, but they take significant practice to be able to perform consistently.

Flip pass

Players can use a *flip pass* when an obstacle lies between the passer and receiver. This obstacle can be a hockey stick or a player who has fallen to the ice. The flip pass involves having the player raise the puck off the ice to make the pass.

To teach a flip pass, have the player pull the puck back in the same fashion as in a normal forehand or backhand pass. The forward motion of the stick starts out the same as well, but in the flip pass, the player opens up the stick blade earlier as the puck rolls toward the toe of the blade so that the blade gets under and lifts the puck. Follow through with the blade rising up, rather than rolling over and close to the ice surface. The higher the blade, the higher the puck should go. See Figure 9-6 for an illustration of the lifting action.

Figure 9-6:
Up and over.

Players use the same adjustments in opening the blade and lifting the follow-through to make a flip pass while on the backhand.

Check that players maintain the proper skating stance with good knee bend while they execute forehand and backhand flip passes.

Snap pass

The snap pass is used when a player wants to make a very long pass that needs more power behind it.

Have players begin the snap pass as they would the normal forehand pass by pulling the puck back behind the back leg, shifting weight to the back leg, and keeping an eye on the target. They then shift their weight forward and draw the puck forward as in the forehand pass, but as the puck approaches the center line of the body, have players briefly slow the forward motion of the stick so that the puck slides slightly ahead of the blade. As they do so, players should pivot the heel of the stick up by rolling their wrists back. The toe of the stick remains in contact with or very close to the ice. Then have players bring the blade down hard on the ice just behind the puck and snap the wrists forward to release the puck in the desired direction. The release should be complete before the puck gets to the front skate. See Figure 9-7 for an illustration of the snap pass release.

Figure 9-7:
Powering
a pass.

Follow-through should be short, low, and closed to the ice, just as in the forehand pass. *Closed to the ice* means that the player rolls the blade face of the stick over and down toward the ice as he follows the puck's flight away from the stick.

Check that players keep the toe of the stick close to the ice when the puck slides ahead and that there is no backswing motion with the stick at that point.

Shooting and scoring

As much as players and coaches would like to have these skills come naturally, shooting and scoring has to be taught. You'll find a wide range of shooting and scoring abilities on any team, but we have a few tricks to share that can help any player improve.

Scoring principles

Just as you have techniques for learning how to shoot well, you also have tricks for learning how to score well. Coach your players in, and use drills that adhere to, the following principles to improve their chances of scoring with their shots:

✔ Care about accuracy — hit the net.

✔ Practice accuracy before power.

✔ Keep shots low (within 6 inches of the ice) to have the best chance of scoring.

✔ Always follow your shot for a rebound.

✔ Don't shoot at the goaltender, shoot for the holes.

✔ Practice quick release — don't give the goalie time to get into position.

✔ Mentally visualize where your shot is to go, but keep your head up and look at the net overall so that you don't tip off the goaltender.

✔ Study opposing goalies to take advantage of their weaknesses.

Low shots are nearly always more powerful than high shots. They are also more accurate. Coach your players to focus on these more effective shots.

The main point to stress in shooting and scoring is to hit the net! Often players will shoot the puck and not be concerned that the shot went wide of the net. Players have little opportunity to score when a shot does not hit the net. So set specific targets for all shooting instruction and practices. That target could be something as simple as a scuff mark on the boards.

Make sure players realize that when you say, "Hit the net," you actually mean hit the target, ideally a hole in the goalie's coverage. You are not telling them just to make contact with the net, although aiming to hit the inside back of the net isn't a bad plan.

Intermediate players should master four fundamental shots: forehand and backhand wrist shots plus snap and slap shots. Regardless of the shot that you're teaching or a player is practicing, emphasize that players keep their heads up looking at the target, not down at the puck.

Forehand wrist shot

The forehand wrist shot is really just a hard forehand pass. Have players pull the puck back behind the back skate and transfer their weight to the back skate. They should also put the puck to the heel side of the center of the blade. They then bring the puck forward firmly with their wrists cocked back as they transfer their weight onto the front skate. Players should uncock the wrists to release the puck when the stick blade is at a right angle to the target. See Figure 9-8 for the release of a forehand wrist shot. The more aggressive the weight transfer and release, the harder the shot will be.

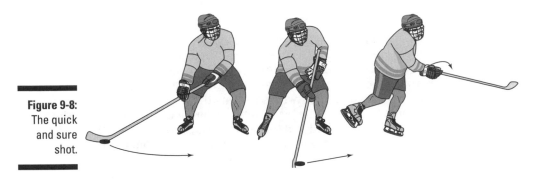

Figure 9-8:
The quick
and sure
shot.

Keep most shots low. This is done by having players follow through with the blade low to the ice and closing the blade over the puck. To raise the shot, the blade needs to follow through higher and open.

Backhand wrist shot

As with the forehand shot, the backhand wrist shot is basically a hard backhand pass. Players should pull the puck behind the back skate and transfer their weight to the back leg. The puck should be to the heel side of the center of the blade. As they pull the puck vigorously forward, their weight should transfer to the front skate. Have players release the puck with a firm snap of the wrists when the stick blade is at a right angle to the target. See Figure 9-9 for the backhand release.

Figure 9-9:
The secret
is in the twist
of the wrist.

As in the forehand shot, players are to keep the stick follow-through low and the blade turned over the puck for a low shot. They can open up the blade and follow through higher for a high shot.

Snap shot

The snap shot is a quicker and more forceful shot than the wrist shot. Execution of the shot requires finer coordination and timing. First, review the instructions presented earlier in this chapter for the snap pass. Then instruct players to initiate the shot as though for a wrist shot, but as they bring the puck forward, they curl their wrists causing the heel of the blade to lift away from the puck. The toe of the blade stays in contact with the ice. The heel is then snapped down behind and through the puck to make the shot, using the wrists. Contact and release should be made before the puck gets to the front foot. See Figure 9-10 for the contact on a snap shot.

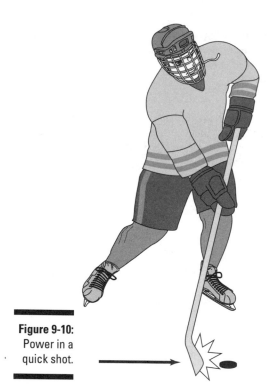

Figure 9-10:
Power in a
quick shot.

Be sure players shift their weight from back to front legs through the shot.

Work on smoothness of timing first, and then add a little power before focusing on accuracy. When accuracy gets consistent, greater power can be added.

Slap shot

The slap shot, like the snap shot, is a coordination and timing shot. Players are to keep the top hand on the stick close to the body while the lower hand slides down the shaft so the lower arm remains straight. The puck is positioned slightly behind the front skate.

Have players pull the stick straight back as they lock the lower elbow, raise the stick no higher than shoulder height, cock their wrists to roll the stick backward, and keep their weight on the back skate.

As they shift their weight forward, have players bring the stick downward to contact the ice, then the puck, with the heel end of the blade. See Figure 9-11a for the proper back swing and Figure 9-11b for the contact and release of a slap shot.

a

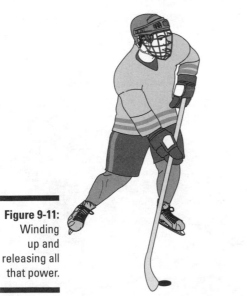

Figure 9-11:
Winding up and releasing all that power.

b

Follow-through begins with a snap of the wrists on release to roll the stick blade over the puck. Then, follow-through continues low, keeping the blade of the stick close to the ice. The stick blade should end up pointing in the direction of the shot.

Stickchecking and puck stealing

Stickchecking and puck stealing move intermediate-level hockey toward a more competitive part of the hockey game. Players like to have the puck and will work hard to get it from opposing players. You need to keep safety as a priority when teaching these skills. If taught correctly, the risk of injury is minimal.

Body position is the most important focus when stickchecking. Instruct players to skate close enough to the player they want to check so that they can execute the check correctly without reaching. If they can't skate to the best position, tell them not to try the check. In addition, help players develop spatial awareness, that is, a sense of where their body is in relation to the puck, the net, the opposing player, and that player's options. This will help them place their bodies in position to execute checks from the best distance and angle. Then each player and your overall team will check more effectively.

Poke checking

The *poke check* is a stick check that is most often used by a defenseman skating backward in a one-on-one situation. Have players place their stick on the ice in front of their body with only the top hand on the stick and keeping the free hand close to the body. The objective is to poke the puck off the opponent's stick. Players do so by extending their stick arm so that the blade of their stick deflects the puck away from the opponent. See Figure 9-12 for an illustration of a poke check.

Figure 9-12:
Poking the
puck away.

Players can also do this check while skating forward to check a puck carrier.

Be sure that players only extend their arm to poke the puck away and that they do not have forward motion of the shoulder and upper body. This could throw off the player's balance.

Hook checking

A *hook check* is a stick check that is used when the defender is behind the puck carrier. Have players extend their stick forward, with the shaft close to the ice surface and the blade as flat as possible on the ice. To do this, players must bend one leg to the point where the other knee is on or almost on the ice. From this position, the objective is to hook the puck to himself using the blade of the stick. See Figure 9-13 for an illustration of a hook check.

The hook check is a low-percentage checking tactic. You're better to coach players to work on getting into a quality defensive position and only use the hook check as a last resort.

Figure 9-13: Hooking the puck away.

Sweep checking

The *sweep check* is another low-percentage stickchecking tactic, which is performed from behind or to the side of the puck carrier. Again, have players lower their body and keep the stick low to the ice with the blade as flat as possible. The objective is to try to knock the puck off the opponent's stick using a sweeping action. See Figure 9-14 for body position on a sweep check.

Figure 9-14:
Sweeping
the puck
away.

No attempt is made to control the puck in a sweep check. The checker must exercise care not to take herself out of the play.

Stick lift 'n' press

Players can only stickcheck using the stick lift or stick press if they get good body position on the puck carrier. The objective is both to gain possession of the puck and to prevent the opponent from doing what she wants with it. Players take a position between the opponent and the net they are defending, then lift the shaft of the puck carrier's stick or press down on the shaft to limit what she can do with the puck before trying to hook the puck away. Contact for both the press and the lift is made near the bottom of the shaft for greater control. Both hands are on the stick to lift or press. Figure 9-15a shows the lift position, and Figure 9-15b shows the press position.

Lifting   a

Figure 9-15:
Lifting and
blocking the
stick to steal
the puck.

Pressing   b

Timing is important in the lift or press if the player is to gain possession of the puck. Players must constantly be aware of the puck's movement so that they can time a hook for puck control immediately following the lift or press.

Protecting the puck

The skill of protecting the puck becomes important as players start playing games, either in practice sessions or in competition.

Body positioning is where puck protection starts. Instruct the puck carrier to keep his body between the puck and the checker. Players need to have strength on their skates and weight on their sticks so that they are not easily pushed off the puck. They achieve that by maintaining proper posture: knees bent, forward lean at the waist, and feet approximately shoulder width apart.

Protecting the puck along the boards requires the same body positioning as open ice protection. The only difference is in movement. Along the boards, the puck carrier may have to shuffle in his desired direction as he protects the puck.

In open ice, the puck carrier must use quick foot movement to position his body between the puck and the checker as he constantly changes position to protect the puck in response to the checker moving to try to get it. Players should typically use two hands on the stick when protecting the puck for better puck control. However, one hand can come off the stick and be used to restrict the checker by acting as an additional obstacle, if necessary.

Use one-on-one drills or small ice area scrimmages, such as three-on-three, to practice puck protection.

Taking Face-offs

Teams that win more face-offs than they lose typically have more success. That's because if your team starts play from each face-off with possession of the puck, you have a definite control advantage. At an intermediate level, all players should learn how to take a face-off because they typically still rotate positions in games.

Players also need to learn what to do when not taking the face-off because all players have a role to fulfill in the winning or losing of face-offs. Each player needs to know the difference in his role if his team wins or loses the draw. The roles for non-face-off takers are presented in Chapters 10 and 11, according to whether the face-off is offensive or defensive.

To begin teaching the skills of taking face-offs, have players in groups of three with one acting as the referee to drop the puck. Rotate this role so that everyone gets to practice taking a face-off. Also, emphasize that players are to drop the puck flat, not drilled at the ice. Instruct each player facing off to concentrate on the puck and have his stick on the ice while standing in the ready position.

All face-offs begin the same. Have the face-off taker (we'll call him *the center* because that's usually who takes the face-off) look around to make sure all his teammates are in position and ready for the face-off before he gets set for the puck drop. Then have him adjust his skates to a wider stance than shoulder width to allow for directing more body weight to the stick, and then move the lower hand down the shaft of the stick to put more weight on the blade. This position makes it more difficult for the opposing center to lift your player's stick or push him off the puck.

When ready, players must place the blade of their stick parallel to and ahead of their skates on the nearest edge of the face-off dot. This signals the official that they are ready. At that point, intermediate level players can use four face-off techniques to try to win the face-off: between the skates, spin and draw, tie up, and going forward. You don't need to teach all four at once. Have your intermediate players learn the first two techniques for initial games. The tie up can come later. The going forward technique is a more advanced offensive move that you can teach after players reach a higher level of game sense.

Between the skates

The objective of this play is to have the center draw the puck back between her skates. Have players concentrate on the puck leaving the official's hand. As the puck is dropped, instruct the center to scoop the blade of her stick toward the far side of the face-off circle, so the blade lies across the top of the circle horizontal to her body and behind the opponent's stick. Then have her quickly pull the blade along the ice toward her body, directing the puck to continue sliding backwards between her skates for a teammate to retrieve.

Spin and draw

The objective is for the center to *spin* in front of his opponent and *draw* the puck back to a teammate. Start with concentration on the puck. As the puck is being dropped, have the center knock the opponent's stick away from its intended direction and rotate his body to a position between the puck and the opponent. You can make this face-off strategy effective more easily if your center spins so that the opposing center is on his forehand and then uses his stick or skate to direct the puck back toward a teammate.

Tie up

At times, the center may just want to neutralize the other center cleanly by "tying him up." This happens when the other center has won the majority of draws all game and, instead of trying to beat him, the objective is just to stop him from winning the face-off cleanly. In this case, as the puck is being dropped, have the center put his stick on the top of the opponent's stick to prevent him from pulling the puck back. At the same time, he skates forward and pushes the opponent away from the puck. Prior to the face-off, have a teammate designated to move into the circle to gain possession of the loose puck while your center is tangled up with the opponent.

Going forward

The objective of *going forward* is to draw the puck forward to make a play. This technique is used in the offensive zone if the center wants to take a shot on goal off the draw. In the neutral zone, this play is used to set up a forechecking situation. Again, have the center concentrate on the puck. As the opposing center tries to draw the puck backward, have your player move his stick in the same direction to put more power behind the puck. For a shot on goal, your center needs to be able to take a forehand shot. That means, for face-offs to the goalie's left, the center should be a right shot. To the goalie's right, the center should be a left shot. To create a forechecking situation, the center needs to send the puck at an angle up ice where the winger can race to get it and continue toward the goal.

Set aside time in practices to allow players to work on face-off techniques. Be sure proper technique is being used. Also, have the person dropping the puck do this as gamelike as possible.

Chapter 10

Coaching Offense to Intermediate Players

. . . .

In This Chapter

▶ Teaching play with and without the puck

▶ Moving the puck through the three zones when on the attack

▶ Taking offensive face-offs successfully

. . . .

When your team is in possession of the puck, you are *on offense*. Players on offense either have the puck on their stick or a teammate does. In either situation, offensive concepts apply. These simple principles help teams control the puck and get it up ice into a good scoring position. Your use of the offensive concepts presented in this chapter will allow you to coach offense successfully and give you easy references to use with your players in practice and game situations throughout the season.

Keys to Teaching Good Offense

Good offense means much more than just having goal scorers. A team's players need the skills to control the puck while they get out of their own end, go through the center ice area, and get in position to score. In the offensive end, the cornerstones of being effective offensively as a team include having good puck movement, playing well with the puck, and playing well away from the puck. Intermediate players should be ready to learn these concepts.

Keeping the puck on the move

Young players tend to bury their heads when they get the puck on their stick. To coach good puck movement, you must begin by reminding players to constantly look for opportunities. Use drills that give them no option but to develop a heads-up habit.

With their heads up, you can then coach players to think quick passes all the time. Use drills that allow quick puck movement, or structure drills so that you can encourage players to move the puck quickly from their stick to a teammate's. For example, have small scrimmages during which players move the puck to the first available teammate. A short quick pass is the goal. If all players do this, you eliminate the fear some players have that if they pass the puck, they won't get it back again.

One way to assure that everyone stays involved in the action is to stress *give and go* in practice sessions. This play involves a player *giving* a pass to a teammate and immediately *going* away from that teammate to where he is clear to receive a return pass. Reinforce the concept of making a pass and *not* spending time admiring the pass. You want players to skate continually and present an option for the puck carrier.

To help players understand the value of becoming a good passing option, teach them to embrace the concept of *skating to open ice*. Open ice is any area without an opponent, so the player is free to receive a pass. See Chapter 13 for puck movement drills in which you can focus on short, quick passes and skating for open ice.

Playing with the puck

The player with the puck on his stick is the one charged with making something positive happen offensively for the team. Again, with intermediate players, you'll likely have to remind them to keep their heads up so that they can read the ice and see what their options are. Make sure your practice drills encourage heads up when handling the puck.

When you run puck-handling drills, raise your glove in the air and get the players to look up at the glove. Or ask, "Where's my glove?" as you touch your head, your shoulder, your elbow, or your hip and slowly skate through the players as they do the drill.

As soon as you see that players carrying the puck consistently keep their heads up, you need to get them moving! Sometimes, the player with the puck will be able to pass the puck immediately. More often, he needs to start skating to open ice as he looks to see what options are available. Options may be to keep the puck and attack, to pass to a teammate, or to dump the puck into the opponent's end. Whatever the option, if the puck carrier is moving, he creates more options and makes it more difficult for opposing players to limit his options.

Teach the notion that the puck is to always be moving. If a player is stationary and has possession of the puck, he has two choices: start skating with the puck, or pass the puck. Select or design practice drills with this in mind.

Playing away from the puck

The whole focus of players without the puck is to try to become a passing option for the puck carrier. To do this, have players without the puck look for open ice that will allow a clear passing lane between them and the puck carrier. If an opposing player stands between the player and the puck carrier, encourage the player to move to another area of the ice that eliminates the ability of the opposing player to intercept any attempted pass. See Figure 10-1 for examples of open-ice options.

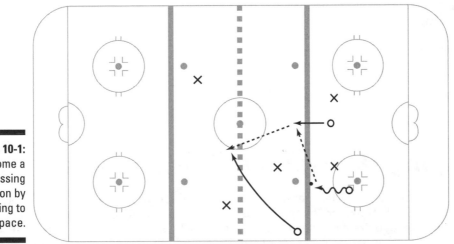

Figure 10-1:
Become a
passing
option by
moving to
open space.

Coach players to be conscious of using all the ice that is available for this purpose. For example, the winger farthest away from the puck carrier can try to find open ice on that wing near the boards. This play often puts players skating away from the puck and not toward the puck, which opens up more space. This allows your team to utilize the entire width of the ice surface to make offensive plays and forces the opposition to cover more area. This practice is known as *creating width* to offensive play.

Players without the puck can also make use of the length of the ice surface. Such players can skate up ice, away from the puck carrier to create options, as long as they recognize the limitations of *offside passes* (refer to Chapter 2 for more about offside infractions). This practice is known as *creating depth* to an attack. See Figure 10-2 for examples of players without the puck creating width and depth to offensive options.

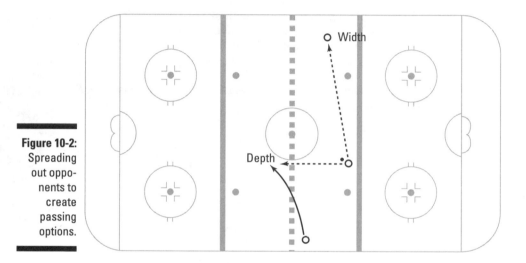

Figure 10-2:
Spreading
out oppo-
nents to
create
passing
options.

Moving through the Offensive Zones

Offense can start anywhere on the ice where your team gets control of the puck. However, the typical offensive attack usually begins in the end of the net you're defending after an unsuccessful shot on goal or a good defensive play. In such a case, your team must work through three zones to create an attack: getting out of the defensive zone, getting through the neutral zone, and mounting a final attack in the offensive zone (see Figure 10-3). You can use the drills in Chapter 13 to help players work effectively in all three zones.

Getting out of your own end

When your team has taken control of the puck and wants to move from its defensive zone into the neutral zone, the situation is referred to as a *breakout*. The most basic breakout technique is to have a player simply skate with the puck into the neutral zone. If the path is clear, this is a reasonable option. However, while carrying the puck, a puck carrier is often an easy check.

A quicker option that's more difficult to stop is to pass to a teammate who has moved to open ice. Short, quick forward passes are most effective. Cross-ice passes are easier to intercept, which gives the opponents an advantage. Use drills that develop the habit of looking for, and getting open, for short, quick passes on breakouts.

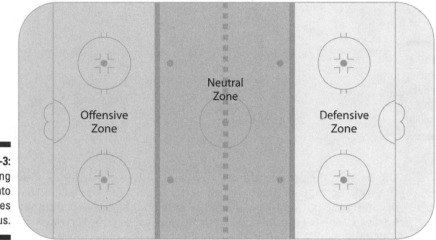

Figure 10-3:
Dividing the ice into three zones of focus.

Emphasize the importance of good passing to make the breakout successful. The first pass has to be on.

Getting through the middle

No matter how your team gets the puck out of the defensive zone, when your players get to the neutral zone, you want your puck carrier to move up the middle of the ice. Two teammates, usually wingers, should skate up ice with the puck carrier, but stay close to the boards, one on each side. This means your team is using the whole width of the ice in the neutral zone.

The second purpose for bringing the puck up the middle of the ice in the neutral zone while wingers stay near the boards is to draw the opponent's defensemen toward the middle of the ice to cover the puck carrier. This movement, called a *wide entry,* allows your team to pass the puck at the last moment to a winger as she enters the offensive zone along the boards. If this neutral-zone pass is timed well, it creates difficult lateral movement for the defensemen and opens more space for offensive play. See Figure 10-4 for an illustration of movement through the neutral zone with a wide entry.

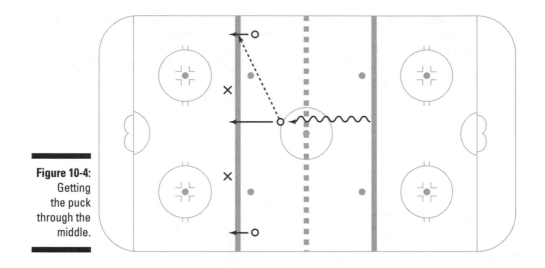

Figure 10-4:
Getting
the puck
through the
middle.

Offensively, the options through the neutral zone, in order of preference, are the wide entry; carrying the puck up the wing, which is easier to check; or dumping the puck into the offensive zone. Make sure that dumping the puck into the zone is your last option because, unless your forwards are very fast, it usually results in turning the puck over to the opponents.

Attacking and scoring

Once your team gets the puck into the offensive zone, the objective is three-fold: to create a scoring chance, to get off a quality shot on goal, and to score. This is usually accomplished by quality (quick and accurate) puck movement and smart positioning away from the puck. If this offense is all that you teach intermediates, you are sure to have decent success.

However, beyond these basics, an effective strategy that you can teach to intermediate players is to look to create an outnumbered situation. To do this, the puck carrier and at least one teammate overload an area that only one opponent is trying to defend. With solid puck movement, your players can create this kind of 2-on-1 situation against an opponent. Have the supporting skater get in position to receive a pass as the puck carrier is about to be checked by an opponent. If the opponent moves to check the support player, he can return the puck to the original puck carrier who would hopefully be free then to take a shot. See Figure 10-5 for an example of overloading an opponent (the right winger has moved to overload the right defensive player).

Figure 10-5:
Outnumbering an opposing defensive player.

Remind players that a weak shot on goal is a better chance to score than no shot on goal. Have practice drills focus on getting the shot away rather than over-passing the puck when a clear shot on goal is an option.

Winning Offensive Face-Offs

Intermediate players need to know the basic face-off alignment. All players must stand on their defensive half of the circle to begin the face-off. Wingers stand at the hash marks on either side of the face-off circle. Defensemen line up at the back of the circle (behind the center) toward the blue line and 10–15 feet apart. See Figure 10-6 for a basic face-off alignment.

Figure 10-6:
Lining up for face-offs to create good options.

The face-off taker is usually your center. He stands in the middle of the circle preparing to pull the puck backwards toward one of his defensemen using one of the techniques explained in Chapter 9. He aims to get the puck to a defenseman because they are in the most protected area during a face-off. That leaves them open to the greatest number of options for setting up an attack.

The defenseman who receives the puck off an offensive face-off has the option to shoot the puck on goal or to make a pass to a teammate. For the latter option to be good, his teammates must get to open ice so that they are free to receive a pass. Looking for open ice becomes each player's job after a teammate takes control of the puck on an offensive face-off.

Check that all players have their sticks on the ice and are in the ready position before the puck is dropped. All players must be prepared to get control of the loose puck, if it comes to their ice, and look for a clear pass or shot. If it does not come their way, but goes to a teammate, all should break immediately for open ice to become a pass option. If the opposition wins control of the draw, your players immediately take defensive positions, which we explain in Chapter 11.

Walk players through face-off alignments in practice. Go over what each player should do in different scenarios. Instead of dropping the puck like the referee would for a face-off, stand on the center dot and toss the puck to an area as though the center drew the puck to that spot. Then talk through the responsibilities of each player. Repeat this for different possible face-off scenarios.

Chapter 11

Coaching Defense to Intermediate Players

*W*hen the opposition team has the puck, your team is on *defense*. The object of defense is to stop the opposition from going where they want with the puck and to stop them from shooting on the net. To do so, defensive players may be responsible for the player who has the puck on his stick, for another player on the offensive team, or for protecting an area of the ice.

In this chapter, we give you tools to teach your team defensive concepts that will help them play good defensive hockey, which means knowing who they are responsible for and when and what to do about it. You can identify reference phrases to use with your team during practice sessions and in game situations to reinforce the defensive concepts.

Keys to Teaching Good Defense

Good defensive play is actually quite simple if a few fundamental principles are followed consistently. Although you should teach intermediate players these principles, players will take some time before they can perform the skills consistently. The keys are position, knowing what to do with the puck, and knowing what to do without it. The ultimate goal of good defense is to gain possession of the puck and go on offense. Teach players to be patient and use disciplined team and individual play to make this happen.

Position! Position!

If a player is in the proper defensive position, then 90 percent of her defensive job is already done. The best defensive position is when the player is between her net and the offensive player she is responsible for. See Figure 11-1 for the best defensive positions. The defending player's stick should be on the ice between the puck and the opponent, if the opponent is without the puck. If the opponent has the puck, your player's stick should be between the puck and the net.

Figure 11-1:
Assuming a position that inhibits the opponent from receiving the puck.

Having players focus on getting into position to place their stick between the puck and the opponent — or the puck and the net — allows the defensive player to discourage opponents from passing to a teammate. It also allows the defensive player to use some form of checking technique on the offensive player before that player can create an offensive play against your team. This position usually puts the defensive player on the defensive side of the puck as well as the opponent, which may provide an opportunity to steal or poke the puck away.

Instruct defensive players to always keep their sticks on the ice to reduce ice space available to the offensive team to make passes. This habit also increases the possibility of intercepting a pass. The concept or phrase to use here is to *take away passing lanes*. In practice sessions, emphasize taking away passing lanes as the players perform defensive drills.

Passing drills such as monkey-in-the-middle (refer to Chapter 7) are great opportunities to work on taking away passing lanes. Be sure to verbally remind the "monkey" to keep her stick on the ice as the drill is going on.

Covering the puck carrier

The job of the defensive player who is covering the offensive player with the puck is to quickly put pressure on the player to limit the time she has to make a pass or some other play with the puck.

Instruct players to skate quickly toward the offensive player who gets the puck, keeping their sticks both on the ice and to the side of their bodies that takes away the best passing lane for the offensive player (the pass that poses the greatest scoring threat for your team). See Figure 11-2 for a good defensive position on the player with the puck.

Figure 11-2:
Cutting off a puck carrier's best options.

By keeping their bodies in position and their sticks on the ice, players also take space away from the puck-carrying player, leaving her fewer skating and passing options. It also gives the defensive player a better opportunity to stickcheck the opponent and possibly to steal the puck or poke it loose.

Walk through a variety of player-with-the-puck offensive scenarios explaining how to take the best body and stick positions. Have players play one-on-one and two-on-two to get the feel of adjusting to good defensive positions.

Defending away from the puck

Every player is responsible for one opponent defensively when teams have even numbers of players in play (see Chapter 18 for details on how to defend in uneven situations). That clearly means that only one player needs to be on the puck carrier. Everyone else's job on the team is to make it difficult or impossible for the puck carrier to use the player they are responsible for. If all members of the defensive team do their job well, it leads to weak attacks, frustration, impatience, and turnovers by the opposition. This is good!

See Figure 11-3 for examples of good defensive positions on players without the puck.

Figure 11-3:
Making nonpuck carriers useless.

Defensive players are most effective when they keep their feet moving so that they can constantly adjust to the movements of their opponent. Teach your players to be moving at least as fast as the player they are covering defensively. Have them make adjustments that allow them to legally shadow the player without the puck so well that he doesn't present a good offensive option for the puck carrier. This means the players must constantly be between the opponent and the net they are defending while their stick takes away passing lanes from the opponent they are checking.

Players can only check one player at a time. Don't let them go from one offensive player to another as situations change. Encourage players to concentrate on the one offensive player that they are responsible for checking. Repeat the mantra: Stay with your man (or woman).

Moving through the Defensive Zones

Defense can start anywhere on the ice when your team loses control of the puck. However, this most often occurs after your team has had an unsuccessful shot on net. In this case, your defensive players have three zones to defend to prevent opponents from having a scoring opportunity and to try to get the puck back. These are the same three zones listed in Chapter 10 for mounting an attack, but on defense you move through them in reverse order: offensive zone, neutral zone, and defensive zone.

To play defense effectively, players must keep their heads up at all times so that they know where the puck is. They must continuously adjust their position and that of their stick relative to the movement of the puck and their opponent. Playing defense is never static.

Stopping opponents from getting started

The technique used to stop opponents from getting out of their end of the rink (your offensive zone) is called *forechecking*. Forechecking is when your team puts pressure (by player position and presence) on the opponents immediately to make it difficult for them to control the puck and play. Teams who don't forecheck tend to skate to their defensive zone and wait for the opponents to come on the attack, which gives up two zones of defensive opportunities.

To teach forechecking, have the player nearest to the puck carrier give quick pressure by cutting off the puck carrier's passing or moving options. The coaching phrase used in this case is "on the puck!" At the same time, instruct your remaining players to have their sticks on the ice out to one side of the body and to skate into open ice positions that cut off potential passes to other opponents (see Figure 11-4). This makes it much more difficult for the offensive team to complete passes and increases your team's opportunity for intercepting a pass and regaining control of the puck.

Figure 11-4: Pressuring opponents in their own end.

As your team practices forechecking, your players will begin to anticipate the offensive team's options and get better at working together to eliminate them.

When coaching beginners, you'll be doing enough defensively by having players simply skate back to their defensive zone after losing the puck in the offensive zone. Players don't have the skating and checking skills to stop opponents from coming out of their zone, so concentration is rightly placed on getting to the defensive zone to protect the net.

Coaches of intermediate teams can phase in forechecking by having the two defensemen head down ice while the nearest forward immediately pressures the puck carrier and the other two forwards retreat to the neutral zone. If the puck carrier successfully passes the puck to a teammate, the next nearest defensive player pressures the new puck carrier and so on through the offensive and neutral zones. This three-man forecheck usually only slows down the offensive team and only occasionally creates a turnover. But it serves as a useful step toward learning full-team forechecking. Remind forwards in the three-man forecheck that, if the opposition does break through, they must race down the ice to get into good defensive positions in their defensive end. As players develop their speed, skating skills, and fitness, they will be ready for full-team forechecking.

Defending the neutral zone

When your opponents get the puck into the neutral zone, your team defends using a technique called *backchecking*. A backchecking defense exerts pressure on the opponents as they try to come through the middle ice area so that it is difficult for them to move and control the puck.

To teach backchecking, instruct players to skate at the same pace as the offensive team and to get into a good defensive position on the opposing player that they are responsible for. That position is one where your players can cut off passes or restrict movement. Most teams try to advance the puck up the middle of the ice (refer to Chapter 10 for more about an offensive perspective). On defense, your team tries to take this ice away by occupying the middle of the ice and taking away angles the offensive players want to use. This play forces the players to move the puck out toward the boards as they move through the neutral zone — which eliminates passing options for the offensive team as they enter your defensive zone. It also makes them easier to check. See Figure 11-5 for an example of a backchecking formation.

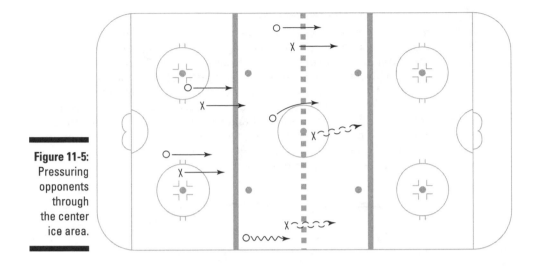

Figure 11-5:
Pressuring
opponents
through
the center
ice area.

Protecting your net

After the opposition successfully moves into your defensive zone, your priority is to protect the net. Fundamentally, instruct players to keep their sticks on the ice and to take up one of two positions:

- ✔ **When checking an offensive player without the puck,** players position themselves between their opponent and the puck as they use their sticks to take away passing options.

- ✔ **When checking an offensive player with the puck,** players place themselves between the opponent and the net to take away scoring options.

However, you need to consider a few additional elements.

Hedging your position

Selecting the best position is not always a clear either/or decision. Often a player must take up a position that covers more than one threatening option at the same time. In these cases, players should hedge their best coverage for the angle that presents the most dangerous opponent's action. See Figure 11-6 for an example of hedging.

In this illustration, the obvious risk for the defenseman on the puck carrier is a shot on goal, so her best position would be between the puck and the net. But you also face a significant risk of having the opponent cut around her right side to drive in on the net, thereby creating a higher percentage shot. So the defenseman wants to *hedge* her body position (give a little) on the puck, using her stick to help cover the puck, and position her body to discourage a move around and in on the net. Note that the defenseman away from the puck is between the opponent and the puck, using her stick to take away the best passing option while hedging to keep her body in position to defend the net (higher risk) if a pass succeeds in getting through or the opponent tries to go around her toward the net.

Figure 11-6:
Hedging for harmless action only.

Preventing an outnumbered situation

Offensive teams often try to create a numerical advantage against a defensive player using the puck carrier and at least one other player. Therefore, you must coach your defensive team to try to keep all defensive situations even numbered. Teach them to do this by having each defensive player constantly maintain good defensive position on the opponent he is responsible for. This makes it very difficult for the offense to create any outnumbered situations.

Have players verbally communicate with each other on defense. They can call out which player they are checking to avoid having two players on the same player and allowing another to go unchecked. Players simply call the number of the player they are checking.

Defending when you are outnumbered

When defensive players actually are outnumbered due to a penalty or a lagging player, the rule of defensive play immediately changes from being responsible for one opponent to being responsible for an area of ice. Have players mentally divide the defensive zone into quarters with each player responsible for anyone who comes into their quarter. This is called playing a box. See Figure 11-7 for the areas of responsibility.

Players must play the opponents by staying between the net and the player(s) in their quarter. Their objective is to force passes and limit movement rather than allow shots. They can watch for an opportunity to create and get control of a loose puck, but this objective is secondary. Patience is key.

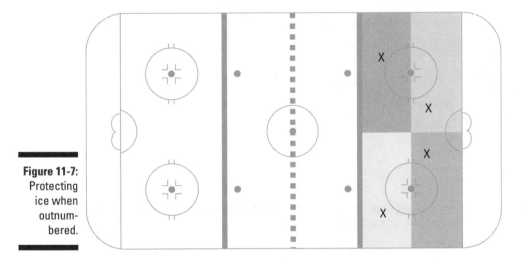

Figure 11-7:
Protecting
ice when
outnum-
bered.

Winning Defensive Face-Offs

Players need to know the importance of face-offs in the defensive zone. If the defending team loses the face-off and gives possession of the puck to the attacking team, it becomes one more scoring opportunity for the other guy.

To maximize your chance of winning defensive zone face-offs, change from the basic face-off alignment (illustrated in Chapter 10) to putting the winger in whose lane the face-off is to take place next to the hash marks nearest the boards with the center standing at the face-off dot. The defenseman in whose lane the face-off is taking place stands at the back of the circle or at the goal line slightly toward the net side. The second defenseman takes the hash mark position nearest the net, and the second winger stands beside him in front of the net or on the circle according to where the best opposing shooters are located. See Figure 11-8 for an illustration of defensive zone face-off alignment. All players should be in the ready position with their sticks on the ice and know who is to receive the puck.

Have the center draw the puck back toward his defenseman. As he gets possession of the puck, the other defenseman moves to provide a pass option. Meanwhile, the center and wingers momentarily step into the circle to become obstacles opponents must skate around if they want to get to the puck, then move quickly up ice to provide pass or breakout options.

Figure 11-8:
Protecting
your net on
defensive
zone
face-offs.

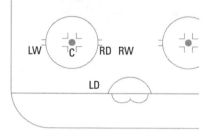

If your team loses the draw, all players immediately move to cut off options for the player each is responsible for.

Chapter 12

Teaching Goaltending Basics

*G*oaltending may just be the most unique position in any sport — period. Goaltenders (or *goalies*) wear lots of bulky equipment; they are confined to an area sometimes referred to as a cage; and people shoot hard rubber objects at them all the time! Why would anyone want to be a goalie?

But they do. Usually at some point during intermediate play, players begin to sort themselves out by preference and ability. As a coach, you can watch for the unique talents required for goaltending, such as agility, focus, and good eye-hand and eye-foot coordination, and you can encourage players with these talents to consider playing the position. More often, you'll see the glint in some kid's eye whenever he gets to play in net. Those are the kids you help become better goaltenders.

Coaches need to have a goaltending segment in every practice plan at the intermediate level. Even if you rotate all players through the position, the basic skills are useful to all — and it's good for skaters to understand the position to better play against it and in support of it.

Goaltenders should be properly warmed up for practices and games. Make sure that they do the skating and passing drills that the other players do at the beginning of practice, then allow them a couple of minutes to do additional agility and stretching preparation in their crease area. Finally, use long shots as the first shots on them in a practice with the shooters instructed to just get the puck on the net, and allow the goaltender to get a feel for the puck. Gradually have players increase the intensity of the shots by allowing them to shoot from closer to the net.

Instead of using all your players to do shots to warm up the goalie, you can designate one of your better shooters to take a number of pucks and position himself 10 to 15 feet in front of the goaltender. The shooter then shoots easy shots to designated areas, such as ten shots along the ice, then ten shots to the blocker, and then ten shots to the catching glove.

Building good goaltending for your team is a special coaching challenge. Goaltenders must have good skating skills, and they must learn to understand playing angles. They also need a unique temperament because pressure and responsibility can weigh heavily on young goalies.

We provide step-by-step instruction for teaching and developing goaltending skills in this chapter. Turn to Chapter 13 for some excellent drills for practicing these skills.

Knowing How to Stand

Young goaltenders often emulate the styles of play used by top NHL goalies of the day. Some play standing up, some have a deep crouch, and others fall and smother the puck. Coaches need to let young goalies find their own style through natural development as they learn to stop the puck. However, just as skaters need one, goaltenders must also have a basic *goaltender ready position,* regardless of style. This position provides the best chance of making the most saves and is fundamental to a goalie's ability to protect against rebounds. So, to teach good goaltending, start with the ready stance.

To teach the goaltender ready position, have goalies stand with their feet shoulder-width apart with an exaggerated bend in the knees and their weight on the balls of their feet. Their backs are straight so that their shoulders line up over their knees and toes. The catching glove is up and to the side of the body and open forward. They need to grip the stick with the blocker just above where the paddle narrows to the shaft. The stick blade should lie on the ice between 3 and 6 inches in front of the skates at a slight angle toward the pads. See Figure 12-1a and Figure 12-1b for front and side views of the goaltender ready position.

a

b

Figure 12-1:
The front and side views of a goaltender who is ready to stop the puck.

Guiding Goalie Gymnastics

Anyone who watches hockey knows that goalies are required to perform some amazing leaps, twists, and turns in their attempts to prevent goals. These feats begin with having the skating skill to stay on, get back on, and move well on their feet. Beyond skating, goaltenders need to learn stick, hand, and body-positioning skills.

Skating skills

Like all hockey players, skating skills are the foundation on which a goaltender builds all other puck-stopping skills. In fact, goalies need to be the best skaters on the team. For these reasons, goalies should do all the skating drills that other team members do. The team skating drills reinforce edge control, striding, balance, and agility. Goaltenders then need additional skating drills to work on coordination, reflexes, and mobility around the net.

Three basic skating movements, used on a regular basis, allow goalies to get in position to make saves. All three movements have one important element in common: The goalie must always try to remain *square to the puck*. This means the goalie must position his body so that the highest percentage of his body's surface area faces the puck and stands between the net and the puck. This gives the goalie the broadest coverage for stopping (or getting hit by!) the puck. See Figure 12-2a for an example of a goalie standing square to the puck, and then note all the holes that players can shoot pucks through when a goalie is not square to the puck, as shown in Figure 12-2b.

Figure 12-2:
A goalie should stand square to the puck.

a

Right

Figure 12-2:
Continued.

b

Wrong

When players understand what playing square to the puck means, teach young goaltenders the three skating skills they need to use around the net to get into position to stand square to the puck. These include the shuffle, lateral T push, and forward and back motion.

The shuffle

The shuffle technique is a series of short sidesteps that allow the goalie to quickly move laterally over a short distance, such as when he needs to quickly reposition in the goal mouth. If going left, for example, goalies step sideways with the left foot, then, keeping the feet parallel, bring the right foot parallel to the left and repeat the step-together pattern until repositioned. They want to keep their weight on the balls of their feet for best mobility. Goalies are to remain in the ready position while they make the quick steps and minimize the amount of time the leg pads are apart. Advise players to move the stick with the lead pad to help cover the temporary gap that occurs between the pads as they step laterally. The objective is to maintain the goalie stance as much as possible while they stay square to the puck.

Lateral т push

The lateral т push allows goalies to move a longer distance than the shuffle, such as when they need to go from one goal post to the other. Have goalies turn the skate on the side they want to move to in the direction they want to go, so it forms a т with the other foot. Then have them push off with the inside edge of that back skate. Have players keep their stick blade on the ice covering the gap that opens between their legs. Their catching glove stays in the ready position and the shoulders stay as square as possible to the goaltender ready position and the puck. See Figure 12-3 for good position during the lateral т push.

Forward and back

Good goaltending requires goalies to be able to move forward to cut down on shooting options for attackers, but then to quickly move back closer to the net in case a pass or rebound creates another option. To move forward, instruct goalies to do a quick push off the inside edge of the driving skate, then glide forward in the ready stance keeping their stick on the ice ahead of and between their skates. Have them use the snowplow to stop. To go backwards, instruct them to do a quick c cut for the drive, then to glide in the ready position and stop by pressing the toes out. Both forward and back drives are short and quick to maximize the time they present the ready stance to the puck.

Use specific goaltender drills to improve agility and mobility. These drills can be as basic as simulating goalie moves used in making saves, such as having the goaltender perform a repeat sequence of quick in-net maneuvers including shuffle left, lateral т right, forward, back, and down-up. Reverse the left and right actions on the next repeat.

Figure 12-3:
Getting
across the
net quickly.

Making saves

When goalies can skate effectively and move into the ready position quickly, they'll begin to make some saves automatically, by virtue of their body being in the way, if nothing else. Then you can begin to add the finer skills of goaltending, starting with helping them understand the areas of the net that must be protected.

Protecting spaces

A goaltender must protect five areas of the net, which are often referred to as *holes*. See Figure 12-4 for an illustration of these five areas.

When a goalie uses the goalie stance, he presents as much of his body and equipment as possible for shooters to hit with their shots. When shooters go for the holes not covered by the goalie stance, the goalie has a variety of options according to which hole the shooter aims for. He can use his body, stick, gloves, and pads to defend these five areas. Following is a list of what works most consistently to protect each of the five areas of the net:

✔ The #1 hole is low on the stick side of the goaltender. This is where most goals are scored. The goalie's best save option in this area is the leg pad, skate, or blocker, according to the puck's elevation and distance from the goalie's body.

✔ The #2 hole is low on the glove side of the goalie. The best save options in this area are the stick, leg pad, or skate. Catching low with the glove is difficult to do, although if the puck rises to knee height, the glove becomes an option.

✔ The #3 hole is high on the glove side. Stops in this area are best made by the catching glove, especially when standing in the ready position.

✔ The #4 hole is high to the stick side of the goaltender. The blocker best protects this area. The goalie must be in the ready stance to cover the top corner.

✔ The #5 hole is the space between the goalie pads. This area is vulnerable for a goaltender because it opens up every time he moves. The best protection is to keep the stick on the ice to minimize the size of the hole and to keep the pads together as much as possible to minimize the amount of time a hole is available, which is best achieved by making movements as short and quick as possible.

The concept of presenting the goalie stance square to all shots is referred to as *playing big*. Make young goaltenders aware of this mental tip while in goal. Reinforce playing big in practice as your goalies work in shooting drills. As the drill is running, simply ask the goalie, "Are you playing big?"

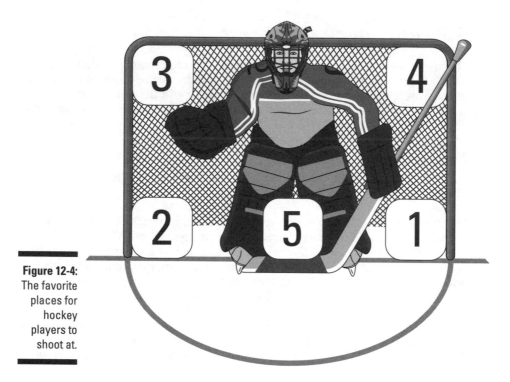

Figure 12-4:
The favorite places for hockey players to shoot at.

In intermediate hockey, most goals are scored from the knees down because players cannot yet raise the puck accurately for shots. Therefore, you should concentrate on teaching goalies to protect the #1, #2, and #5 holes first. As shooters learn to raise shots, begin work on protecting the #3 and #4 holes.

Stopping pucks

Following is a list of fundamental concepts to teach beginning goalies to help them make saves consistently, regardless of their style or skill level:

- Goalies must keep their heads up and their eyes on the puck at all times, even if the puck is in the other end of the ice.

- Goalies must present their ready stance to all attacks so that, at worst, pucks can hit them. Saves don't have to be fancy; they need to be effective.

- Goalies must position themselves on the puck (square to the puck and between the puck and the net), not on the body of the shooter.

- When you have two attackers and only one defenseman, goalies must play the puck carrier as usual, positioning themselves square to the puck and between the puck and the net. The defenseman's job is to prevent a pass to the second attacker.

✔ Have goalies keep their eyes on the puck, following it into their glove, stick, or body, and then give with, or cushion, its contact. This gives them control over rebounds.

✔ Instruct goalies to keep their stick and gloves slightly in front of the body, not against it, so they can cushion incoming pucks. Avoid "lazy" gloves that drop below the waist.

✔ Have goalies minimize dangerous rebounds by redirecting the puck away from the traffic flow or by smothering the puck with the catching glove. Goalies must learn to feel the angles of their stick, skate blades, and blocker for redirecting pucks effectively.

Playing Specific Shots

After goalies get consistent with the fundamental concepts, you can begin to teach some more specific save techniques that are used for certain types of shots. The most valuable of these techniques is called playing the angles, which is often used in combination with another technique, poke checking. Goaltenders also need to learn the butterfly technique and, finally, stacking the pads.

Playing the angles

Playing the angles means presenting the goalie stance square to the puck, regardless of what angle the puck is coming from. But playing the angles also goes one step further to include moving into positions that cut down openings that the shooter has on the net. The type of movement that does this best is called *telescoping*. When instructing and in early drills, don't be concerned about goals being scored against your goalie. Just have her work on sorting out angles. Use telescoping, shuffling, and side-to-side movements as necessary to adjust positioning so that she can play square to the puck.

Telescoping is when the goaltender moves out from his net to face a shot. The purpose of this technique is to give the shooter less of the net to see or hit with his shot. This also gives the goaltender a greater chance of being hit with the puck and making a save. The risk the goalie needs to balance is the chance that the shooter could stickhandle around him or pass the puck off and get an open shot on net. The basic rule is once you move out, stay out; no running back to the net mid-play. To do this safely, have goalies move out quickly to the optimum position, then make adjustments as necessary to maintain an optimum position (one that continues to cut off the angles) on the puck. Remind goalies when telescoping to stay square to the puck, to maintain the goalie ready stance, and to minimize holes as much as possible.

To telescope effectively, goalies must work on developing an awareness on the ice of where they are relative to the net and what view they are blocking. Coaches can teach this by attaching ropes to each of the goal posts and extending them out to where the puck is on the ice. Then have a goalie start in the crease between the posts and slowly move out toward the puck. Have her stop at different distances from the net to see what gaps exist between her body and the ropes. This will show the goaltender what portion of the net she is protecting and not protecting at different spots as she telescopes out to make a save. Repeat this with the puck in different locations, such as those illustrated in Figure 12-5. The Xs in this figure represent some of the stop-and-see positions for the goalie. This is a great visual for your goalies!

Goalies can adjust their speed of movement to suit the situation. If the shooter is far out, their movement can be slower. If the shooter is close, they must quickly get out of the net to cut down the amount of net available to the shooter.

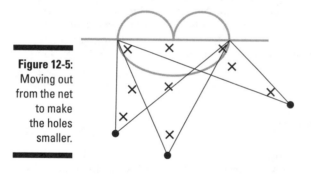

Figure 12-5:
Moving out
from the net
to make
the holes
smaller.

Advise goalies that although they should usually go out to cut off the angle, they do not always go out. The general rule is that if the puck is in front of the net, go out; if it is behind or in the corner, stay in the net.

To play a shooter who is coming out of the corner, the goaltender must hold a position tight to the goal post, making sure no holes exist between the post and the goalie's body or pads. The stick blade is on the ice as square as possible to the puck. See Figure 12-6 for good post position. The goalie should also anticipate an opportunity to use his stick to prevent a pass going to the front of the net. If the shooter wraps around behind the net, the goalie uses the parallel T push to quickly get to the other post where he resumes the same tight position against the post.

Poke checking

The *poke check* is a quick, straightforward action made with the blade of the stick lying almost flat on the ice. Teach goaltenders to extend their elbow to a straight arm and not to lean forward with the upper body when performing the poke check. Also advise goalies to avoid using a sweeping action with the stick. This movement is usually too slow and often results in the goaltender losing his balance. After executing the poke check, goalies immediately resume the ready stance.

Figure 12-6: Closing holes when playing at the side of the net.

The poke check can be an effective deterrent in the telescoped position or with players cutting near the crease (we talk about telescoping in the previous section). The poke check is also effective when a shooter attacks the net with no defenders present, such as on a breakaway. In this situation, teach the goalie to be patient and to let the shooter make the first move. He may then get the opportunity to use a poke check to knock the puck off the shooter's stick.

At the end of the goal stick, have goalies use tape to build up a knob. This stops the stick from sliding out of the goaltender's hand when he is using the poke check.

Butterfly

In the butterfly save technique, teach goalies to keep their chest and upper body upright and square to the puck. When the shot is released, goalies drop to their knees with their pads and feet fanned out so that their toes point toward the goal posts. Instruct them to keep their sticks on the ice to cover the #5 hole between their knees. See Figure 12-7 for a good butterfly position.

This technique is effective against low shots, especially in high traffic, such as on screen shots, when the goalie may not be able to see exactly where the puck is. It provides wide coverage of the ice surface and puts the catching glove in a good position to catch the puck or smother rebounds.

Stacking pads

The stacking pads technique is a desperation technique for goaltenders. This technique is used when the goaltender is at one side of the net and a shot comes in from the opposite side too quickly for him to move over square to the puck. The goaltender literally throws his pads toward the path of the shot like a slide into home plate in baseball.

Teach players the move by having them start with the parallel T push across the crease toward the incoming puck. As soon as they push off, the players drop to the knee of that driving leg and let the gliding leg slide off the ice as they extend the lower knee to stack their pads two high across the crease, forming a wall to block the shot. The catching glove stays ready above the hip and the stick covers the ice surface above the head. See Figure 12-8 for the stacking pads drop (a) and end (b) positions.

Figure 12-7: Covering as much ice surface as possible.

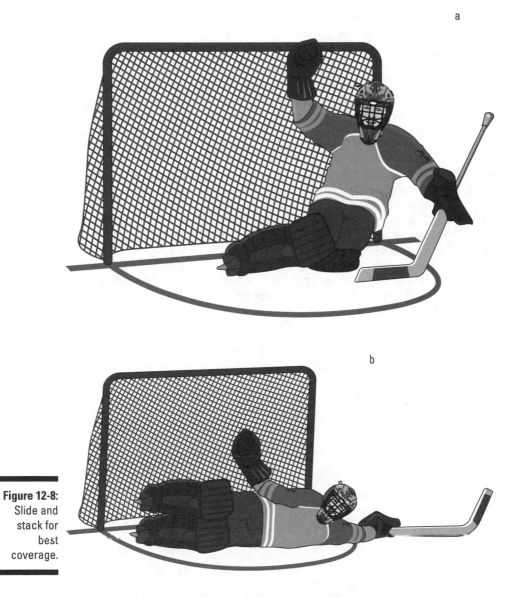

a

b

Figure 12-8:
Slide and
stack for
best
coverage.

Priming for the Mental Game

Goaltenders come in all sizes, shapes, and mental packages. All must have a
positive attitude about the position. Goals are scored against all goaltenders.
Goaltenders need to learn to be able to determine why the puck got past
them, make adjustments, and move on. Be sure to reinforce the practice of
refocusing on what they can do after the opponents score.

Goaltenders require courage. Pucks sometimes miss the protective padding — and they can hurt. Players often skate toward the goal at high speeds that can result in a player falling down and crashing into the goalie. The goaltender must have the courage to hold his position and stay focused on the puck.

Confidence is important to every player. However, goalies may need more than most. They need to believe in their skills so that they do not second-guess their performance when a goal is scored on them. Preparation is a major source of this confidence. Therefore, as coach, you must spend regular, quality practice time with your goaltenders, or bring in an assistant who can.

After a goal against, make it a routine for your goaltender to quickly assess why the goal was scored, make the necessary corrections mentally, and then get back to the game at hand.

Temperament is a big factor in the goaltending mental game. A goaltender cannot possibly play at a consistently high level if he doesn't have control of his emotions. He can't let anger influence his play; he can't blame others for goals against, even when they may have made things more difficult. Teach goalies that everyone makes mistakes. What makes a goalie good is when he can learn and move on.

A positive attitude is the only attitude that makes playing goal tolerable. Coaches can help cultivate this positive attitude in general by curtailing anger and blame in their own actions and body language and instead, helping players view mistakes as learning opportunities and carry on with the positives. Goaltenders can have a lot of pressure put on them, either by themselves or by others. A positive attitude will allow them to cope with the pressures and stay focused on what needs to be done to be a successful goaltender.

Chapter 13

Drills for Intermediate Players

· ·

In This Chapter

▶ Using drills to develop players' skating skills

▶ Improving puck skills through drills

▶ Designing drills that combine skills in gamelike situations

▶ Developing offensive reading abilities

▶ Cultivating a sense of position through defensive drills

▶ Developing goaltending skills

· ·

As players master the basic skills of skating and puck handling, coaches can begin to shift the focus from technique to speed and quickness in these skills. You also need to introduce more complexity in the drills so that players begin to think more about gamelike situations. Intermediate players are also ready to shift from individual to team focus by using simple offensive and defensive concepts in drills. Finally, this is the level at which players discover that they really like or dislike goaltending, so those who want to tend goal should begin to master those specific skills.

To serve these needs, the drills in this chapter are divided into skating, puck skills, and then combination drills for more complexity. Then we offer specialty drills for practicing offense and defense, followed by a section of drills for developing goaltenders. See the cheat sheet at the front of the book if you are not familiar with the symbols used in the drills.

Skating Drills

The following drills help develop the intermediate skating skills of lateral movement, pivoting, and turning. After your players master technique, emphasize quickness and agility.

Face the clock

This drill lets players work on both forward and backward lateral movement to both the left and right as they skate the perimeter of the ice.

How it works: Players skate the perimeter of the ice, facing one end (such as toward the score clock) of the rink for the entire drill. Skaters move at an angle laterally three strides right and three strides left as they progress forward going down one side of the ice, and then three strides right and three strides left as they skate backward up the other side of the ice. Halfway through the drill, change directions. You can add pucks in this drill when skill execution allows.

Coaching pointers: Always check that players maintain good skating posture. Specifically, check that they keep a good bend at the knees so that their bodies aren't moving up and down during the crossovers.

Skate the circles

This drill is to help players become proficient at skating both right and left on forward turns. This skill is essential for overall skating efficiency.

How it works: Using the two circles in each end zone, have players skate a figure-eight pattern around the outside of each circle. Emphasize that they must keep striding as they skate the turns. See Figure 13-1 for the skating pattern. Use neutral zone dots for a third group if necessary.

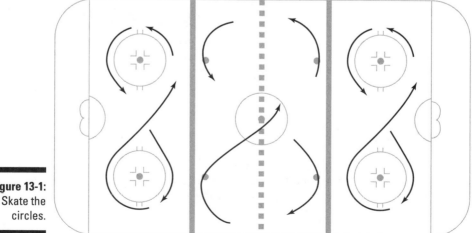

Figure 13-1:
Skate the
circles.

Coaching pointers: When turning, check that players keep their sticks on the ice and to the inside of the circle. This means that one hand is on the stick on one turn and two hands on the other. Also make sure that players push from the hip as they skate the turns. See that players continuously stride all the way around each circle.

Whistle pivots

This drill helps players develop the ability to pivot both to the right and to the left. If players cannot pivot both ways, their lack of mobility can be exploited in game situations.

How it works: Have players skate the perimeter of the ice. On the first whistle, they pivot from forward to backward, on the second whistle, they pivot backward to forward, on the third whistle, they pivot forward to backward, and so on. Halfway through the drill, go in the opposite direction.

Coaching pointers: Make sure that players have two hands on the stick when pivoting forward to backward and backward to forward and one hand on the stick when skating forward and backward. Check that they keep the stick on the ice at all times. Also make sure that players stay in the proper skating posture all the time, with knees bent, and that they do not straighten up as they pivot.

Puck Skills Drills

The drills in this section help players develop the intermediate skills of more advanced passing, shooting, and scoring. Work on accuracy first, slowing the drills down, if necessary. Then begin to emphasize quickness and power.

Flip-snap drill

Passing skills make plays work. This drill lets players practice passing over an object on the ice and making long, hard passes when required.

How it works: Have players skate in pairs around the ice surface. Place sticks on the ice at the blue lines, as illustrated in Figure 13-2. As the skaters come to the sticks, one flips a pass over the stick to her partner who then carries it to the next stick where she flips the puck back to the original carrier. Have them make wrist passes as they go on either side of the net as indicated in the illustration. Coming back the other side of the ice, the puck carrier releases a snap pass as she reaches the bottom of the first circle which should be received by her partner at the blue line. The new puck carrier skates to the center line and releases a snap pass, which her partner is to receive at the top of the next circle. After a few repeats, reverse direction of the drill.

Coaching pointers: Make sure players open up the stick blade to make the flip pass and close the blade over the puck when making the snap pass. In both cases, be sure that the receiver presents his stick blade as a target. Eventually, help players incorporate the passes into a smooth skating rhythm, though initially, they will likely need to glide to focus on making the passes.

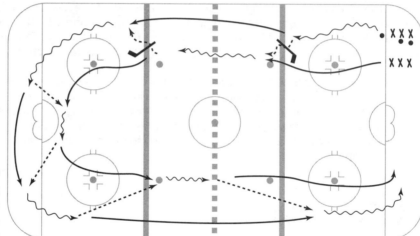

Figure 13-2:
Flip-snap
drill.

Figure-eight passing

This is a good concentration passing and receiving drill that features quickness, accuracy, and timing. The figure-eight skater has to be sharp to receive and complete all the passes, while his stationary partner has to have good timing with his passes. The drill also works on footwork and pivoting skills.

How it works: Have players work in pairs. Place two pylons or gloves six feet apart. The first player stands with a puck between and in front of the pylons. The second player skates a figure eight around the pylons, pivoting so that he always faces the first player. This skater keeps his stick on the ice as he skates so that he can receive and return ten passes from the first player as he enters the center of the figure eight. See Figure 13-3 for the drill pattern. Have players switch positions after ten passes. Coaches can specify or mix passing requirements, such as forehand wrist pass, backhand wrist pass, or flip pass.

Coaching pointers: Help the stationary players focus on timing their passes to meet a moving target. Check that the figure-eight skater stays in proper skating posture throughout the drill. Make sure both players keep their sticks on the ice all the time. Confirm the mechanics of whichever pass you are using, especially the wrist action and location of puck release relative to their body.

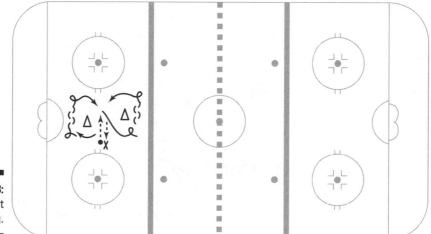

Figure 13-3: Figure-eight passing.

Hot-spot shooting

This scoring drill for shooters helps build confidence in players' scoring ability. In addition, as a saves drill for goaltenders, this drill provides coaches with a clear opportunity to focus on save techniques.

How it works: Using both end zones, have players pick their *hot spot,* which is their favorite scoring spot. Assign numbers to each player and have players shoot in sequence. See Figure 13-4 for an example. Go right to left (for the goaltender) one time and left to right the next round of shots. Coaches can specify the type of shot, such as a forehand wrist shot, backhand wrist shot, or snap shot. For slap shot practice, pick favorite long-shot hot spots.

Coaching pointers: Time the shots so that the goaltenders can get in position and have a chance to make a save. Tell shooters to shoot to score as opposed to simply making the goalie move. Watch shooters' and goaltenders' techniques closely for an opportunity to provide improvement tips.

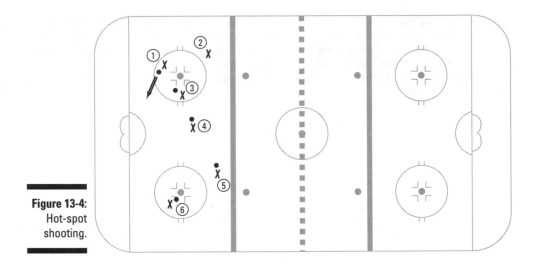

Figure 13-4:
Hot-spot
shooting.

Figure-eight shooting

This is a great drill that combines passing, quick shot, puck control, and foot-work skills for the skaters. The drill is also a challenging saves drill for the goaltender.

How it works: See Figure 13-5 for starting player and pylon placement. As X1 skates a figure-eight pattern through the pylons, always facing the net, X2 and X3 alternate passing to X1 for a shot on net. After six shots, have skaters rotate positions. On each shot, have the goaltender go to the post on the side the pass is coming from then out to play the shot.

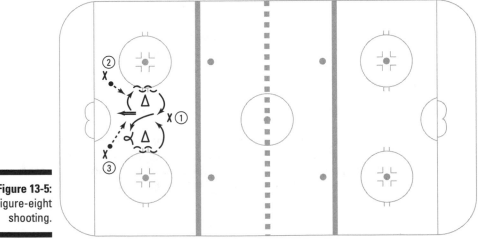

Figure 13-5:
Figure-eight
shooting.

Coaching pointers: Make sure all three skaters have their sticks on the ice all the time. Insist on quality passing that is accurate to the best time and place for the shooter. Check that shooters make a quick release and hit the net with a legitimate scoring attempt each time.

Circle shooting

The three different drills presented here are to let players practice three common types of shots frequently used in the game. The drill also helps players learn to go for rebounds.

How it works: Use the four end-zone circles and face-off dots for the skating path, as illustrated in Figure 13-6. Have players work out of all four corners to go in for their shot and stay for the rebound from the next shooter. Do only one of the three illustrated drills at a time. Use pattern A to practice shots from the slot, pattern B for low shots, and pattern C for wide shots.

Coaching pointers: Make sure players focus on hitting the net with legitimate scoring chances with each shot. Encourage players to keep striding when they shoot rather than stopping to shoot. Also remind players to stay at the net to play the rebound with their best scoring effort.

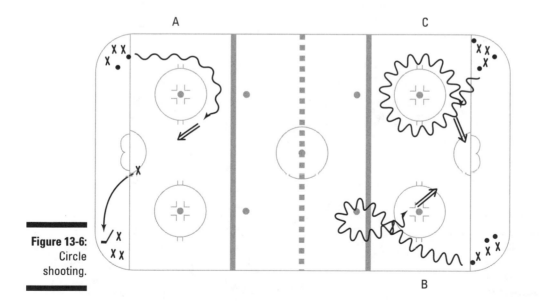

Figure 13-6: Circle shooting.

Neutral zone shooting

This is actually two drills. The first works on helping players learn to shoot as they skate down the boards into the offensive zone with the puck. The second lets them practice shooting after receiving a pass as they skate down the boards into the offensive zone. Both drills have players practice staying at the net and getting rebounds.

How it works: Have four lines of players along the walls at the blue lines, as illustrated in Figure 13-7. Have a player skate down the wall for a shot on goal as in A of Figure 13-7, and then stay at the net for a rebound from the next shooter. The player then goes to the end of the line on the opposite side of the rink. Alternate shots from each side of the rink. To increase the challenge of the drill, add a pass from the middle line as in B of Figure 13-7. Players should be in three lines closer to the center line so that they are moving across the blue line when receiving the pass. The passer goes to the end of the line he passes to and the rebound player goes to the center line. Alternate shooters from left and right wings.

Coaching pointers: Help players look for and create holes in hitting the net from the board angle. Remind them to shoot on the fly. After the shot, make sure they go to the net to play the rebound. When the pass is added, have the player receiving the pass call for the pass (helps on-ice communication) and check that passers focus on timing and accuracy so that the shooter doesn't have to stop skating to receive the pass.

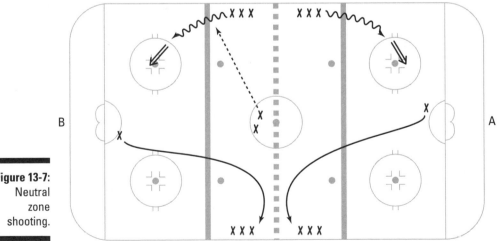

B

A

Figure 13-7:
Neutral
zone
shooting.

Pairs keep-away

This is a puck protection drill in which players practice using their body to protect the puck. It also works on agility and legal stickchecking.

How it works: Have players work in pairs spread out over the ice surface. One player in each pair has a puck on his stick. Have players stay within a 6-foot radius. See Figure 13-8 for the drill pattern. On the whistle, the puck carrier pivots and uses his body to protect the puck as his partner tries to gain possession of the puck. Go six to ten seconds, blow the whistle, and then have players switch puck possession and repeat.

Coaching pointers: Encourage puck carriers to use tight turns and keep their feet moving. See that checkers focus on short, quick stick action, and quick skating to get around the puck carrier in trying to gain possession of the puck.

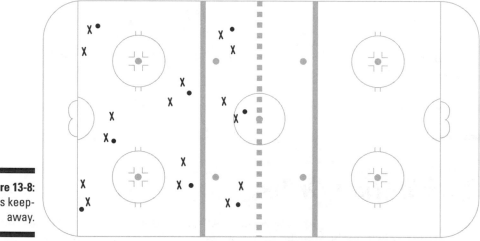

Figure 13-8:
Pairs keep-away.

Neutral zone keep-away shot

This is a gamelike drill for checking and protecting the puck. All players are involved and the goaltender has to be alert against a variety of shots.

How it works: Pair players up in the neutral zone and assign each pair a number. On the first whistle, all pairs start to play keep-away. See Figure 13-9 for the starting line-up. On the second whistle, the #1 keep-away puck carrier goes in for a shot on goal with the partner trying to legally prevent a shot. On the next whistle, pair #2 goes for the shot, and so on. Pairs rejoin the keep-away group after a shot. Remind players to use poke, hook, sweep, or lift and press checks to prevent shots.

Coaching pointers: Check that puck carriers keep their body between the puck and the checker to protect the puck. Make sure checkers skate into good body position on the puck carrier before they use their stick to try to get the puck. Have the goaltender focus on finding the shooter each time, then challenging the shot.

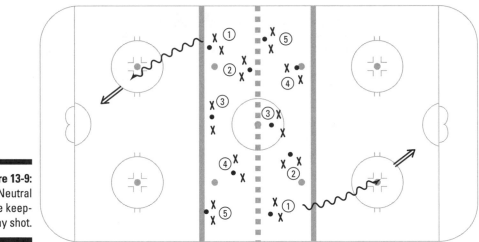

Figure 13-9:
Neutral zone keep-away shot.

Combination Drills

When players are learning certain skills, their development is quickest if they focus just on the specific skill. However, once they become somewhat accomplished at the skill, it needs to be put in context with other hockey skills. In other words, they need to practice using the drill in more mixed, gamelike conditions. This is the purpose of combination drills such as those that follow.

Four-corner mobility drill

This drill works on a number of skating techniques: forward and backward skating, lateral movement, and pivots. It can also be used as a skating and puck-handling drill.

How it works: Start with an equal number of players in each corner. On the signal, one player from each corner skates forward to the center ice dot and stops. Each player does a crossover to the side face-off dot, pivots and skates backwards to the blue line, and then pivots and skates forward to the opposite corner. See Figure 13-10 for the skating pattern. The second player from each corner leaves when the first player crosses the blue line. This drill can be done without pucks to emphasize skating, then with pucks to emphasize puck handling.

Coaching pointers: Stress proper body position and technique as each skating skill is executed. Watch especially as players get tired; there is a tendency to straighten the legs and not maintain proper skating posture. For this reason, it can be useful to do this drill late in a practice with teams that have the basic technique.

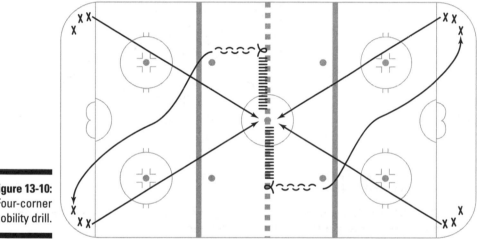

Figure 13-10:
Four-corner
mobility drill.

Pylon course shot

Skating, puck handling, agility, and shooting are all elements of this drill.

How it works: Set pylons to allow for good lateral movement as players skate the length of the ice with the puck and then shoot on net. See the pattern illustrated in Figure 13-11. Have players in two lines in opposite corners of the rink. The second player leaves when the first player gets to the first blue line. After shooting, have players stop at the net for their own rebound and the rebound from the next shooter. Then go to the end of the line in the near corner. Coaches can specify which shots to practice, such as forehand wrist shots, backhand wrist, snap, or slap (from inside the top of the circle).

Coaching pointers: Stress strong skating as the players go through the pylons. Make sure players keep their heads up all the time. Also remind them to hit the net with a determined shot at a hole and to stay for a serious rebound attempt off the next shooter.

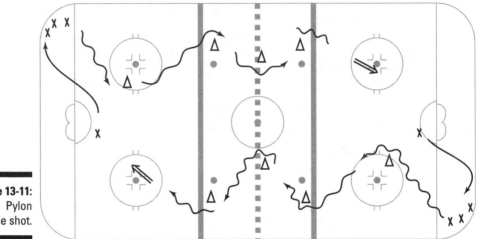

Figure 13-11:
Pylon
course shot.

Deke drill

This drill helps develop two skills: deke to the right and to the left and pass off the boards to get the puck by a defender.

How it works: Have two lines of players starting in opposite corners, each with a puck (see Figure 13-12). At the first pylon, the player passes off the boards as she approaches the pylon and retrieves the puck as she goes outside the pylon. At the second pylon, she fakes right and goes left. At the third pylon, she fakes left and goes right, and then goes in for a shot on goal. The shooter stays at the net for her and the next shooter's rebound.

Coaching pointers: Make sure players keep their heads up when carrying the puck. Advise them to experiment with the strength of the chip off the boards for the board pass and to vary the angles to find out what is most effective. Have players make each deke a quick fake one way and then back in the opposite direction.

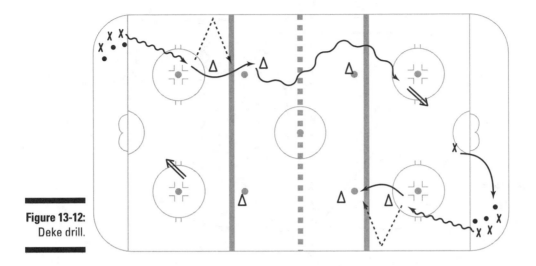

Figure 13-12:
Deke drill.

Offensive Drills

These drills are designed to help intermediate players begin to develop a sense of teamwork on offense and to develop the art of using teammates to make an attack happen. Coaches should also use these drills to gradually develop speed and accuracy on offense.

Three-man weave

This drill helps players understand the advantage of using the entire width of the ice to make good things happen offensively. Players also learn to react to each other and to fill offensive skating lanes.

How it works: Start with three lines at the goal line. The first player in each line leaves with the midline skater carrying a puck. The puck carrier passes to an outside skater and follows the puck to exchange lanes with that skater. The new puck carrier heads toward the middle and passes to the opposite winger, and then follows the puck to exchange lanes with that player. The skater who has the puck as they cross the offensive blue line goes in on goal for a shot. See an illustration of the skating pattern in Figure 13-13.

Coaching pointers: The key is to have players pass and follow their pass. Stress that the puck carrier goes in front and the skater filling the lane goes behind. Have players pass to the next player as soon as possible and focus on anticipating the place to pass so the receiving player does not have to slow up or chase the pass.

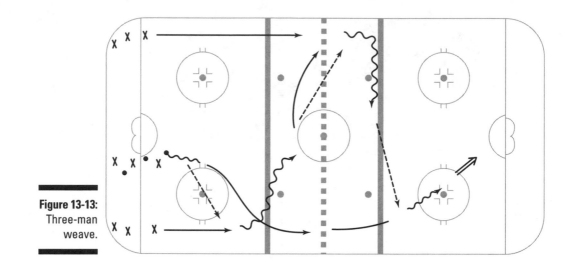

Figure 13-13:
Three-man
weave.

Give and go acceleration

Going to open ice is a concept that all good teams stress. This drill helps
players understand the idea of passing the puck and then skating to open ice
to get a return pass.

How it works: See Figure 13-14 for starting player positions. X1 and X2 leave
with a puck. While skating the length of the ice, X1 passes alternately to X3,
X4, and X5. After each pass, X1 accelerates to open ice to get the return pass.
After receiving X5's pass, X1 goes in for a shot on goal and rebound. Rotate
players through the X3, X4, and X5 positions.

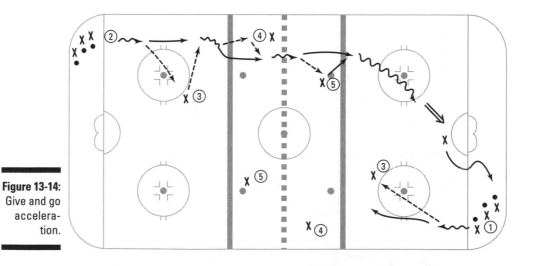

Figure 13-14:
Give and go
accelera-
tion.

Coaching pointers: Stress acceleration after passing the puck. Make sure players have their stick on the ice for the return pass.

Neutral zone go to open ice

This drill works on passing, receiving a pass, acceleration, and shooting, as well as the concept of passing the puck and then going to open ice for a return pass.

How it works: Have players in four lines, as illustrated in Figure 13-15. X1 passes to X2 and accelerates to open ice through the center ice circle for a return pass. X1 goes for a shot on goal and rebound and then stays at the net for the next shooter. X3 passes to X4 next, then the X2 to X1 line, and so on. When skill allows, have X1 and X3 start at the same time, then X2 and X4. Players return to the opposite line on the same side of the ice.

Coaching pointers: Stress quality passing, acceleration to open ice after the pass, and attacking the net aggressively for a shot.

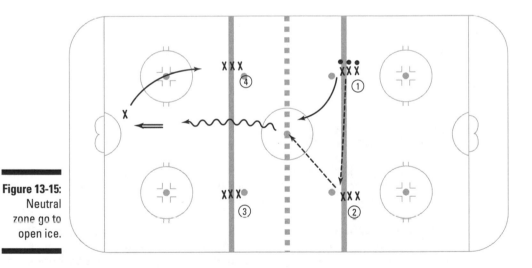

Figure 13-15:
Neutral zone go to open ice.

Offensive regroup drill

This drill is designed to help players without the puck to skate aggressively, regroup, and get back into play to create a shot on the net. Quality passes are also an important element in this drill.

How it works: See Figure 13-16 for starting player positions. X1 passes to a stationary X2. X2 passes to a stationary X3. X1 and X2 quickly go into the neutral zone and return to the offensive zone so that X3 can pass to X4. X1 and X4 then go for a shot on goal and possible rebound. Rotate players through the X2 and X3 positions.

Coaching pointers: Encourage skaters to go as quickly as possible and not to slow down to receive the return pass. Have the stationary players make strong, quick passes. Help all players anticipate good pass placement.

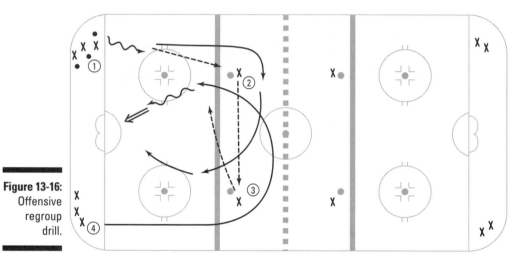

Figure 13-16:
Offensive
regroup
drill.

Cross-ice 3-on-3

This cross-ice drill helps players learn to read off teammates in offensive and defensive situations, helping them develop game sense. The drill also works on agility and puck-handling quickness.

How it works: Move the nets to the side boards in one or two zones, as illustrated in Figure 13-17. Have players play 3-on-3 across the ice. The players' objective offensively is to move the puck quickly, get to open ice without the puck, and execute quick-release shots. Use 20- to 30-second shifts before switching in new players.

Coaching pointers: Encourage movements offensively that create scoring options and defensively that limit the offensive team's options. Make sure both sides use quick puck movement. Also encourage verbal communication among teammates.

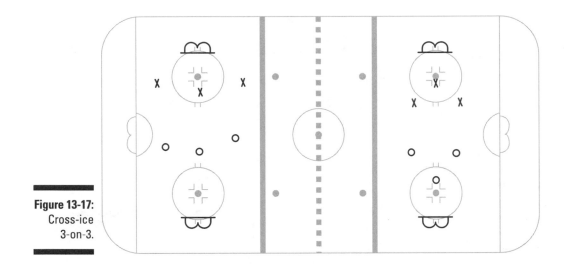

Figure 13-17:
Cross-ice
3-on-3.

Defensive Drills

These drills are designed to help intermediate hockey players develop a sense of position while playing defense. When each player can place their body and stick where they should be, they'll begin to play solid defense as a team.

Defense 1-on-1

One-on-one situations constantly arise in a hockey game. This drill helps prepare players to be successful defensively in 1-on-1s.

How it works: Line players up, as illustrated in Figure 13-18. F1 passes to D and gets a return pass as he skates forward. D skates backward keeping F1 on the board side using good backward-skating posture. He works on slowly closing the gap between himself and F1. He should not stop skating backward and should always keep his stick on the ice, trying to neutralize F1's options to pass or get around him.

Coaching pointers: Make sure the defenseman positions himself so that the forward is on his outside shoulder side (board side) by the time the 1-on-1 reaches the defensive blue line. Also check that the defenseman's stick is on the ice and that he maintains proper backward-skating posture.

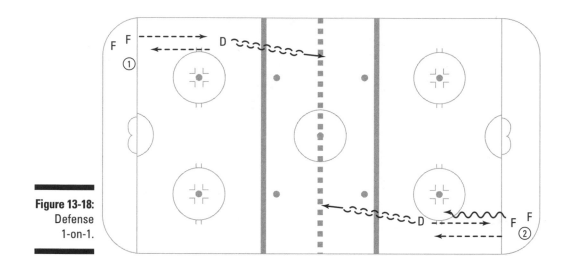

Figure 13-18:
Defense
1-on-1.

2-on-1 from center

This drill is designed to help a lone defenseman learn how to position herself between two forwards and not give the forwards time to create a lot of options.

How it works: Have players in lines, as illustrated in Figure 13-19. The inside forward line starts with the puck. F1 passes to D to start the drill. D passes the puck to F2 and all start skating toward the net. D skates backward between the forwards, trying to maintain position between and in front of the forwards. At the same time, D tries to eliminate any forward-to-forward passes.

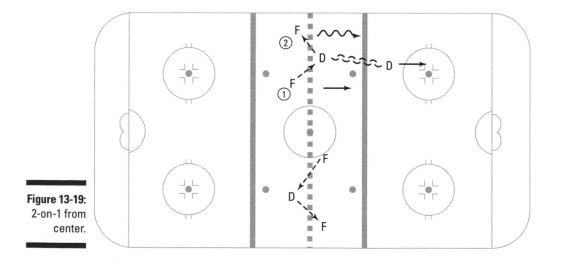

Figure 13-19:
2-on-1 from
center.

Coaching pointers: Check that the defenseman maintains proper skating posture and uses her stick to eliminate passes by the forwards. The forwards should be able to create a shot on goal, so advise the defenseman that her goal is to force the least dangerous (wide) forward to take the shot.

2-on-2 defense

This cross-ice drill helps defensive players work together to eliminate offensive opportunities.

How it works: Place the nets for cross-ice play in two or three zones, as illustrated in Figure 13-20. Play 2-on-2 games with the focus on defense. The objective defensively is to be on the defensive side of an offensive player, take away time and space from the offensive player with the puck, and take passing options away from offensive players. Use 20- to 30-second shifts before changing players.

Coaching pointers: Encourage verbal communication between the defensive players. Have them skate aggressively to eliminate time and space for the offensive players as opposed to being passive and backing in on their own net.

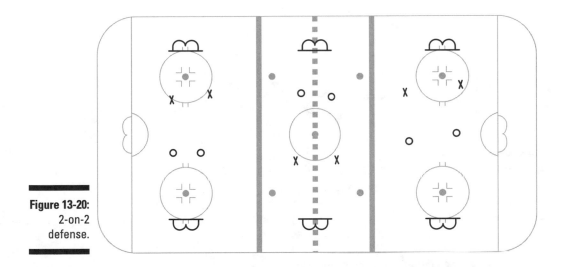

Figure 13-20:
2-on-2
defense.

Goaltending Drills

The following drills are designed to help young goaltenders learn and practice getting into position, moving efficiently, playing the angles, and making saves. Coaches should initially conduct the drills slowly and talk goalies through the saves. As the goalies become more proficient, add harder shots and shoot to all areas of the net.

Forward-back drill

This drill helps goaltender awareness of their position on the ice relative to the net. It also helps develop forward and backward agility.

How it works: Have three lines of shooters in the neutral zone. Set up pylons on the players' side of the end zone face-off dots. See Figure 13-21 for the set-up. Have the goalie start at the post and angle out to play a shot from the first player in line #1. The player skates in for the shot. After the shot, the goalie goes back to the goal line, and then angles out to play a shot from the first player in line #2. Repeat for a shot from line #3. Then repeat for lines #3, #2, and #1.

Coaching pointers: Check that the goaltender maintains his goalie stance throughout the drill. Encourage him to be aggressive, learn from making mistakes, and try new tactics to find out what works and what doesn't.

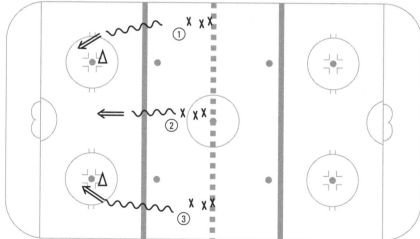

Figure 13-21:
Forward-
back drill.

Lateral movement

Goaltenders have to be able to move laterally across the crease and still be in position to make a save. This drill helps goalies develop lateral movement across the net.

How it works: Have two lines of shooters just inside the blue line, as illus-trated in Figure 13-22. The goalie starts on the post and moves laterally across the net with the shooter to make a save, staying square to the puck. Have shooters alternate from opposite sides. Always allow the goalie time to start at the post.

Coaching pointers: Make sure the goaltender keeps his stick on the ice and maintains his goalie stance as much as possible. Advise goalies that their speed needs to mirror the speed of the shooter as closely as possible. Their focus is on presenting the fewest holes for the briefest period possible.

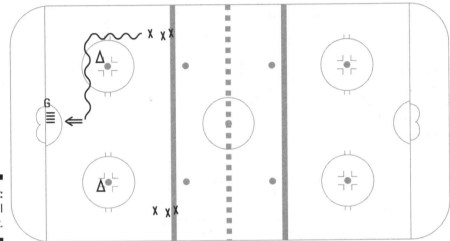

Figure 13-22:
Lateral
movement.

Follow the play

A pass from the corner leading to a shot from the slot is a common play that goaltenders face in game situations. This drill prepares goaltenders to defend against this situation.

How it works: Have skaters line up in both corners with pucks, as illustrated in Figure 13-23. X1 leaves the corner without a puck and skates around the top of the circle. X2 passes to X1 in the slot area. The goalie starts at X2's post and follows the pass to play the shot. X2 leaves without a puck and receives a pass from the next player in the X1 line. Shooters return to the opposite line.

Coaching pointers: Have the goalie tight to the post to start the drill. Help goalies time their movement from the post so that they are square to the puck when the shot is taken.

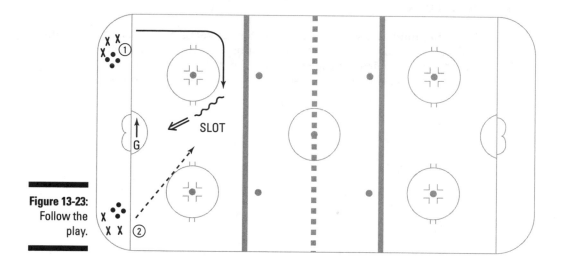

Figure 13-23:
Follow the
play.

Semicircle five puck drill

This drill helps goaltenders work on being square to the shot and knowing where they are relative to the net.

How it works: Five players have pucks and are in a semicircle in front of the goalie, as illustrated in Figure 13-24. The goalie squares to X1's puck and X1 shoots. The goalie squares to X2's puck and X2 shoots, and so on. Let the goalie get set on each puck before each shot. Go left to right for the first round of shots, and then go right to left for the second round. Coaches can vary the shots from mid-high, high, low, left, right, and top corners, according to the skill level of the goalie.

Coaching pointers: Make sure goalies are square to the puck in a solid goalie stance for each shot. If a lot of shots are going into the net, give the goalie time between shooters to actually look and see where he is relative to the net and adjust accordingly.

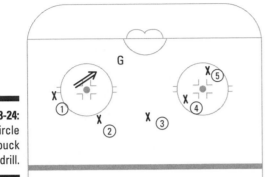

Figure 13-24:
Semicircle
five puck
drill.

Shots off wing

This drill gives goaltenders a clear understanding of their positioning and how to eliminate holes as they move out to stop shots. It also works on agility on rebounds.

How it works: Shooters start in a line outside the blue line, as illustrated in Figure 13-25. All shooters in line #1 go in on goal one at a time, allowing space between each shot as the goalie moves out to play the angle and back in to the net in case of rebounds. Then all players from line #2 similarly shoot on goal.

Coaching pointers: Make sure the goalie stands square to the puck and out of the net enough to take away scoring opportunities. Remind her to maintain a proper goalie stance with her stick on the ice. Watch for pucks going through the goalie. If this is happening, identify the holes she needs to eliminate.

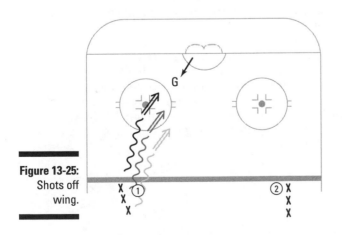

Figure 13-25:
Shots off
wing.

3-line shooting

This drill works on lateral movement, maintaining a quality goalie stance, playing angles, and making saves.

How it works: Have three lines with pucks outside the blue line, as illustrated in Figure 13-26. Lines should alternate shots with line #1 taking a wide shot first, line #2 taking a wide shot second, and then line #3 taking a midlane shot.

Coaching pointers: Watch that the goalie adjusts positioning appropriately. Encourage her to show energy as she moves to play the outside shots, and then back to the middle. Also check posture.

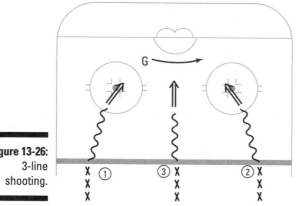

Figure 13-26:
3-line
shooting.

Walk-outs

This is a great drill for goalies to work on lateral movement and controlling the rebound after the shot.

How it works: Have two groups of shooters in opposite corners with pylons placed as illustrated in Figure 13-27. The first player in line #1 starts against the side boards, skates toward the net, and shoots between the pylons. The goalie starts against the post on the line #1 side and moves laterally to stay square to the puck to make the save. The first player in line #2 allows the goalie to get to the post on his side, after playing the shot, before the player from line #2 leaves for his shot.

Coaching pointers: Check the goalie's stance. Watch how the goalie adjusts to the speed of the shooter; he wants to be square to the puck in his ready position by the time the shot is released. Give the goalie time to control the rebound from each shooter before the next shooter goes.

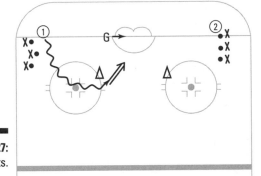

Figure 13-27:
Walk-outs.

Chapter 14

Refining Your Coaching Strategies

. . . .

In This Chapter

▶ Evaluating and assessing skills

▶ Figuring out your team's strengths and weaknesses

▶ Matching players with the best position for them to play

▶ Fine-tuning team dynamics

▶ Checking up on your own performance

. . . .

The more you coach, the more your coaching skills (or habits) develop, whether you plan it that way or not. We advise you to plan your development, which helps you to develop in a positive direction. Players need you to develop as a coach because they are getting better, and so should you.

If your goal is to grow as a coach, one technique for doing that is to pause periodically through the season and look objectively at how you are doing. This technique allows you to refine your coaching techniques so that both you and the players can get better. This chapter walks you through some exercises you may want to include in your coaching practice that will help you develop your coaching skills.

Evaluating Individual Skills

As you coach intermediate players, you teach more complex skills and use more complex drills to reinforce proper technique. Evaluate your players' skills to ensure that they continue to improve — in other words, make sure that what you're doing is working.

One way to evaluate player skills is to conduct game-condition drills that simulate situations players will be put in during games, such as playing 3-on-3. Give clear instructions for how the drill is to be conducted, then have assistants run the drill so that you can concentrate on evaluating individual performance.

If you have to do things to keep the drills going, such as blowing whistles and dropping face-off pucks, you'll compromise your ability to do quality evaluations.

To conduct the evaluations, list each of your players down the left side of a page and list the skills you've been emphasizing across the top of the page, such as passing, shooting, heads-up play, getting to open ice, or defensive positioning. As the players play 3-on-3, assess each player on each skill using a quick 1-to-5 scale in which 1 is excellent and 5 is horrendous.

The evaluation chart is not for players to see. You use the chart to decide who individually needs work on what and whether any patterns are emerging team-wide that may indicate players have missed the message. Perhaps almost all players on your team just shoot wildly at the net, which may suggest that you need to revisit the segment on looking for the holes in shooting.

This type of chart may also draw your attention to individuals who are mastering certain skills at a higher level than what stands out to you in normal practices and games. This may give you more options on who to play in specific positions as players begin to specialize and you start to change from rotating all players through all positions.

Assessing Team Strengths and Weaknesses

Team play becomes more of a focus at the intermediate player level, giving you the opportunity to evaluate how you're teaching team concepts in addition to individual skills. Too often, coaches tend to make team assessments based on game results, but this is rarely an accurate way to assess the strengths and weaknesses of your team. The emotion involved typically clouds your judgment. Emotion can be managed by putting some time between the game and the time you assess the team's play. Wait until the next day to go over game notes and to talk formally with assistants about what the team did well and what they did poorly. Identify individual weaknesses only for the purpose of targeting who needs individual work in upcoming practices. Focus on team performance, on issues such as offensive and defensive play, passing and shooting accuracy, and team discipline. For each issue, you would have set goals before the season started. Base your assessment on these goals. Prepare a checklist of team goals ahead of time and rank the performance (1 is great, 5 is awful) after each game. Look for consistent patterns in performance.

Your team is bound to have good games and poor games. Focus on the goals you set at the beginning of the season. This will help you avoid going through a series of highs and lows during the course of the season that are based on winning and losing, rather than on real accomplishment.

Another way of assessing your team's strengths and weaknesses is by comparing your team within the league you are competing. How does your offense compare to the offense of other teams in the league? Is your team on a par with other teams in the area of defensive play? Are the shooting skills of most teams in the league comparable? These questions are all part of the assessment process. If your team is way behind in some skill, you have some work to do.

Be sure to take into consideration the talent level and ages of your players compared to your opponents. If your players are comparable, then your team should have its share of success. On the other hand, if you have a relatively young team with less experience, adjust expectations accordingly. Don't let the score of the game color your assessment of true team strengths and weaknesses.

Assigning Positional Play

Players at beginner levels of hockey are typically rotated through all positions. They'll eventually gravitate to a specific position, based on the success or the fun they've had at each position.

However, each position has unique qualities that require a certain skill set to play the position successfully. You can encourage intermediate players to experiment with positions for which they seem best suited and which may provide the greatest success. The following sections offer the key talents required at the different positions used in the game.

Defensemen

Defensemen can play either right defense or left defense. Often a *right-shot defenseman* (one whose forehand shot goes off his right side) will play right defense and the *left shot* (a player whose forehand shot goes off his left side) will play left, but this is not a requirement. Defensemen are commonly capable of playing either side. Key defensive talents include the following:

- ✔ **Backward skating:** Above-average backward-skating skills are necessary for all defensemen. Agility and mobility may vary, but defensemen have to be the best backward skaters on the team. As players advance, it becomes important for defensemen to improve agility and mobility.

- ✔ **Passing:** Above-average passing skills are required to play defense. Often, defensemen are the players who make the important passes as their team tries to break out of their defensive zone. Associated with these quality passes is the ability to read the play and move the puck to the right areas.

- ✔ **Coming up with the puck:** Defensemen have to become good at battling for and retrieving loose pucks, which requires a combination of skating ability, strength, and the ability to read the play.

- ✔ **Being in the right spot at the right time:** Strong positional play makes defensemen stand out above all others. Being in the right position on the ice during play makes any defenseman more effective.

Forwards

Forwards play either left wing, center, or right wing. Forward-skating skills are important in all three positions. Beyond skating, talents that forwards need include the following:

- ✔ **Competing on face-offs:** Centers need strong face-off skills. This involves developing hand-eye coordination.

- ✔ **Anticipating the play:** Centers are usually the creative ones on the forward line, with the ability to read the play and move the puck to teammates to create offensive opportunities.

- ✔ **Defending:** Centers are often the forwards who give first support to their defensemen in the defensive zone, so centers need good defensive positioning skills.

- ✔ **Fighting for loose pucks:** Wingers need to be strong to fight for loose pucks along the boards. This strength provides numerous play opportunities for the team.

- ✔ **Shooting on the move:** Wingers need to be able to shoot the puck off the wing and on the fly.

- ✔ **Backchecking:** Defensively, wingers are usually responsible for covering the other team's defensemen. They need to be able to backcheck hard to get on the defensive side of the defenseman.

Goaltenders

Goaltending is often referred to as the most important position on the team. The position often attracts a special personality in addition to unique talents. Key goaltending abilities include the following:

- ✔ **Intestinal fortitude:** Goalies need to like the challenge and pressure of being the one player who can make *the* difference in the outcome of the game.

- ✔ **Skating:** Goaltenders are usually the best skaters on the team. To be effective, the goalie has to be good at a variety of difficult skating maneuvers that provide great agility and mobility.

- ✔ **Visual coordination:** Goalies need good eye-foot and eye-hand coordination.

If you see a goaltender who seems to flinch or straighten up when a shot is coming, you need to consider a couple of things. First, his equipment may not be protecting him properly and the puck may be hurting him. If this is not the case, and the goalie isn't comfortable with some shots, goaltending may not be the right position for him.

Taking the Pulse: Team Dynamics

Just as your doctor routinely checks your heart as part of a standard medical examination, as the coach, you want to do the same for your team. Being able to read team dynamics is an essential tool for a coach.

Your team will communicate with you. You need to pick up on the verbal and visual forms of communication they send your way. If players look down or away when you speak to them, they're blocking you out. Find a positive way to catch their interest. Sometimes a simple question will do, such as, "What do you think would work best in this situation?" Always be observant and listen to what the players are saying.

Be careful about cliques that may form within the team. Along with this, watch for any player being excluded from the main team group. Naturally, certain players will spend more time together, but this can't be at the expense of cohesive team dynamics.

Certain players will evolve into team leaders. Sometimes the best players are looked up to by their teammates simply because of their superior play. Other times, a certain type of personality rises to become the natural leader. As the coach, recognize these leadership roles and work with these players to make them better, positive leaders for your team.

Over the course of a season, you will see positive behavior as well as negative behavior from your players. How you react to both will influence team dynamics. Negative behavior needs to be addressed immediately, and you need to make clear to the players that this type of behavior will not be tolerated. Positive behavior needs to be reinforced in a way that the players involved, and all their teammates, know that this is the type of behavior that will be rewarded.

Finally, look at the energy level of your team. How is the energy in the dressing room in pre-game and post-game situations? Are players talking? Joking? Involved? Players should be positive regardless of the score. Be sure to be listening. Casually walk through the room or catch the essence of player conversations from outside the room. Silence, in a dressing room, on the bench, or on the ice, is not golden.

Coach's Scorecard

What were the goals you set for your team at the beginning of the season? What were the goals you laid out for yourself? Draw up your checklist, then approximately a quarter of the way through the season, objectively rank how well you are doing on a scale of 1 to 5. Be honest. No one need see this checklist but you.

Don't expect to be perfect; but do pat yourself on the back for the jobs well done and adjust on the items that are the most urgent weak spots. If you're not sure how to make adjustments, contact your coach-mentor, consult your assistants for ideas, attend a coaching clinic and ask questions, or consult a good hockey coaching book like this one, *Coaching Hockey For Dummies*.

When you coach intermediate-level players, some items that should be on your scorecard include the following:

- **Communication skills with players:** Are you listening to player feedback? Are the players getting the information you are presenting?

- **Skill improvement:** Include both individual and team factors in your assessment. If the weakest kids aren't getting any stronger, perhaps you are not meeting their needs. Remember, some kids are late, but spectacular, bloomers.

✔ **Respect from parents:** Do you get parents who repeatedly create problems? Do parents contribute to the positive chemistry of the team? A positive score here makes your job considerably easier.

✔ **Fun:** Are the kids laughing, talking, learning, and feeling satisfied? Are you? None of you will stay at hockey very long if you're not having fun.

Part IV
Coaching Advanced Players

The 5th Wave   By Rich Tennant

RICHTENNANT

"Hey – at least wait until the puck comes down before you criticize my slapshot."

In this part . . .

This part provides techniques for instructing players who are ready to play at higher levels of hockey. We include body contact, teamwork on offense and defense, and special teams. We also provide drills for reinforcing these skills in practice, and then present strategies for coaching advanced players and games.

Chapter 15
Teaching Advanced Skills

· ·

In This Chapter

▶ Giving checks and taking hits

▶ Performing at a faster pace

· ·

As players advance in hockey, they come to a level of the game that can be intimidating both for players and their parents. This level is the introduction of contact hockey, when *body checking* (hitting) becomes part of the play. As a coach, you can be extremely influential in taking the reluctance and risk out of body contact. Start by providing thorough instruction in how to check an opponent properly and how your own players are to take a check. At the same time, educate your players on the purpose of checking and on having respect for other players. If you do this, body contact becomes a normal, safe part of the game.

A second factor that figures prominently if players want to achieve success as they advance in hockey is speed. You need to coach advanced players to take quick advantage of opportunities that arise and to avoid lapses in their own play that provide their opponents with opportunities they can take quick advantage of, such as during line changes, when pouncing on loose pucks, or on turnovers to offense or defense.

Advanced players still need consistent work on the basic skills of skating, passing, and shooting, but with greater emphasis on speed and quickness. Then for new skills, focus on body contact and quick exchange and intervention. This chapter works you through that information.

When Hitting Is Legal

Many hockey players look forward to the time that they can start to hit their opponents, just like they see in the big leagues. However, many young hockey players are small for their age or lack the aggressive edge that is often associated with hitting in hockey. So they shy away from hitting. Or they duck checks. Or, at worst, they drop out of hockey at this stage, even though they like the game, because they aren't comfortable with body contact.

As a coach, be aware of your players' attitudes when you introduce body contact, then conduct all instruction and drills using a positive and constructive approach. Body checking is not for annihilating an opponent; it is a technique for getting the puck away from an opponent. Nothing more; nothing less. Safety is key, whichever end of the check a player is on. Players need to know that's your approach.

Body checking

Start to teach body checking by reminding players that at no time in hockey can players legally body check an opponent who doesn't have the puck — the purpose of body checking is to gain possession of the puck. More specifically, the goal is to separate the puck carrier from the puck and then have your team gain possession of the puck.

Secondly, remind players that along with physical contact comes some risk of injury. Players must be taught to respect that risk by learning how and when to body check. For example, checking from behind is very high risk, especially along the boards, and must never be condoned. Coaches must establish one rule at the outset: Checking from behind is never acceptable for a member of your team, beyond the penalties imposed under the rules of the game. Similarly, players must be advised that aiming to strike at an opponent's knees or other reckless intent to injure is not acceptable. After you establish these clear ground rules, you can then provide thorough instruction for delivering and taking body checks safely and intelligently.

We explain two common body checks in this chapter: the rub-out and open-ice body checks. Other contact checks exist, such as the hip check, but because of the skill required to execute it properly and the risk of injury, we do not recommend instruction at this level.

The rub-out check

The *rub-out check* is the most common body check used in hockey and is the most effective form of body contact. The check is used on a puck carrier who is skating up ice along the boards.

Instruct the checker to skate with, but slightly ahead of, the puck carrier so that he can angle the puck carrier toward the boards. The checker must keep his head up and lead with his stick on the ice and two hands on the stick.

Have the checker take a wide stance for stability and slide his stick under the puck carrier's stick. At the same time, the checker leans toward the puck carrier, pushes off his outside leg primarily, and thrusts his shoulder and side of his trunk into the chest of his opponent, making contact slightly off center. This momentarily turns his opponent's body into the boards. As the puck carrier is turned off balance, the checker steps between the player's knees, which puts the checker in front of and in control of the puck. This action temporarily pins the puck carrier against the boards. See Figure 15-1 for the body position on the rub-out check.

Figure 15-1:
Rubbing out
your
opponent.

Remind checkers to pin for only a moment, then release and join the play. The idea of the pin is to separate the puck carrier from the puck. Either the checker or a teammate should gain control of the puck and continue play. Also remind checkers to keep their heads up with their eyes on where to contact the opponent's chest. Ensure that they keep their elbows down (stick on the ice) or penalties and injury may result. Reinforce the notion that they do not lead into contact with the head or the top of the shoulder, which can invite injury. Instead, make contact with the whole side of their shoulder, upper arm, and trunk.

Open-ice checks

Open-ice body contact requires timing, balance, and strength. The technique for *open-ice checks* is the same as for the rub-out check, but it is more difficult because players don't have the boards for assistance.

Have checkers put two hands on their stick and keep their sticks on the ice. Then instruct them to first get themselves in a position that has their shoulder lined up directly with the opponent's chest. They then execute the contact slightly off center, as in the rub-out check, using forceful knee extension, but they must regain balance by landing on both feet in a wide stance. In the moment the opponent is off balance, the checker takes or passes the puck to a teammate. Again, remind checkers to keep their head up, knees bent, elbows down, and hit with the full-shoulder side of the upper body. They must clearly avoid any contact with the opponent's head.

Taking a check

Learning to *take a check* is as important as learning to check and it requires practice as well. By providing sound instruction in taking checks, you create conditions on the team that leave players unconcerned about being checked. They understand that they can handle a check safely, so they regard checking as a natural part of playing the game.

First and foremost, instruct players to keep their heads up. Players must always be able to anticipate the possibility of being checked. If a player sees that he is about to be body checked, he can prepare for it.

To prepare to take a rub-out check, instruct players to widen their stance, bend their knees, and lean into the check while keeping two hands on the stick. Have the players extend their upper arms toward the boards and use the upper arms and shoulder area to absorb or cushion the check. They should relax or eliminate any tensing up while being checked and as they cushion against the boards. Teach them also to roll with the direction of the contact in cushioning the hit.

When a player is digging a puck out along the boards, rather than skating along the boards, he has to keep his head up for potential checks. This position is dangerous because the boards are too far away to be used as a cushion and the player runs the risk of the check sending him into the boards head first. In this case, advise players to turn their side to the check and lean into it as they see it coming. That way, they can absorb the check with the side of their body and cushion against the boards as much as possible as they roll out of the check.

For open-ice checks, instruct players to add more bend at the knees and slightly more forward lean into the check with the upper body. Ensure that their stick stays on the ice and their head stays up. Have them extend their knees pushing up and into the check as contact is made, ideally with their whole shoulder side, if they have time to position themselves to that angle.

In open-ice hits, players should actually seem like they are checking back against the opponent as they are being checked. Players should still roll with the force of the check, if off-center, and land with as wide a stance as possible for greater stability.

Practice taking checks in slow motion first so that players clearly experience the cushion with the whole side of their trunk and the roll with the force of the contact. This should make most players comfortable and safe with taking body contact.

When Speed Defines the Game

As the game of hockey advances by level, quickness becomes an increasingly important factor in a team's success. Beyond performing skills at a faster pace, players can learn some team tactics that help quicken their performance. These tactics include changing on the fly, improving strategies for loose puck play, and smoothing out the team's transition game.

Changing on the fly

By the time players reach the advanced levels of recreational hockey, they no longer play shifts of a league-required duration, complete with whistle stops to allow everyone to change. Line changes made during play, as opposed to on whistle stops, are called *changes on the fly*. These line changes can be opportunities or liabilities for a team, and as such, should be taught and practiced.

Changing on the fly starts with good communication. The coach must clearly identify which players are up next. Be consistent in how you do this. Have players on the bench watch the play and be aware of where the player is that they will be replacing. Remind them to focus in advance of the change so that, as soon as they step on the ice, they are ready to join in the play.

Call out forwards who are to change in the same order each time, such as left wing, center, and right wing. Then call out defensemen in the same order, such as left D, right D. Finally, have players identify the player on the ice they are replacing. They can actually call out the name so that everyone on the bench knows "I've got Reynolds" or "I've got MacAdam."

Players should ideally change as a unit. Tell players that when a forward sees a line mate change, then he needs to get ready to change at the next opportunity. The same is true for defense partners. This instruction also helps with bench management by keeping lines and defense pairings together.

Prescribing shift length

Shift length has an impact on the performance of your team. Players need to become aware of how long they have been on the ice during a shift. Be clear about how long you want shifts to be. A common range is 30 to 45 seconds. Players who stay out longer than 45 to 60 seconds simply aren't able to perform to the best of their abilities. Fatigue is a limiting factor when speed counts.

Let players know that in addition to letting fatigue hurt the team, a player who continually stays on the ice for extended shift lengths takes ice time away from a teammate. This attitude is selfish, putting oneself above the team, regardless of talent, and is not to be tolerated. Bench time usually fixes the problem. Make sure that players know why they are sitting.

A good rule to have for your team is that changes are to take place only when the puck is on the opponent's side of center, especially if your team has possession of the puck. Then one line or pair of players changes at a time, keeping enough players on the ice to control the puck.

Make sure that when players leave the ice, they skate quickly all the way to the boards and exit the ice through the bench doors. Have players who are going on the ice go over the boards to avoid traffic jams that slow down changes at the bench doors. Younger players not strong enough to climb over the boards will need to use the doors to get on and off the ice. In this case, designate one end of the bench for going on and the other for coming off.

Conduct short-shift scrimmages to practice changing on the fly. Two blasts of the whistle means both teams change at the next best opportunity, so players have to think it through.

Focusing on loose puck play

In advanced recreational hockey, loose pucks are an opportunity for possession, and the team with the greatest time of possession usually wins. When the puck is loose and up for grabs by either team, usually the most alert and quickest skating team gains possession. What can you do, short of yelling, "Stay alert!" to help your players come up with loose pucks?

Train your team well in positional play. Good positional play puts at least one of your players near the puck at any given time. Positional play is based on forwards having a lane they should be skating in and each defenseman having his half of the ice to cover. See Chapter 16 for more detail on lane work. With players covering these areas of the ice, your team should be able to retrieve more than their fair share of loose pucks.

Secondly, coach players to keep their heads up for loose-puck possibilities. When they can anticipate loose pucks, they have the jump on getting there first. You want to eliminate any hesitation or debate.

Two techniques are useful when going for loose pucks to ensure a positive outcome regardless of whether your player gets to the puck first:

- ✔ When possible, have players take the defensive side of the puck. This helps eliminate possible offensive opportunities for the opponent if your player doesn't get possession of the puck.

- ✔ If your player arrives at a loose puck at the same time as an opponent, teach him to lead with his stick and poke the puck away from the opponent in the direction your player is skating. That creates a second chance for your player to get to the loose puck. Alternately, if players can't get to the puck first and gain possession, advise them to try to poke or tip the puck in the direction of a teammate.

With practice, players become more automatic and quick at performing these options.

Players battling for loose pucks require a certain level of bravery. Be sure to use practice drills that simulate gamelike loose puck situations (see Chapter 19). Such drills make young players more comfortable when they face loose puck battles in games.

Managing transition play

Hockey is a game of constant turnovers. Teams continually switch between playing offense and playing defense. Often, the more quickly they can do this, the more scoring opportunities they can create or stifle.

Players need to understand both offensive and defensive positional play to make transitional play effective. Then to be successful, they have to work together as a single unit, whether switching from offense to defense or the other way around on turnovers.

Teach transitional play by first walking players through the following offensive and defensive turnover scenarios so that they get a feel for the adjustments required to switch. Then gradually speed up the drills.

Offense to defense turnovers

When your team has possession of the puck and your opponent forces a turnover, you must teach players to get into their defensive positions as quickly as possible. To do this, they must be aware of the position of the puck and of the position of the player they are responsible for defensively. Then they immediately step into a position that cuts off pass opportunities to the player they are defending against or they check or go between the puck carrier and your net.

A turnover in the defensive zone creates the greatest sense of urgency. Because the opponent is so close to your goal, he can often create a scoring chance from a turnover. Instruct all players to get back inside the defensive blue line when a turnover occurs in the defensive zone. Then the nearest defenseman to the net covers the front of the net while his defense partner either gives quick pressure on the puck carrier or supports a forward who is pressuring the puck carrier. If a forward is pressuring the puck carrier, then each of the other two forwards becomes responsible for covering an offensive defenseman.

On a turnover in the neutral zone, instruct players to take away passing lanes and disrupt your opponent's attempts to create an attack on your defensive zone. Your nearest player needs to put quick pressure on the puck carrier as the other players establish good defensive positioning on their nearest opponent. If a forward gives pressure on the puck, then his line mates must cover the two offensive defensemen. If this happens, both defensemen need to move up on the play to cover the two remaining offensive forwards.

When your team turns over the puck in the offensive zone, you allow the other team to set up a breakout. Regardless of the type of breakout, instruct your players that the nearest forward must pressure the puck carrier. The other two forwards move to the defensive side of their man and, if a pass is to be made to their man, they must give immediate pressure. In both pressure situations, teach the checker to stay with their check rather than chase after the puck if their man passes to a teammate. Both defensemen should be inside the blue line and ready to play defensively in any loose-puck situation.

Defense to offense turnovers

When your team forces a turnover and gets control of the puck to go on offense, instruct all players to create offensive options. The puck carrier needs to gain clear control of the puck and, if possible, get it moving up ice with an eye for a quick pass. Other players need to race to open ice and be available for a pass.

Train players to skate to open ice away from the puck carrier. Skating toward the puck carrier almost always makes the player a poorer passing option for the puck carrier.

On turnovers in your defensive zone where your defenseman gets the puck, one option for controlling the puck is to bring the puck back behind the net while teammates set up for a breakout play. This option slows the play, but allows set-up time. Regardless of the breakout used, instruct players to get to their designated positions on the ice quickly and to become part of the breakout. They must find open ice in an area that makes them a passing option. If the opponents forecheck, players need to learn to read the forecheck used by the defensive team and repeatedly move to open ice where short, quick passes or one clear, longer pass can evade the forecheck.

After a turnover in the neutral zone, direct offensive players to use speed and quickness to get free from their checker. Have them use short and quick passes that spring a player loose to attack the offensive zone. One effective technique to teach so that players get free in the neutral zone is to have forwards change skating lanes to create options. Another technique, especially if forward progression seems to be cut off, is to have defensemen back off slightly toward their own goal and offer a clear passing lane to the puck carrier to make a play back, which buys some set-up time or offers an alternate play option.

A turnover off the forecheck in the offensive zone can often be turned into a scoring chance. Instruct players that, if a forward gains control of the puck, a second forward immediately goes to the front of the net looking for a pass. The other forward stays above the top of the face-off circles as a support player. Both defensemen need to be inside the blue line and ready for a pass and possible shot on goal.

Chapter 16

Coaching Offense to Advanced Players

....

In This Chapter

▶ Executing offensive teamwork successfully

▶ Breaking out from the defensive zone

▶ Maximizing offensive opportunities in the neutral zone

▶ Staying in motion in the offensive zone

▶ Getting creative with offensive zone face-offs

....

*W*e can't overstate the importance of quality puck movement for successful offensive team play. Quick, accurate passing is the trademark of every successful team at every level. The best passers are nearly always the best players on a team. Successful coaches spend a great deal of practice time on quality passing so that passing can be a strength of the team and each individual player on the team.

Assuming that you continue to work on perfecting players' passing skills, the focus of coaching advanced players turns more to teamwork, making all the individual talent on your team work together so that the opposition always has to worry about six players on the ice, not just one or two. In this chapter, we discuss some basic concepts or strategies that you can teach to players to cultivate offensive teamwork. Once players begin to use these concepts, you can start to teach specific offensive plays. Some of the most effective basic offensive plays are presented in this chapter.

Coaching Teamwork Strategies

We recommend four key concepts to teach advanced players to help them execute offensive teamwork successfully. They have to do with positioning, width, depth, and an ability to read the play.

Positioning for offensive attack

Advanced players on offense need to have foremost in their minds the concept of getting to open ice and becoming a passing option. Becoming a passing option is the priority for every player without the puck. The puck carrier, on the other hand, has to have his head up and be ready to move the puck quickly to the best, often nearest, available teammate. Quick puck movement is a very difficult offense to defend against. However, if a good option is not available to the puck carrier, he must know to skate with the puck and help create an option for himself either by repositioning to where he is free to pass or shoot or by protecting the puck as he buys time until a teammate gets open for a pass. In either case, forward progress is preferable to standing still with the puck.

If a player cannot make eye contact with the puck carrier, then he is likely not positioned to be a good option to receive the puck. Have players use this notion as their guide to getting in good position.

Filling lanes

Advanced-level players need to be aware of the concept of *using lanes,* which is important in adding width and depth to an offensive attack. More importantly, they need to be prepared to switch lanes to create options. This makes it very difficult for the defensive team to counteract the offense.

The ice offers three lanes for forwards: the mid-lane and two outside lanes. The mid-lane is the ice that the center typically skates on, and the two outside lanes are where each of the wingers normally skate. See Figure 16-1 for an illustration of the forwards' lanes. Defensemen split the ice down the middle with half of the ice surface for each.

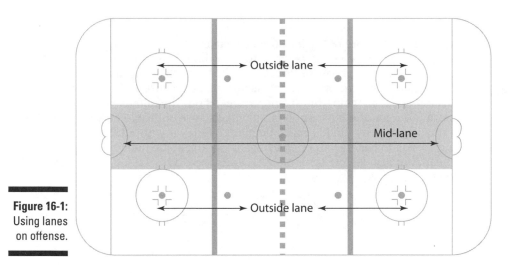

Figure 16-1:
Using lanes
on offense.

Adding width to the offensive attack

The concept of creating width to offense means to have as much cross-ice surface available as possible to make plays. To do this, instruct players to keep all lanes filled to create offensive options. That does not mean that players are locked into one lane. If a winger skates to the mid-lane to be open for a pass, the center should skate to the outside lane vacated by the winger, a tactic sometimes referred to as switching lanes. See Figure 16-2 for an example of switching lanes. By filling each lane, players utilize the whole width of the ice, which is an excellent way to spread out the defensive team, leaving more room to maneuver on offense.

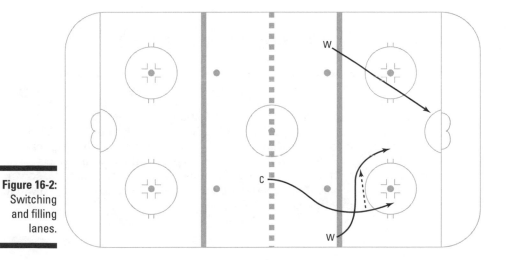

Figure 16-2:
Switching
and filling
lanes.

Adding depth to the offensive attack

You can make more of the ice surface available to your offense by using the length of the ice, which is referred to as adding depth to offense. To do this, have an offensive player *stretch skate*, which means go up the ice away from the puck carrier and his own defensive end. See Figure 16-3 for an example of stretch skating. Again, this strategy spreads out the defensive team, leaving more room for offensive options. Just make sure offensive players know the limits imposed by offside rules. Remind the player without the puck that his purpose is to become an offensive pass option, so he must not just skate ahead, but also get clear for a pass. Lanes should be refilled immediately following the pass.

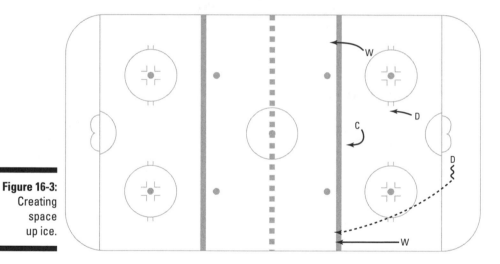

Figure 16-3:
Creating
space
up ice.

Reading the opponent's defense

As players gain experience playing hockey, they begin to understand what the defensive team is trying to do against them in given offensive situations. A coach can help players look for tendencies in the play of the defensive team and help them work together to exploit any weaknesses. For example, you may notice an opposing defenseman who cannot pivot to his right. So you'd advise your forwards that they should pass or drive with the puck around to his right at every opportunity to take advantage of his weakness. Or you may notice that the opponent's defense is slow to turn and go, so you could advise your players to send the puck past the defense and try to win a foot race to retrieve the puck.

Secondly, alert your offensive players to the idea that defenders will try to limit an offense's time to make plays and space to work in, so the offense needs to take quick but accurate advantage of opportunities that do open up to make plays. For example, have players pass as soon as they see a teammate open up rather than delaying the pass. Or you may note that your opponents are lazy (give plenty of space) on their forecheck, in which case you can advise your players to move through the zones to quickly take advantage of the open space.

Sometimes your offense just won't have a good play available. In that case, advise the puck carrier that his responsibility is to move the puck to an area of ice where he and his teammates can get a chance to restart a play safely. Remind players that they never need to force a play and risk losing the puck.

Creating Offense from the Defensive Zone

At advanced-player levels, breakouts from the defensive zone can be made more effective with the addition of motion. For example, players can change lanes to maintain width or add depth and be creative. Help players understand that by creating organized motion, in keeping with width and depth concepts and getting to open ice, they work together, which usually results in a successful breakout.

In this section, we describe two breakout patterns suitable for advanced recreational players.

Simple is usually better. Success on the breakout is based on the execution of plays and not on how complicated the plays are. Match the plays to the skill level of your players.

Center circle breakout

A defenseman usually has the puck to start the breakout. Have his defensive partner cover the front of the net. Instruct players to create motion by having the center circle into one corner and skate up the boards. At the same time, the winger on the same side skates into the mid-lane. The winger on the other side of the ice stays wide and skates up the far boards leaving at the same time as his teammates. See Figure 16-4, the "a" option, for this play. Having the center and winger switch lanes gives width to the breakout. You can add depth by having the winger skate up the boards and into the neutral zone before skating into the mid-lane, as illustrated in Figure 16-4, option "b."

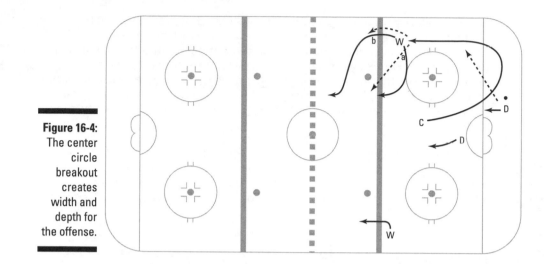

Figure 16-4:
The center circle breakout creates width and depth for the offense.

D to D breakout

This breakout adds the option of a pass between the defensemen. Start with having the center circle behind the net, rather than into the corner. This time he doesn't receive the puck as he goes by the defenseman who has it. Have the defenseman who is protecting the front of the net go to the opposite corner from the direction the center is circling to get the pass from the defensive partner with the puck while the center pulls up to protect the front of the net. The puck receiver immediately passes back to the first defenseman who has cut up ice on the same side. See this breakout illustrated in Figure 16-5. This type of fake then give-and-go provides a great deal of motion that is more difficult for opponents to break up.

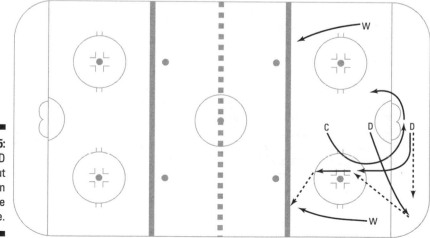

Figure 16-5:
The D to D breakout adds motion to confuse the defense.

Direct players to have the puck carrier pass the puck to the first available teammate or get moving himself. The puck has to be moving to have an effective breakout.

Generating Offense through the Neutral Zone

Play in the neutral zone has to be an extension of the breakout play. All players need to be available to join in the play to maximize opportunities. This means that defensemen move up with the play and forwards have all three lanes filled in the neutral zone. The keys to neutral zone offensive success are to get the puck into the middle lane, move with speed, and set up for a wide offensive zone entry.

Advancing the puck in the mid-lane

More options are available on offense if the puck is brought through the neutral zone using the mid-lane. The puck carrier can pass to the right and to the left rather than having just one option. This also tends to draw the opponents more toward the center of the ice, which opens more space for your wingers. Show players how to get the puck to the mid-lane either by passing to the open man there or by carrying the puck and switching position with a teammate. See Figure 16-6 for examples of these two options.

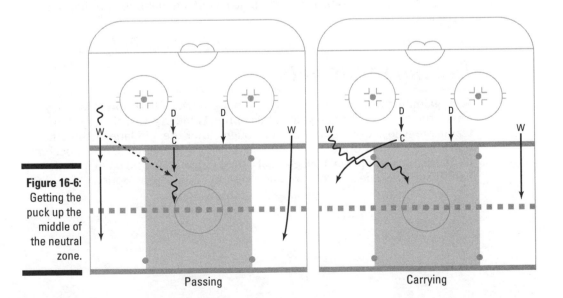

Figure 16-6: Getting the puck up the middle of the neutral zone.

Passing   Carrying

Moving with speed

Encouraging your players to move the puck quickly through the neutral zone makes any offensive play harder for the defensive team to defend against. Speed also makes it necessary for the defensive team to back in over their blue line, which allows the offensive team easier access to the offensive zone.

Going wide into the offensive zone

Ideally, your team's first play into the offensive zone is along the boards, assuming your team gained the mid-line in the neutral zone. This play is known as *making a wide entry*. If your winger makes a wide entry with efficient speed, the defensive team will find it difficult to keep up with the play because they must move laterally. That creates offensive options both for the puck carrier and those away from the puck. When the puck is sent to a winger about to enter the offensive zone for the wide entry, the next closest player to the zone should drive straight toward the net looking for a pass or rebound while being careful not to go offside in the process.

Attacking in the Offensive Zone

When your team gains the offensive zone, instruct all forwards to move in deep and stay in constant motion, with one player always cruising in front of the net (the actual individual in front of the net can constantly change). Instruct defensemen to be inside the blue line and to get open on their half of the ice.

Driving to the net

After gaining the offensive blue line, the puck carrier's first option is to try to attack the net for a shot on goal. If this option is taken away, she looks for the teammate who is driving to the net through either the mid-lane or the other outside lane. If that option is cut off, the third forward should by then become an attacking pass option. If all else fails, defensemen must be open for a pass back inside the blue line to start a new series of attack pass options.

Joining the rush

If the puck carrier has no forward options when she gets into the offensive zone, then she can pass back to a defenseman who has also gained the offensive zone. Instruct defensemen to follow the play up the ice trying to stay no more than half a zone behind the puck so that they are available quickly for offensive play. Occasionally, a defenseman may be in a better position to drive toward the net on the rush than the third forward, in which case she should join the rush and the third forward must cover her defensive position.

Remind players that when the offensive team has possession of the puck in the offensive zone, all five skaters should be inside the blue line and available to contribute to the play.

Creating a moving triangle

When an initial rush into the offensive zone does not result in a goal, your team must regroup to attack the net again. The most effective concept for such follow-up play is to have the three players closest to the net form what is referred to as an *offensive triangle*. In principle, teach players to have the puck carrier and one other player attack the net while a third player stays high, relative to the two attackers, to create passing or late-man-in options. See Figure 16-7 for one offensive triangle formation.

Figure 16-7:
Creating offensive motion with a triangle formation.

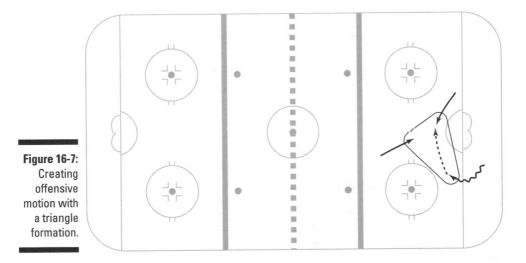

Remind players that none of the players or positions in the triangle are static. They should constantly switch positions to re-create offensive triangle attacks from a variety of angles until they are successful.

Although forwards run this offense, the two defensemen must cover their half of the ice inside the blue line, being ready for a pass if the triangle needs to regroup — or being ready to jump into a triangle formation, in which case the off-position forward would move to cover that player's defensive area.

Coaching Advanced Offensive Face-off Techniques

As players advance in hockey, you can begin to make use of unique skills to win offensive face-offs. For example, you might have a defenseman who has a great shot. You could use a modified face-off alignment in which your center tries to get the puck to that defenseman.

Another time for a change from the basic alignment is when you want to exploit a weakness in the defensive team. An example is when the other team's face-off alignment has left an area of the face-off ice unprotected. Your team may want to move the puck toward that area to gain a quick attack option.

Some other face-off realignment options to consider, according to the talents on your team, include the following:

- **Switch wingers:** Use this option to put a right-shot winger on the left side of the center and a left-shot winger on the right. This alignment lets your center get the puck to either winger for a quick shot on goal because, in these positions, both wingers have a better shooting angle on the net.

- **Switch defensemen:** Use this option to move a left-shot defenseman to line up inside the blue line to the right of the center and a right-shot defenseman to the left. Again, this improves the shooting angle for the defensemen when the center gets either of them the puck.

- **Move defenseman up on the circle:** In this alignment, the board side defenseman is moved up to the edge of the face-off circle from his regular blue line position. This allows him to get to the puck quicker, which is useful if he has a quick-release shot. His defense partner would maintain his normal position inside the blue line.

On face-offs, sticks should be on the ice, all players should know each others' roles, and all players must be ready to quickly battle for a loose puck.

Chapter 17

Coaching Defense to Advanced Players

*W*hen players advance defensively, you need to continue to work on improving skating and passing skills, which are the tools for playing sound defense (refer to Chapter 16 for similar information regarding offense). Beyond these individual skills, teamwork takes on more importance at this level. Teamwork starts with players knowing where they should be relative to their opponents and where they can expect their teammates to be. When they master these skills as a group, your team will be able to effectively shut down opponents' options in all three zones of play and during face-offs (check out Chapter 10 for more about the zones of play).

After you cover the basics of coaching defensive hockey, we recommend that you follow a particular order to developing more-advanced defensive play. Initially, the emphasis is on individual positional play. Next, work on getting defensive zone coverage down cold. Then develop solid forechecking, followed by neutral zone backchecking.

Ganging Up on Your Opponents: Defensive Teamwork Strategies

Defensive teamwork requires players to work together as one unit to limit the time and space their opponents have to control the puck. Positional play is the foundation of such teamwork. Players need to learn to read what opponents are doing offensively so that they can shut them down as a unit.

Maintaining solid positional play

We mention in Chapter 11 that positional play is essential to playing successful team defense. You need to teach players to position themselves on the defensive side of the opponent they are responsible for. That means your player must be between the opponent and your net. For the player whose opponent is the puck carrier, she must be on the defensive side of the puck as well. The following list highlights three specific techniques for improving team defensive play:

- Checkers can enhance their defensive positioning by skating what is called an *inside-out pattern,* which means approaching the opposing offensive player from the middle (inside) of the ice and skating toward the boards (out). This inside-out pattern reduces the options of the offensive player simply by limiting the ice she has available to make a play with the puck because your player — the defender — ends up occupying the best ice space.

- Players can improve their defensive positioning by always having their heads on a swivel, constantly looking to stay aware of where the puck is and where other players are. With this technique, your players are able to assess situations and then adjust accordingly. This technique also helps your players continually look around the whole ice surface all the time, rather than just focusing on the puck or the player they are responsible for.

- Advanced players can learn to stay with the offensive player they were checking after the puck is passed. Rather than following the puck after the pass, you want your players to remain close enough to the passer to eliminate her from joining the attack again. To prevent her from doing so, your player skates with her on the defensive and best pass-option side, or, if contact is allowed, finishes the check on the passer, which means leaving her sufficiently off balance that she is temporarily out of the play. Make sure players know the difference between legally and illegally restricting an opponent from joining the play.

Coach players to read off each other, not just the opposition, when they have their head on a swivel. Players should understand each teammate's role so that they can read what a teammate is doing in given situations in a game and react accordingly. For example, when a defensive player goes into the corner in a fight for the puck, she needs to know where her nearest teammate will be coming from so that she can direct the puck to that player. That teammate needs to understand that her responsibility is to get open to receive an outlet pass while also maintaining a defensive position in case the opposition comes up with the puck. The next nearest teammate covers any defensive hole created by the first two in their attempt to get control of the puck.

Taking away time

The more time an offensive player has to make a play, the more likely he will make a good one. So a defensive team's job is always to work toward taking away as much time from the offensive team as possible. *Taking away time* means reducing the amount of time a player has to make a play with the puck.

To prepare your team for time-stealing defense, emphasize getting quick pressure on the puck carrier. Quick pressure on the puck carrier comes first from good defensive positioning and then from eliminating hesitation in getting on the puck. The moment your players lose control of the puck and go on defense, the nearest player to the puck carrier immediately gets on the puck. His job is to try to separate the puck from the puck carrier so that the puck carrier has no time to work with it. Have all other teammates immediately move to cut off pass options to the opponent nearest to them and to position themselves on the defensive side of the opponent. When a defensive team acts together quickly in this formation, they don't allow the opposition any time to make a good play.

Taking away space

The more space the offensive team has to work with, the greater the opportunity they have to make a good play. *Taking away space* means eliminating open ice area between the puck carrier and her teammates. Instruct your team to use *inside-out skating* (starting near the mid-lane and skating at an angle toward the boards as they come up the ice against an opposing player — the objective being to force the puck carrier into the boards to limit his offensive options) to eliminate the space your opponents have to work in. This helps take away ice that the puck carrier can use to initiate a play.

Players away from the puck should also be close enough to their opponent to eliminate the ice they have available to work with. Teach players to position themselves on the defensive side of their opponent, slightly to the puck-carrier side, so that they can place their stick in the ideal passing lane to take away space for that option. This makes it more difficult for the passer to find an open man to pass the puck to. To accomplish this, have your checkers use the head-on-a-swivel technique to know where the puck and their opponents are at all times. They must also realize that they have to constantly adjust to maintain this position as the opponent tries to move up ice.

Use practice drills that help players get a feel for time and space. A simple warm-up drill is to have all players skate randomly with a puck, using the whole ice surface. Then gradually limit the ice available to them, first to just half the ice (from the center line to one end board), then to between the blue lines, and finally to just the ice between a blue line and the center line. The lesson is for players to find out how much more quickly they have to maneuver the puck when less space is available — which is a good offensive lesson — but also how limiting time and space can force weak plays, making such play an effective defensive strategy.

Reading offensive options

As your checker takes time and space away from the puck carrier, her teammates need to read the ice to find out what options are still available to the puck carrier. When players begin to read these options, they can make necessary positional adjustments that reduce opportunities for the opposition to take advantage.

Reading these options from the defensive or offensive side of the puck is referred to as *reading and reacting.* Run read-and-react drills frequently in practice sessions to help your team work quickly and together to play tight defensively, which makes it difficult for any offense to work effectively.

Defending Your Offensive Zone

Defense starts the moment the puck is turned over to the opposition in the offensive zone. Whether your opponents get control of the puck off a rebound, an errant pass, or a steal, your players must immediately switch to defensive play. In the offensive zone, the key to good defensive hockey is solid forechecking.

A successful forecheck requires that all players remain up ice, involved in the play, and aware of each other's responsibilities. Each player must know who she is responsible for and immediately play her tight. Have players check using the inside-out technique to take away passing lanes and have them keep their sticks on the ice on the side of the opponent's best pass-receiving option. Instruct the nearest player to the puck to take away time and space by putting quick pressure on the puck carrier. Ultimately, ensure that players know that their objective is to remove the puck from the opponent's possession using an appropriate check.

Challenging Opponents in the Neutral Zone

Emphasize with your forwards that they must backcheck through the middle of the ice. To teach this, have your puck-side defenseman always take the puck carrier. As soon as she puts pressure on the puck carrier, have your forwards find the nearest opponent without the puck. Your forwards must be confident that the puck carrier is covered. As the forwards take an opponent, have them identify who they're covering so that you have no duplication or open player. Then have your forwards quickly get on the opponent's defensive side. A quick and loud "My man! My man!" is an easy way to tell teammates who they are covering.

Have players use inside-out checking with the objective again being to separate the opponent from the puck. If your team does not succeed in getting control of the puck, you must ensure that you have synchronized your system for backchecking in the neutral zone with the system you want your team to use for defensive zone coverage.

Defending Your Net

The first rule of defensive zone play actually starts just outside the zone. Teach your defensemen to never back in to the zone; you want them to force offside instead. The best ways to do that are to use the rub-out or open-ice checks as the opponent approaches the blue line (refer to Chapter 15 for more about these checking techniques).

When the checking opportunity doesn't exist as the opponents enter your defensive zone, basic defensive zone coverage starts with the puck-side defenseman playing the puck carrier as the puck enters the defensive zone. Instruct the other defenseman to take the forward nearest the net, an action known as *net-front protection*.

Instruct forwards to pick up the remaining players away from the puck in the following sequence:

 ✔ The first forward back in the defensive zone picks up the offensive forward who is not covered by either of the defensemen.

 ✔ The second forward is responsible for the defenseman on the puck side of the ice.

 ✔ The third forward covers the other defenseman.

For instructional purposes, identify the forwards as F1, F2, and F3. Then you can say F2 covers the puck-side point. This will have your players thinking defensive positioning and not being confused with the usual labeling of center and left and right wing.

Walk players through the defensive set-up initially. Then gradually speed up the drill. The more quickly players can pick up the appropriate opponent and cut her off from becoming a useful play option, the more successful your team will be defensively.

Executing Advanced Defensive Face-off Techniques

Your defensive face-off alignment should be based on two factors: your players' strengths and the alignment of the offensive team. Opponents normally line up for the face-off with the intention of using their strengths to get control of the puck. So your alignment needs to be able to neutralize the opponent's preferences.

One way to do this is to have your defensemen line up next to the opposing wingers and your wingers line up with the opposing defensemen. For the most part, this aligns your players with the opponent they would normally be responsible for defensively. Whatever alignment you use, be sure that your goaltender has a clear view of the puck as the linesman drops it. Have your center attempt to pull the puck back toward the bottom of the circle or toward the corner where the risk of opponents getting to the puck first is the lowest. On a defensive zone face-off, your team's clear priority is puck control.

When your center wins the draw, designate a player who is to retrieve the loose puck. All his teammates need to know who that player is so that they can hold their positions momentarily to stop opponents from giving quick pressure on the puck. Make sure your center knows he is responsible for the

opposing center. Then after your team gains possession of the puck, all players break for open passing lanes.

If your center loses the draw, make sure all your players immediately get to
their check and are ready to cut off passing lanes or to pressure the puck. To
do this successfully, your players must know going into the face-off who they
are responsible for. Have them clarify to each other before the face-off to
avoid any confusion. As a rule, your defensemen cover the opponent's
wingers and your wingers take the opponent's defensemen. Two alternative
and effective defensive zone face-off strategies for advanced players follow: D
(defenseman) on the wall and winger on the wall.

D on the wall

When your opponents put a winger on the board-side hash marks, line up a
defenseman opposite that winger. When your center wins the draw, you want
this defenseman to retrieve the puck. See Figure 17-1 for the alignment and
initial play. The other defenseman stands on the circle at the net-side hash
marks with a winger on either side of him. As the wall-side defenseman gets
the puck, his defensive partner moves to cover the front of the net in case of
a turnover and to offer a pass option. The center and wingers break for open
ice pass options.

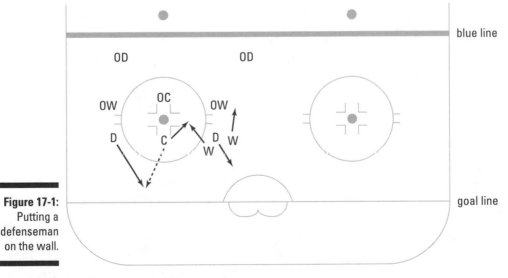

Figure 17-1:
Putting a
defenseman
on the wall.

O = opposing player

Winger on the wall

Sometimes the offense puts a defenseman instead of a winger on the hash marks by the boards and moves their winger to a position on the net side of their other winger at the hash marks.

The adjustment to make in this case is to place a winger at the hash marks with the opposing defenseman on the boards. One of your defensemen stays lined up with a winger at the hash marks on the net side with the other winger lining up next to him, as in the D-on-the-wall alignment. Put your second defenseman to the net side of the back of the face-off circle where he is closer to the opposing winger, who is his responsibility to check if your team loses the face-off.

The play from this alignment is to have the defenseman at the back net-side of the face-off circle retrieve the puck when the center wins the draw while the defenseman at the hash marks moves to protect the net in case of a turnover or to offer a pass option. The center and wingers break for open ice after temporarily detaining the opposition. See Figure 17-2 for this alignment and initial play.

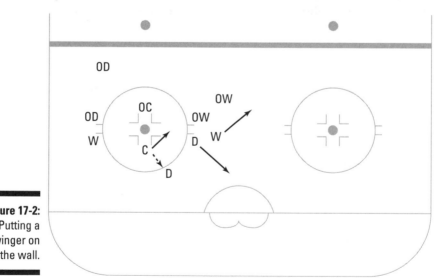

Figure 17-2: Putting a winger on the wall.

Chapter 18

Special Teams

● ●

In This Chapter

▶ Selecting players for special teams

▶ Putting power in your power play

▶ Killing penalties effectively

● ●

Special teams are an important part of a team's success. A *power play* is your team's chance to take advantage of an improved scoring opportunity — you get more players on the ice than the other team. *Penalty killing* allows your more aggressive defensive players to really shine — to come out even or ahead when the other team has more players on the ice. In addition to mastering the strategies of power play and penalty killing, you want your players to acquire attitude — or call it hunger — to give high performance for the team when assigned to either special team. Some players have this drive naturally; some need to be encouraged.

At beginner hockey levels, all players should have the opportunity to play on special teams. Simply use the next players who are up in your regular line rotation to give all players some experience playing on the power play and penalty-killing units, as well as to give you a chance to find out who rises to the challenge.

Somewhere between the intermediate and advanced levels, greater emphasis is placed on having success with special teams, so you then have to choose who to play. At those levels, you also have to select which power play or penalty-killing strategy to use based on the talent you have available. We discuss those strategies in this chapter.

A word to the wise before we go further: Be sure to monitor shift length on special teams. Make one-minute shifts on the power play the maximum. This length allows you to use two different units and to keep players fresh because speed is important on a power play. Penalty-killing shifts are usually shorter, especially if you use a pressure style of play. Shifts of 30 to 40 seconds allow you to use three or four units of fresh players.

Determining Who Should Play on Special Teams

Early in the season, try all players in special team situations. As the season progresses, you may want to put the most effective players on the special team units. Players who are good in these types of pressure situations will soon be clear to you, and they will want to be on the ice for these challenges. Players who struggle under pressure will not want to be out on the ice in game situations where they may possibly hurt the team's chance for success. That is a fair choice for the sake of the team.

Your challenge may be the player who wants to be "out there" but whose talent does not warrant a position on the unit. Know your team well enough to determine where each player stands and use an assignment approach that keeps some slots on the special teams always open. With open slots on the special teams, players know they can work to improve and get a chance to try again. Be open and specific with players about what they should improve to be a better power play or penalty-killing player and help them work on it.

You can also select who is to play on special teams based on a reward concept. Players could get more special team ice time because of their success in regular 5-on-5 play. The unspoken side of using the reward concept means players get less special team time for poor performance, which can be a useful notion for positive, competitive players who are enjoying their hockey experience. But it can be disheartening for players who are struggling. So use this approach judiciously, keeping the focus on positive reward.

If a player is not practicing or playing with the intensity of the team overall, do not reward him with special team ice time. Doing so sends a negative message to the other players on your team. Be sure to communicate to the player why his special team ice time is being limited so that he knows how he can change things.

At elite levels, some players may be considered to be special team specialists, but this focus or designation is not appropriate at the minor hockey level. Players are there to learn, get better, and have fun at this stage, not sit on the bench. The more players you rotate through the special teams, even at this advanced level, the more players reach those goals. Remember that most kids you are coaching still have 20 to 50 years of hockey ahead of them after they leave your tutelage. That's plenty of time for individuals to specialize.

Coaching Winning Power Play Strategies

Whenever your team has at least one more skater than your opponent, you want to have a strategy in place to help your players take advantage of the situation. Power plays are an opportunity to have greater control of the puck with fewer checkers and more passing options available.

One point to make with players is for them to show more patience when they have the puck so that they can look for the sure play. With only two minutes for them to have an advantage, they don't want to lose control of the puck. At the same time, players must realize this doesn't mean to sit back. Aggressive, quality puck movement is essential for power play success.

The overall number of passes on the power play often increases compared to the same puck possession time at even strength. However, players often have a tendency to over-pass the puck on the power play. Players need to learn the balance between aggressiveness and patience so that they don't turn the power play into a negative by continually passing and not creating a play or scoring situation. Have players focus on purposeful passes, beyond just keeping the puck moving. The objective is to make something positive happen. Make sure they shoot the puck!

One fundamental strategy on a power play is to have the puck carrier and one other player create a 2-on-1 against an opponent. Instruct a second player, usually the nearest teammate, to support the puck carrier to create the 2-on-1. You want your players to never feel compelled to try to beat a defensive player 1-on-1.

Set aside time in practices to work on the power play. Some coaches prefer to work on the power play early in practice when the ice is smoother. This may allow for more effective passing, especially in the early stages of learning the plays. However, game conditions should ultimately apply.

Breaking out of your own end

The simplest choice of a breakout to use on the power play is the same one you use when teams are at even strength. Your players know exactly what to do. And, if the breakout is effective at even strength, it should work when on the power play. To find out about basic breakout plays, see Chapter 16.

Generally, you want whoever breaks out with the puck to try to get to the mid-lane to allow for passing options to either side or up the middle. Following are two additional plays for doing so effectively:

- ✔ The stretch breakout is particularly effective when your team has the man advantage. Have your center curl into the corner, with or receiving the puck as he goes. Have the winger on the same side leave the zone, skating up the boards looking for open ice in the middle to be available for a long pass. See Figure 18-1 for the pattern.

- ✔ The double swing is another common power play breakout. For this play, have the center swing to the corner with the puck as in the stretch breakout. But this time, have the defenseman who is protecting the front of the net skate a pattern that mirrors the center's pattern on the opposite side of the ice. Also have both wingers begin to move up ice when the center and defenseman go to the corners. This results in the center trailing one winger up one side of the ice and the defenseman trailing the other winger up the other side. As the unit skates into the neutral zone, wingers look for open ice in the middle to become passing options. See Figure 18-2 for the skating patterns.

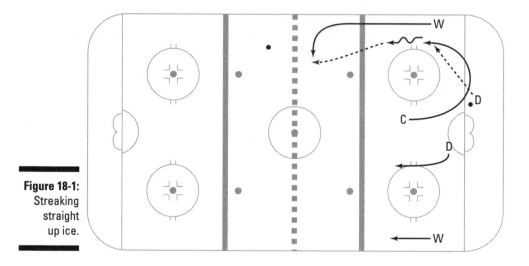

Figure 18-1:
Streaking
straight
up ice.

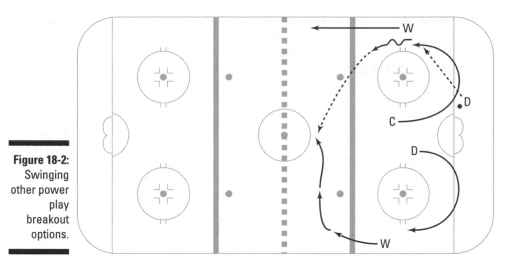

Figure 18-2:
Swinging other power play breakout options.

Powering through the neutral zone

Play in the neutral zone must flow smoothly from the breakout that was used. The objective is the same as in even-numbered situations (when both teams have the same number of players on the ice) — your team needs to get the puck up through the middle of the neutral zone to create the best play options. Also have players accelerate from the controlled speed they used in the breakout to top speed through the neutral zone. This forces opponents to back off and virtually let your team into the offensive zone unobstructed.

If your team lets up or goes more slowly toward the blue line, they will likely be forced to dump the puck into the offensive zone. This typically results in a turnover — a lost opportunity when on the power play. Emphasize that your players use their speed through the neutral zone. As the puck enters the offensive zone, the power play unit should be at maximum speed.

Power playing in the offensive zone

As the power play unit enters the offensive zone, make sure players realize that their first option is to attack the net on the rush. Only if the defensive team doesn't allow this to happen should the power play unit then go to preset plays.

Power play opportunities come in three forms: 5-on-4, 5-on-3, and 4-on-3. In the following sections, we discuss key concepts for playing each.

5-on-4 power play

The principle for offensive zone play on a 5-on-4 power play is *overload*. Overload places all forwards on one half of the ice. Have one forward go to the front of the net (usually your strongest winger), one to the boards near the hash marks (usually your center), and the third forward to below the goal line approximately halfway between the net and the side boards. The puck-side defenseman goes next to the boards and just inside the blue line. His defense partner is also just inside the blue line and lined up with the far post of the net. See Figure 18-3 for the positions.

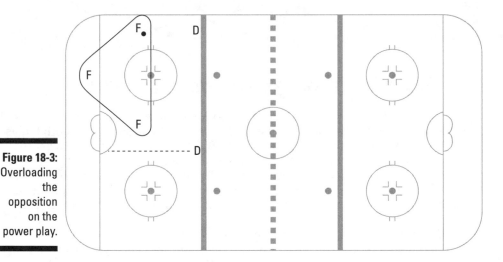

Figure 18-3:
Overloading
the
opposition
on the
power play.

Teach players that these positions are just areas to be occupied, and for the forwards particularly, this doesn't mean that they should stand there. Players should rotate through the positions. Movement confuses the defense. At the same time, you want each position to be filled at all times, just as they use the offensive triangle in even-strength play. Teamwork is a hallmark of an effective power play.

Another effective power play for advanced players is the *umbrella*. The umbrella starts with the overload set-up. The difference is that you put the board-side defenseman at the middle of the blue line and have her partner slide toward the face-off dot on the opposite side of the offensive zone. Have the forward who was originally on the boards by the hash marks move off the boards to the face-off dot on her side of the offensive zone. This typically brings your defensemen more into the play and requires quick, aggressive play-making motion. See Figure 18-4 for the positions.

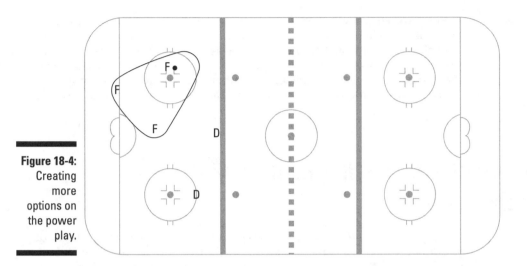

Figure 18-4:
Creating more options on the power play.

5-on-3 power play

Occasionally, your team may get to play a two-man advantage due to penalties. The stretch breakout is particularly useful in a 5-on-3 because of the additional space available. As they get through the neutral zone, have your players carry the puck in over the blue line at full speed and go in for a shot on goal. If they need to set up a play, they can use overload or the umbrella formation. Typically, however, a more effective formation is a 2-1-2. To set this up, position one forward in front of the net to cover the slot area by moving up and back (perpendicular to the net). The other two forwards move up and back (toward and away from the goal line) covering an area from the face-off dots to near the goal line on either side of the net. The defensemen locate between the blue line and the top of the circles, with one above each circle. The objective is to get the puck to a deep forward who looks for a diagonal pass for a shot from the slot. If the shot isn't available, he passes out to a defenseman and they try the play again.

Have the forward on the face-off dot to the goalies' right be a right shot, when possible, and on the left, a left shot when possible. This provides better shooting angles on the net.

One caution here to coaches: Players often tend to over-pass the puck and not shoot in a 5-on-3 because of all the time and space available. Remind them of their focus — a shot on goal.

4-on-3 power play

Occasionally, your team may have a one-man advantage but with only four players on the ice. In a 4-on-3, use similar breakout and neutral zone principles as when playing 5-on-4. In the offensive zone, have players establish a box formation in which the defensemen at the top of the box (who typically start the play with the puck) look for diagonal passing opportunities to the forwards who circle into the slot area from their low box positions. If a forward doesn't get a shot from the slot, he can pass out to either defenseman and the play begins again. The best opportunities for diagonal passes come when the defensemen pass the puck between them forcing the defensive triangle to shift coverage, which opens up space for the diagonal low forward coming into the slot.

Pressuring with Penalty-Killing Strategies

When your team *kills penalties,* you typically play with one fewer player than your opponents. So you need a high-energy unit on the ice to get the job done. Good penalty killers are often players who love the challenge of playing against the man advantage. They thrive on disrupting power plays in all three zones.

The important skills in a penalty killer are skating and an ability to read the play. Players must first recognize which power play strategy opponents are using, and then anticipate what the opponents are going to do. This anticipation is important to be able to quickly disrupt their plans. Also, an active stick is an asset for taking away passing options. This is especially important in the defensive zone.

We suggest two penalty-killing strategies to teach to advanced young hockey players: pressure and passive penalty killing. The pressure strategy requires you to have penalty killers use quick skating to force the puck carrier to rush plays and hopefully cause mistakes or turnovers. Any time the puck carrier might not have complete control of the puck, have players immediately put pressure on him by attempting to get the puck.

Passive penalty killing does not use quick pressure. Instead, instruct players to focus on positioning. In your offensive and neutral zones, the penalty killers must take away the mid-lane. Once in the defensive zone, very little pressure is used to force a turnover. Instead, players must stay in a set alignment, protecting the slot area (between the circles) and forcing the opposition to work outside of the penalty killers. Instruct your players to allow the power play to move the puck freely outside their protection area. The objective of this approach is to force opponents to waste their power play time.

In either system, shift length should be kept to 30 to 40 seconds to allow for fresh skaters on the ice as often as possible.

Your team can use a combination of both passive and pressure penalty-killing strategies. You may want to be passive in your offensive and neutral zones and use pressure when play comes to your defensive zone. Some teams like to use up-ice pressure in the offensive zone to initially try to force a turnover, and then they become passive in the neutral and defensive zones. Another option is to be passive in the offensive zone but look to apply quick pressure in the neutral zone to force offside infractions or turnovers, and then play passive in the defensive zone.

A major factor in choosing between pressure and passive strategies is your players' skills. Skilled teams are usually able to be successful with a pressure style while poorer skating teams will likely struggle. A second factor is the level of your opponents' power play. You should pressure a weak power play, but you may want to play more passive against a strong power play. If your penalty killing is not great, look to limit risk and lean toward a more passive approach.

Experiment in practices to see what works best for your team, and provide experience for your players so that they are familiar with the options and prepared for versatility.

Penalty killing in the offensive zone

Whether you use passive or aggressive pressure on penalty killing, have your forwards inside the blue line and focused on taking away the middle of the ice. Two good positioning options for the forwards exist: side-by-side or stacked.

Side-by-side means that both forwards are parallel to each other in the offensive zone, positioned somewhere between the tops of the circles and the face-off dots. Stacked means that the first forward lines up in front of the net at approximately the hash marks and the second forward is 10 to 15 feet directly behind him. In either case, instruct both defensemen to move inside the blue line and cover the outside lanes.

As the opposing defenseman skates out from behind the net with the puck on their breakout, he should see each of your players taking away ice and passing lanes. Have your players visualize the puck carrier looking at four crests on the fronts of your jerseys.

Penalty killing in the neutral zone

The objective for penalty killers in the neutral zone is to take away the middle of the ice and disrupt the speed of the power play. This forces the power play to dump the puck into the offensive zone or have to regroup and try to go through the neutral zone again.

Have your players focus on positional play and make sure they use their sticks to take away passing lanes. Skating an inside-out pattern also forces the puck to the outside.

Penalty killing in your own zone

Regardless of the numerical disadvantage, as soon as the opposition gets into your defensive zone, have your penalty-killing unit focus on protecting the slot area. This area in front of the net is where most power plays try to get the puck because that area provides the best scoring opportunities.

Instruct players that all penalty-killing skating in the defensive zone is done in straight lines. If a player is going to put pressure on an opponent, instruct her to go straight to the player, stop and check, if appropriate, and backskate to her original position using a straight line as opposed to circling back to the starting position. This prevents players from being temporarily out of position, which is all the opponent may need for a scoring chance when you are short-handed.

Penalty killing comes in three forms: 4-on-5, 3-on-5, and 3-on-4. In all of these situations, impress on your players that active sticks are important to take away passing lanes. Heads on a swivel and verbal communication also make penalty killing more successful.

Boxing out the opposition when 4-on-5

The most useful formation for advanced young penalty killers when playing 4-on-5 is to form a big four-cornered box around the slot area. Each corner of the box is the location of a penalty killer. The box moves as the puck moves, always keeping a penalty killer in front of the puck carrier, and always maintaining the box shape. This means that at times the box may sit square to the goalie, if the puck is centered, but the box will sit with one corner to the goalie when the puck is near the top edge of a face-off circle. See Figure 18-5 for the configurations.

When a power play unit passes the puck around the perimeter of the zone, and you want a passive box, have players use little movement and simply give the outside ice to the power play.

When you want to use a pressure strategy, have the penalty killer nearest to the puck quickly take away ice between the puck carrier and himself. If the puck carrier has less than complete control of the puck, the penalty killer may apply quick pressure in an attempt to gain control of the puck.

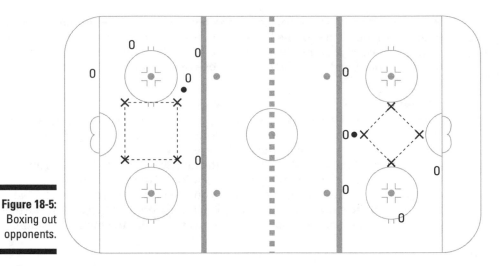

Figure 18-5:
Boxing out
opponents.

Triangle 3-on-5

Occasionally, your team may have to face a two-man advantage. In this case, have the three penalty killers form a triangle in the defensive zone using the box formation with an empty corner. Have one player in front of the puck carrier, as you normally would using the box formation, and have the other two players fill the nearest corners. See Figure 18-6 for two applications of the formation according to the location of the puck. As the power play moves the puck around, have your penalty killers rotate in such a way that the nearest player to the puck takes the puck carrier and the other two players take the corners of the box that flank that checker.

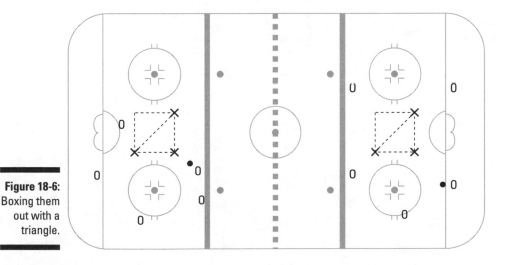

Figure 18-6:
Boxing them
out with a
triangle.

Have players imagine the triangle as the box formation used in the 4-on-5 situation with the corner of the box farthest from the puck always empty. This means that each player only has to skate one side of the box to adjust position when playing 3-on-5; they do not move diagonally.

Triangle 3-on-4

Occasionally, your team may have to play one man short with only three players. In this case, use a modified triangle formation. Have two players on the puck side of the triangle with the third player covering the middle of the triangle, which is actually the slot in front of the net. See Figure 18-7 for two applications of the formation according to the location of the puck. The triangle changes shape with puck movement as your defensive players switch positions to keep the closest player to the puck carrier on the puck and the farthest player from good passing opportunities moves to cover the middle position.

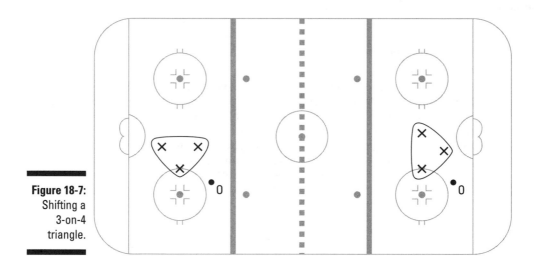

Figure 18-7:
Shifting a
3-on-4
triangle.

Chapter 19

Drills for Advanced Players

● ●

In This Chapter

▶ Dishing out and taking body checks

▶ Exchanging players on the ice for players on the bench

▶ Getting to the loose puck first

▶ Switching from defense to offense

▶ Improving offensive teamwork

▶ Gaining defensive position

▶ Making power plays powerful

▶ Killing penalties

▶ Working on a number of skills at once

● ●

Advanced young hockey players still need to do basic drills that work on the individual skills of skating, puck handling, and shooting. However, at this level you add elements to shift the focus to speed and *pressure* (being checked). Beyond these basics, your coaching focus shifts from individual to teamwork skills. We offer drills in this chapter that help you to work on body checking and the team skills discussed in Chapters 15 to 18. See the Cheat Sheet if you are unfamiliar with the symbols used in the drills.

Observe that you can practice offensive and defensive strategies using the same drills. Select one offensive point to emphasize and one defensive point. For example, use a 1-on-1 drill to have the forwards work on outside speed while the defense works on gap control. Similarly, you can use power play and penalty-killing drills to focus on either unit's play.

Body Checking Drills

Remember to walk players through these drills first, and then gradually increase the speed and force used in contact. Make sure that the players receiving the checks cushion and roll, which we describe in Chapter 15, when contact is made.

Body checking

This drill, a good starting point to teach checking, allows players to focus on the individual parts of the rub-out check (refer to Chapter 15) and to not be concerned about the physical demands of checking or being checked.

How it works: Have players work in pairs. One player skates along the boards and the other player checks his partner, slowly and under control, into the boards. Players then switch positions and repeat. See Figure 19-1 for the checking drill pattern. Have players check each other as they move from the blue line around to the blue line on the opposite side, and then repeat in the opposite direction.

Coaching pointers: Be sure to control the speed of the drill, going very slow initially. This speed allows you to teach proper technique while keeping the drill safe for the players. Changing direction is important and allows the players to practice checking techniques from both the right and left sides.

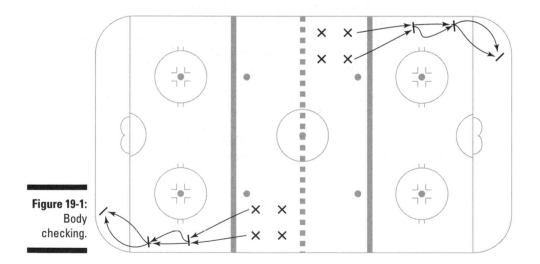

Figure 19-1:
Body
checking.

Angling drill

This drill helps players understand how to use an angled skating path to eliminate ice from the player carrying the puck — that is, to cut him off from his intended path — and check the player effectively.

How it works: Line players up as illustrated in Figure 19-2. Have X1 skate slowly with a puck behind the net. X2 follows and uses his position to angle X1 to the boards and checks him against the boards. Gradually increase the speed of the drill.

Coaching pointers: Be sure to start slowly. Once players understand how to find the proper angle to skate, have the puck carrier attempt to avoid the checker. Stress timing on the part of the checker. Keep sticks on the ice and demand safety all the time.

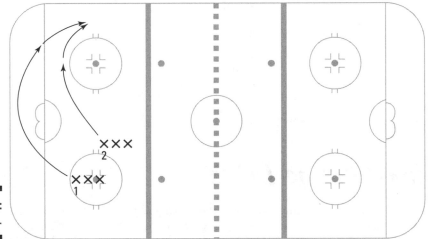

Figure 19-2:
Angling drill.

Mirror and angle

This is a more active and gamelike checking drill than the preceding drill ("Angling drill") because you use more of a game pace in the skating component. Players ultimately need the extra challenge involved.

How it works: Place players in lines as illustrated in Figure 19-3. Have X2 skate down the boards with a puck as X1 mirrors his skating path but inches ever closer. X2 must go below the goal line and then may continue around the net or cut back up the boards. X1 continues to mirror and close the gap between them until he checks X2 to the boards.

Coaching pointers: Have players get a feel for gradually closing the gap with the puck carrier. Emphasize the need for control skating and not rushing or lunging at the puck carrier. Stress safety and the proper checking technique. Also have the puck carrier understand how to take a check using his stick and arms to cushion contact with the checker and the boards.

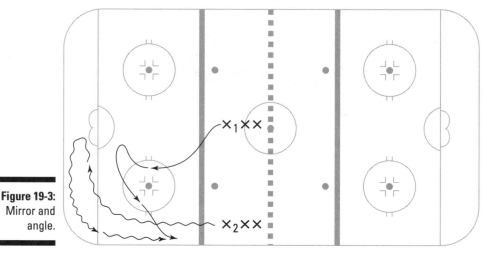

Figure 19-3:
Mirror and
angle.

Quick-Change Drills

When your team needs to exchange players on the ice for the fresh legs of players on the bench during play, you want to be able to do that without giving the opponents any advantage. These quick-change drills can help make your exchanges smooth when game time arrives. When using these drills, remind players where to come off and go on the ice at the bench, as we explain in Chapter 15, to minimize congestion. Watch for players who do not race to the bench or are not ready to get immediately into the play.

Quick change

Changing on the fly may seem like a simple thing for your team to understand. Assume they don't know the small things that can make a big difference. This drill gives all players a clear and simple system to use for all on-the-fly changes.

How it works: Run a scrimmage and designate one team to change. Following the drill pattern in Figure 19-4, have F1 gain center ice and dump the puck into the end boards at the far end. At the same time, have F2, F3, D1, and D2 call out their positions as they skate quickly to the bench. Have F1 forecheck until F4 and F5 join him. At the same time, D3 and D4 take their positions on the ice. F1 then changes as the new unit carries the play.

Coaching pointers: Have players clearly call out their positions when they are coming off the ice. Look for lazy skating from players coming off the ice; all players are to skate quickly all the way to the boards. Doing so makes changes quick and avoids a situation where your team might get called for a penalty for having too many men on the ice.

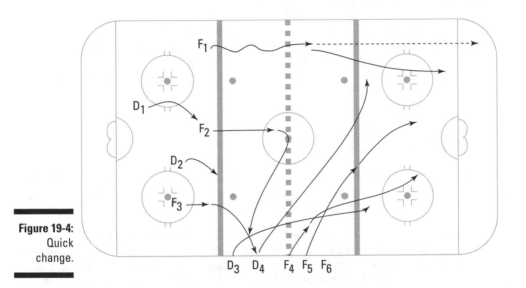

Figure 19-4:
Quick
change.

Quick change scrimmage

This drill gives players a gamelike situation in order to work on effective line changes. The added challenge of finding the right time to change is a good learning scenario for players.

How it works: Conduct a 5-on-5 scrimmage with each skating unit color-coded. Changes can be made only when the play is *live* (no changes during stoppages). Start with, for example, the red unit playing against the white unit. Have the blue unit on the bench ready to change with the red unit and the green unit ready to change with the white unit. If you only have three lines, when blue changes with red, have the white unit take a double shift.

Then white changes with red, and blue takes the double shift. Designate time or call out shift changes but have players determine the precise time to change following the call.

Coaching pointers: Instruct players that the puck has to be controlled by a teammate or be deep in the opponent's zone before a player attempts to change. Stress that players skate quickly all the way to the boards on every change. Players going on the ice are to go over the boards to allow players leaving the ice to use the doors.

Loose Puck Drills

He who gets to the loose puck first, wins. Well, it may not work out to that exactly, but getting to the loose puck first certainly gives your team more chances to do something productive. Don't let your players sit on their heels. Make a competition out of who gets the highest number of loose pucks in the drills or even during games.

Center ice chase

This competitive drill is a fun way to work on loose puck battles. A good time to use the drill is at the end of practice. Players enjoy the competition along with the opportunity to work on puck protection and checking skills.

How it works: The coach stands at the center ice dot with pucks. Have two players line up on opposite edges of the center ice circle on the center line as illustrated in Figure 19-5. As the coach slides a puck over the blue line, both players race for the loose puck. The player who gets to the puck first tries to score on the near goal while the other player tries to gain possession of the puck. Players keep competing until the coach blows his whistle and starts the next pair.

Coaching pointers: Have both players keep their feet moving after one has gained possession of the puck. Sticks stay on the ice throughout the drill. The player with the puck needs to use his body position to protect the puck from the checker. The checker works on his different checking techniques to help him gain possession of the puck.

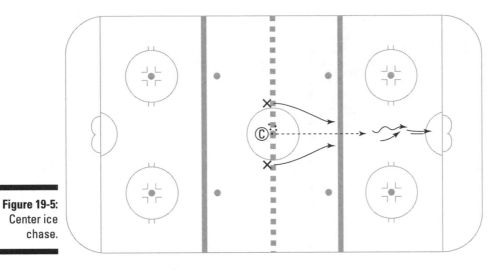

Figure 19-5:
Center ice
chase.

Loose puck out of the corner

This drill lets players work on loose puck battles in a confined space. The drill also resembles a game situation in which the defenseman has to protect the front of the net while trying to get control of a loose puck over a forward — who is trying to get to the puck first and create a scoring situation.

How it works: A defenseman starts in front of the net lined up with the far goal post. A forward starts with one knee in contact with the short-side face-off dot. The coach, with pucks, stands between the players. See Figure 19-6 for the starting positions. The coach slides a puck into the corner as both players immediately try to gain possession. If the forward gets it, he tries to attack the net with the puck while the defenseman tries to stop him. If the defenseman gets control, he tries to gain the blue line while the forward tries to check the puck away. Have loose puck battles last 15 to 20 seconds maximum.

Coaching pointers: Body position is a real focus in the drill; players have to be in the right place to get the job done. The defenseman must be between his net and the forward all the time when not in possession of the puck. The forward must use quick skating and his body to protect the puck from the defenseman. Be sure to let the drill run no longer than 20 seconds to ensure gamelike intensity.

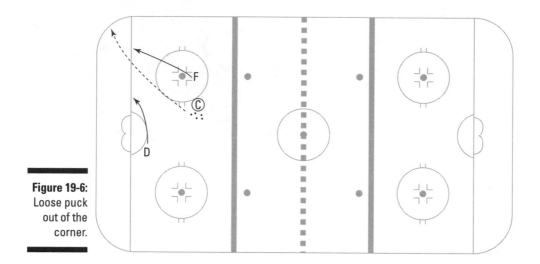

Figure 19-6:
Loose puck
out of the
corner.

Transition Drills

The more quickly your team can switch from defense to offense, the easier it is to catch the opponent off-guard and thereby get a better offensive attack rolling. Similarly, if your team can jump from offense to defense quickly, your players can more effectively limit any advantage the opponents hoped to gain. Quick execution is essential in these drills.

Neutral zone transition

This drill gives players a feel for the basics of transition play. High-tempo skating and quick puck movement reinforce the need for speed.

How it works: Start with forwards in all four corners and defensemen as indicated in Figure 19-7. Have a forward leave from both corners at one end of the ice, one with a puck, and pass and skate into the neutral zone. A defenseman starts on the near blue line and skates backward through the neutral zone. As the forwards reach the center line, they pass the puck to the defenseman and circle through center ice heading back toward the end they started from. The defenseman passes back to the forwards as they return through the neutral zone — have players keep their passes onside. The forwards go in for a shot on goal. Alternate ends for the drill.

Coaching pointers: Stress high-tempo skating and quick puck movement. Forwards have to skate at top speed as they return to their original end and receive the return pass. Don't let your forwards slow down to wait for a return pass. The defenseman has to make the return pass quickly to the forwards. If the return pass is too slow and causes an offside play, have the players repeat the drill correctly.

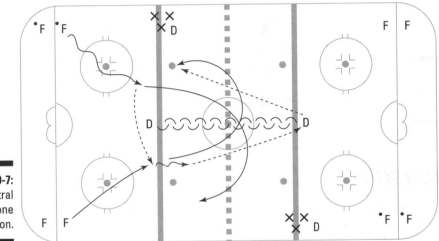

Figure 19-7:
Neutral
zone
transition.

5-on-2 transition

This gamelike transition drill is where all five skaters are involved but with limited opposition.

How it works: A forward line starts at center ice and dumps the puck into the end zone behind D1 and D2 (see Figure 19-8 for an illustration of this drill). Either D gets the puck, and then all five execute a breakout play and attack into the neutral zone against D3 and D4. When the forward line gains center ice, the puck carrier passes the puck to either D3 or D4. The forward line then switches lanes as they reverse direction and attack D1 and D2 while receiving a pass from D3 or D4. D3 and D4 move up on the play to make the attack into a 5-on-2.

Coaching pointers: Coordination of all five skaters is the goal. High-tempo skating by all five has to be maintained as well as quick puck movement. Remind forwards to fill the three forward skating lanes. The defensemen have various passing options but still have to move the puck quickly to a forward.

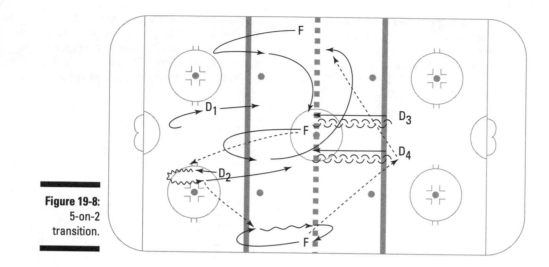

Figure 19-8:
5-on-2
transition.

Offensive Drills

Focus on teamwork in these offensive drills. Start with a moderate pace, and then bring speed and quickness into the drills. If accuracy suffers, ease up on pace until all players are comfortable with and can execute at that particular pace.

Horseshoe

This full-ice skating/passing/shooting drill involves all skaters and goaltenders. You can use this drill as a goalie warm-up drill early in practice or as a tempo skating drill at the end of practice.

How it works: Start with half the players in opposite diagonal corners. A player leaves from each end at the same time and skates up the boards toward the far blue line. A second player starts skating with a puck and passes to the first skater from the opposite line as he skates below the bottom of the center ice circle. This player continues for a shot on goal, and then stops at the net for any rebound from his own shot and the next shooter. See Figure 19-9 for the pattern.

Coaching pointers: Have players "stride" all the time (never standing still) as they receive a pass. Eliminate any coasting as the skater waits for the pass.

The passer needs also to always be striding when making the pass. When attacking the net for a shot, again stress striding while shooting. After the shot, make it a habit for all players to stay near the front of the net to play any possible rebound.

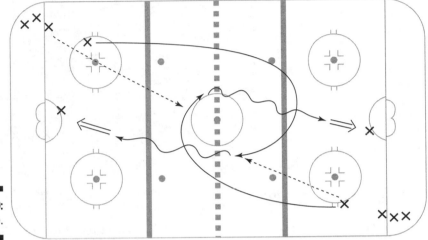

Figure 19-9:
Horseshoe.

Reverse horseshoe

This skating/passing/shooting drill is a variation of the horseshoe drill and is also an excellent warm-up or tempo drill in a practice. You can use this drill to bring tempo back to a practice after a nontempo segment.

How it works: Start with half the players in opposite corners with pucks. The first player from each end leaves at the same time and skates below the bottom of the near side of the center circle and then around the circle. As that player skates up the other side of the circle, he receives a pass from the second skater in line in the opposite corner. Have the puck carrier go in for a shot on goal and stay for his and the next shooter's rebound. See Figure 19-10 for the pattern.

Coaching pointers: Stress skating continuously and maintaining tempo. Making and receiving the pass is done after the skater has skated the turn and is skating away from the passer, as the passing angle is better at this point in the drill. Have players make a quick release shot with the shooter staying at the net to play any rebound from his shot and from the next shooter's shot.

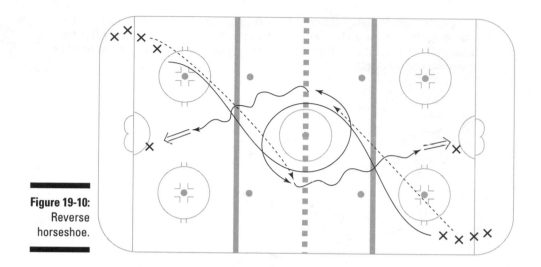

Figure 19-10:
Reverse
horseshoe.

2-on-1 cross

This full-ice drill runs from both ends at the same time. It works on skating/ passing and executing an offensive cross tactic for the forwards. The defense will learn to deal with that unique offensive tactic.

How it works: Have players start in forward and defensive lines as illustrated in Figure 19-11. The first player in each line starts, with F1 and F2 making touch passes down the ice 2-on-1 on a D. When they get to the offensive blue line, the forward on the boards has the puck and cuts across in front of the D and leaves the puck. At the same time, the F in the inside line goes behind him and picks up the puck. Both F1 and F2 drive to the net for a scoring chance. Set up the same drill on the other side of the ice.

Coaching pointers: As the forwards skate the length of the ice, be sure passing is accurate and crisp. On the offensive cross, the forward with the puck is always closest to the goal and the other always has to come from behind the puck carrier. As the cross is being executed, the puck carrier simply leaves the puck and doesn't actually pass it to his partner. Have defensemen continually stay between the two forwards, lining up more to the middle of the ice to encourage the forwards to move the puck to the outside where the danger of a quality scoring option is reduced.

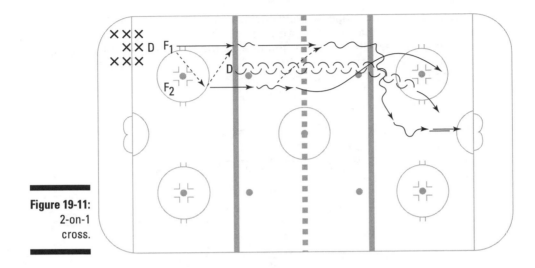

Figure 19-11:
2-on-1
cross.

Defensive Drills

Have players focus on skating to gain defensive position and keeping their sticks on the ice to close off passing options for offensive players. The defensive players' positions on the ice are a major factor in successful defensive play.

Defensive 1-on-1 gap control

This drill helps defensemen work on timing and skating skills to help narrow the gap between themselves and the attacking puck carrier. Backward skating, starts and stops, and pivots are all involved.

How it works: F1, carrying a puck, and D1 start down the ice 1-on-1, as illustrated in Figure 19-12. On a whistle, have F1 turn facing the boards and go in the opposite direction. D1 stops and skates forward in the same direction as F1. On a second whistle, have F1 again turn facing the boards. D1 stops, and then starts skating backward as both resume playing 1-on-1. This time have D1 start to close the gap on F1, trying to control his offensive options by the time he crosses the blue line.

Coaching pointers: Proper skating posture on the part of the defenseman makes all skating maneuvers more efficient. Have the defenseman line up his outside shoulder with the inside shoulder of the forward, discouraging any attempt by the forward to go to the middle of the ice. Always remind players to keep their sticks on the ice.

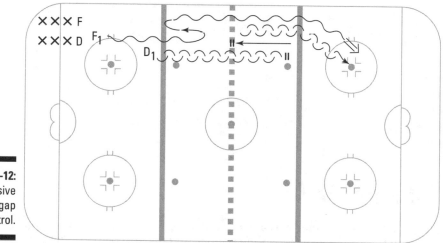

Figure 19-12:
Defensive
1-on-1 gap
control.

2-on-1 walk and shoot

The 2-on-1 situation is a good opportunity to create a quality scoring chance. This drill lets the defense work on getting their point shots on goal, the forwards work on going to the net to play a point shot, and all work on both the offensive and defensive execution of a 2-on-1.

How it works: Line up forwards and defensemen as illustrated in Figure 19-13. Begin with F1 passing to D1, who walks across the blue line with the puck and takes a shot on goal. F2 leaves on F1's pass and screens the goalie on D1's shot. After the shot, F1 and F2 get a pass from the next F in line and attack D1 for a full ice 2-on-1. D1 protects the middle of the ice to force an outside shot.

Coaching pointers: Have F2 screen the goalie and avoid being to the side of the net. F2 is to the puck side and available for a pass from D1. Be sure that F1 and F2 skate aggressively on the 2-on-1. D1 must skate at the same speed as the forwards as he stays in front of them. Have the forwards make frequent passes as they skate down the ice.

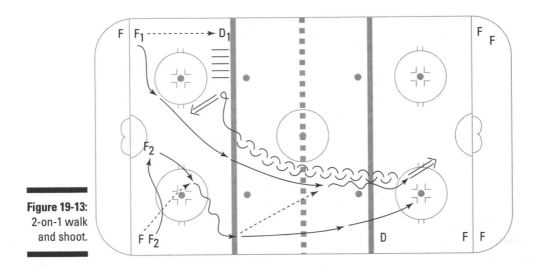

Figure 19-13:
2-on-1 walk
and shoot.

Power Play Drills

Emphasize quickness and accuracy in these drills. Watch players for over-passing; they need to focus on their purpose — scoring.

Power play puck movement

This drill works on puck movement to create a quality shot on goal, which is the basis of a successful power play. The drill has no penalty-killing resistance, which allows the players to experience success.

How it works: Position forwards where you would want them in a 5-on-4 power play overload situation. Place two defensemen on the blue line. See the example in Figure 19-14. The defensemen must remain stationary but the forwards can move based on the location of the puck. The coach sends the puck to a forward to start play. Emphasize quick puck movement by all players and efficient movement to open space. Have players make four passes maximum to set up a quality shot on goal. Be sure to take the shot on goal.

Coaching pointers: Stress quick puck movement. Make sure that the puck is in motion all the time, either by passing or with the puck carrier moving with the puck. Have players shoot when they get in a good scoring position. Players have a tendency to look for the perfect scoring opportunity, often drastically reducing the number of shots and scoring opportunities. Avoid this by having players see the value of taking *high percentage shots* (shots with good odds of scoring).

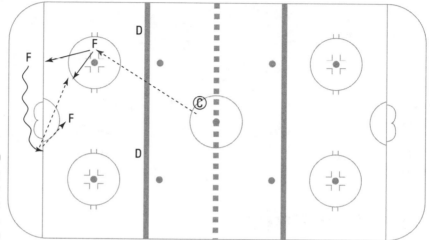

Figure 19-14:
Power
play puck
movement.

Power play hot-spot shooting

This drill helps players feel comfortable and confident when shooting on the power play. When players shoot during this drill, they feel the possibility of success as they perfect their shot from their hot spot.

How it works: Place a five-man power play unit in the offensive zone on the spots they want to be on when they get an opportunity for a shot on goal, such as those indicated in Figure 19-15. Give each player three pucks. Taking turns, have each player shoot all his pucks consecutively before moving on to the next shooter.

Coaching pointers: Make sure that all shots feature a quick release. The shooter's head is up and he's looking at the net. All shots have to be on the net! The first couple of times through the drill, use an empty net before adding a goalie. If players frequently miss the net, add five push-ups for every shot that misses the net. Push-ups are a definite motivator to hit the net!

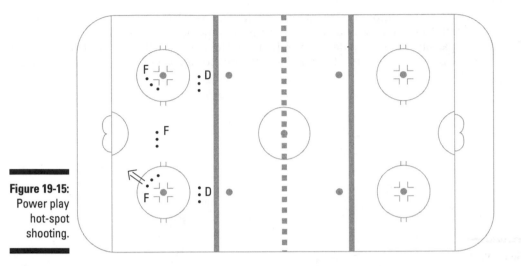

Penalty-Killing Drills

To build an effective penalty-killing team, you must emphasize players' sense of zone coverage while in formation. In other words, each player on the ice must be aware of the area he is protecting relative to the areas protected by his teammates so they can quickly shift their formation as a team in response to the changing position of the puck. Remind players to use active sticks and straight-line skating to cut off passing lanes.

Active sticks penalty killing

This drill helps players to know how to react to each other in the defensive zone in a penalty-killing situation.

How it works: Have four players set up the box formation in the defensive zone. With active sticks and straight-line skating, have the players shift the box formation on a coach who skates randomly with a puck inside the zone. See Figure 19-16 for an example.

Coaching pointers: Start with the penalty killers lined up in a basic box formation. Slowly move down the boards while carrying a puck. Watch for the proper rotation of players and also for the penalty-killing players using their sticks to take away passing lanes through the box. The idea is to only give passing lanes outside the box. Look for the player farthest away from the puck carrier to move into the middle of the box for added penalty-killing coverage.

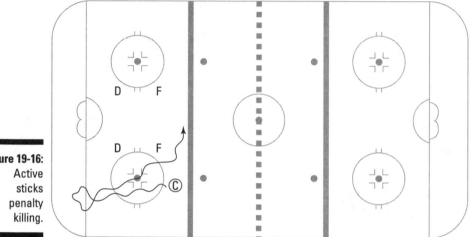

Figure 19-16:
Active
sticks
penalty
killing.

Live defensive zone penalty killing

This gamelike drill adds pressure and urgency to a penalty-killing situation to help players fine-tune penalty-killing skills.

How it works: Set up a box formation with the penalty killers. Then, have a five-man power play unit set up inside the zone as well. See Figure 19-17 for an example. On the coach's pass to a power play player, play becomes live. Instruct the penalty-killing unit to clear the puck out of the zone every time it gets possession. The coach feeds a new puck into the drill each time the penalty-killing unit clears a puck.

Coaching pointers: The first few times through, have the power play unit not be overly aggressive; let the penalty killers have some success. As the penalty killers get comfortable in their roles, have the power play unit get more intense. Look for active sticks and straight-line skating from all penalty killers. When any penalty killer gets possession of the puck, make it a habit that the puck is shot down the length of the ice.

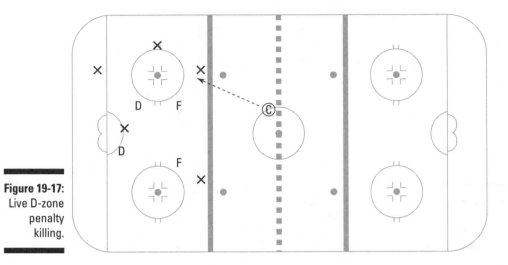

Combination Drills

Combination drills are designed to make drill conditions more gamelike in that a variety of skills are worked on at once. These drills are useful once the basic lessons in individual situations have been acquired.

Pressure shooting

This drill combines pressure shooting by an attacking player and quick defensive pressure from a checker. Use this drill to show the importance of aggressive action: aggressive attacking with the puck offensively and aggressive checking defensively.

How it works: Have players line up as illustrated in Figure 19-18. X1 starts with her knee in contact with the neutral zone face-off dot. X2 stands outside the blue line with a puck on her stick. On the coach's whistle, X2 leaves and races to the net for a scoring chance. X1 chases and tries to cut off X2 or poke the puck away.

Coaching pointers: Create urgency for both players by keeping the length of the drill to ten seconds or less. The shooter shoots as soon as she gets below the top of the face-off circles and continues to drive to the net for a rebound. The defensive player has to move quickly to take away ice from, and be on the defensive side of, the shooter.

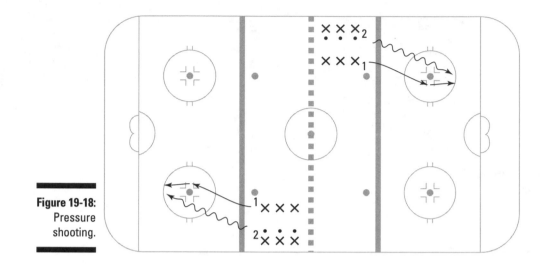

1-on-1 out of corner

This confined space 1-on-1 drill creates an isolated game situation in which both the forward and the defenseman work in a very competitive situation.

How it works: F1 starts with a puck while making contact with the boards in the corner. D1 starts in line with the far goal post. On the coach's whistle, F1 tries to get in a scoring position and D1 tries to take ice away quickly from F1and defend the net 1-on-1 against F1. See the example in Figure 19-19. Both players must stay below the tops of the circles.

Coaching pointers: Have the defenseman take ice away quickly and force the forward toward the end boards by using an inside-out skating path. Have the forward skate quickly and attack the net, trying to get to the slot and get a quick shot on goal. Keep the drill time to less than ten seconds to maintain intensity.

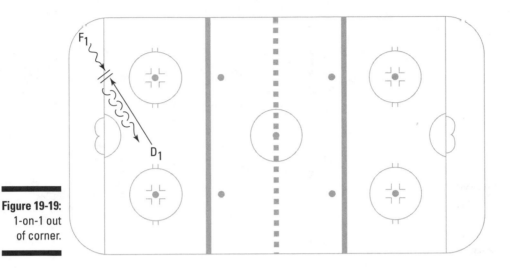

Figure 19-19:
1-on-1 out
of corner.

2-on-2 full ice

This drill lets players work on both offensive and defensive team skills such as quick repositioning and passing.

How it works: Start with two forwards in opposite corners and two defensemen on the blue line with a puck, as illustrated in Figure 19-20. Have all four players leave the zone as D1 passes to F1. The Fs gain the blue line and challenge the defensemen 2-on-2. D1 and D2 try to protect the middle of the ice to force an outside shot and protect the front of the net. Check that D1 and D2 keep their skates pointing up ice when protecting the net and that they leave the shot for the goaltender.

Coaching pointers: Be sure the forwards attack with speed and that passes are accurate. Forwards should use their speed to force the defense to give up the defensive blue line. The defense needs to steadily close the gap between the forwards to force the forwards to dump the puck into the offensive zone. Help the defense learn to read the 2-on-2 as two separate 1-on-1 situations, making them responsible for one forward each. Conduct the drill at high intensity and have each segment last approximately 20 seconds.

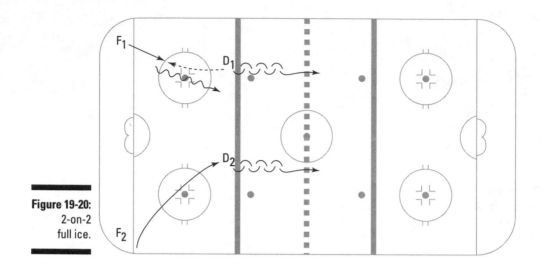

Figure 19-20:
2-on-2
full ice.

Full ice 5-on-3, 5-on-4

This drill is a chance for both the power play and penalty-killing units to work in different scenarios on the same sequence of plays. The power play unit will break out twice, once in a 5-on-3 situation and once 5-on-4.

How it works: Put a unit of five men on the power play and have them start by breaking out of their defensive end. On the breakout, have a three-man penalty-killing unit work against the power play as it comes into the neutral zone. After the power play unit scores or the penalty killers clear the puck out of the zone, the coach shoots a second puck into the defensive zone for a new breakout. Two new forwards replace the original penalty killers. On the second breakout, the power play unit faces a 5-on-4 penalty-killing unit in the neutral and offensive zones.

Coaching pointers: Start with the penalty-killing units being passive to allow the power play units to have success moving the puck. Gradually increase the intensity of the penalty-killing units. Look for quality puck movement from the power play units and active sticks and smart pressure from the penalty-killing units. Keep the same defense on the ice for the penalty-killing unit in both the 5-on-3 and 5-on-4 situations to simplify the drill.

Chapter 20

Further Refining Your Coaching Strategies

*B*y the time you reach advanced-level youth-hockey coaching, your coaching skills will have developed through some interesting learning experiences. If you began coaching at a level where everyone got equal ice time regulated by their association, you focused on having fun and learning the very basics of the game. Even at that level, you presumably set basic attainable goals and came to be consistent in their application. Hopefully you reached the aim of keeping everyone happy and saw to it that all involved had lots of fun. You probably discovered that you just needed to keep things simple, positive, and organized to help players lay a good foundation for their hockey experience.

While you advanced as a coach, you likely discovered that you needed to build a framework to work within where you could evaluate players' progress as they developed their hockey skills both as individuals and as a team. The environment became more structured, requiring your players — and your practice time — to be more disciplined. You began to use game performances to evaluate both individuals and the team.

When you coach advanced hockey players, you encounter further coaching changes. You need to help players begin to concentrate on playing a particular position, so you start to work on improving individual skills unique to the different positions. Teamwork and team dynamics also become more critical to team success, which puts more of a burden on your communication skills. In this chapter, we demonstrate how exciting coaching at this advanced level is. You may even get to work with a budding success story.

Fine-Tuning Individual Skills

Throughout this book, we provide the information you need to equip players with the skills they need to play the various individual positions in hockey. In this section, we present additional details that will help you to help your players be more effective in the particular positions they choose to play.

Goaltenders

A good place to start fine-tuning individual player's skills is with goaltenders. They have the most unique position in hockey and use the fewest cross-over skills compared to other positions. After your goaltenders master the basic skating skills and goaltender maneuvers, their next hurdle (so to speak) is stopping the puck. Your last line of defense against the opposition is your goaltender — a lone position, a one-person job. Use these finer points to help make the goaltender position strong, and then practice the drills in Chapter 13 to fine-tune these points.

- ✔ **Monitor position in the crease.** Young goaltenders tend to stay back on or near the goal line, a position that typically gives up too much of the net to the shooter, reducing the goaltender's ability to make a save. Have your goaltenders use the top of the crease as a reference point, not the goal line.

  Most crease areas are painted blue. Use the phrase "Get out of the paint" with your goaltenders to keep them thinking about challenging the shot and being out of the crease to play the angle.

- ✔ **Emphasize rebound control.** Have your goaltenders work on controlling the rebound after every save is made. The save is the priority, but you also want your goaltenders to be able to direct the puck safely to the corners or to contain the puck to stop play, eliminating the threat of another shot on goal.

- ✔ **Improve puck handling.** This skill is often considered a bonus; if the goaltender is good at it, he can help reduce risk of turnovers, help move the puck in the defensive zone, and he can help with breakouts. Have your goalies do puck-handling and passing drills, when appropriate, with the other players. Goalies often try to do these drills with their gloves off. Don't allow this. Keep the gloves on, just like in a game situation.

If your goaltender doesn't have the puck-handling and passing skills to move the puck effectively, don't make them part of your team plan. Advise the goalie to stay in the net and let his teammates pick up loose pucks.

Defensemen

With advanced-level defense, 1-on-1 gap control and positional play are the two areas that need regular repetition in practice. A significant part of a defenseman's role is simply being in the right position. When checking the puck carrier, have defensive players focus on keeping the puck on the outside ice relative to their position. This position limits opponents' passing and scoring options. In other words, it closes the gaps.

Defensemen should close gaps between themselves and an approaching puck carrier coming into the defensive zone to the point of making body contact at the defensive blue line. Players away from the puck can close gaps by placing their sticks on the ice between the puck and the opponent they are checking. The "Defensive 1-on-1 gap control" drill in Chapter 19 is an effective drill for practicing these principles.

Solid positional play also requires that you stress patience in your defensemen's play. You want the defensemen to have the confidence to maintain their position and force the offensive player to create alternate offensive options.

Wingers

Two of the most valuable skills you can develop in your wingers are to fine-tune their shot off the wing when attacking in the offensive zone and to enhance their ability to protect the puck when it is along the boards.

Use drills that have wingers shoot the puck at the net while they are skating toward the net. Focus on helping them develop powerful, accurate shots on the fly through controlled speed initially, then at increasing speeds. Ultimately, you want to include drills that have them shoot on the fly while being checked. The drill for neutral zone shooting in Chapter 13 is an effective way to practice this action. When ready, you can add checkers to the drill.

In any zone, a winger has to be strong with the puck to maintain possession while being checked by an opponent. Work with wingers to use their body position and their strength to advantage in fending off checkers, protecting the puck, and coming up with loose pucks in *scrums* (battles against one or more opponents for puck possession).

Centers

Centers are your team face-off specialists. They need to practice face-off techniques to the point that they are competent at winning more draws than they lose. Dedicate practice time for centers to work together on draws. Have an assistant drop pucks in gamelike situations so that centers can work on their face-off skills. Or have the centers drop pucks for each other as a routine five-minute session at the end of every practice.

Centers also need to be competent at distributing the puck to teammates; they typically have the puck more often than teammates. Help your centers read how to move the puck to the right place at the right time, anticipating the speed of their teammates and the reach and movement of opponents. Of course they must be technically competent passers. Use the drill for three-man weaves in Chapter 13 with a slight modification to practice these skills. Add one or two defensive challengers who pick up the forward line as they cross into the offensive zone, forcing the puck-carrying player (usually the center) to anticipate and decide which winger to pass to for the shot on goal.

Identifying Team Strengths and Weaknesses

The strength or weakness of your team's offense is often judged by the number of goals your team scores. We suggest that a better way for you to evaluate your team's offense is by the number of scoring chances that they create. If your team is generating plenty of scoring chances, then your offense is being creative, even if it's not scoring as much as you — or your players — would like. Of these two different ways of evaluating offense, you should be far more concerned if your team isn't creating scoring chances. If you identify a concern over a lack of scoring chances, you may have to back up and look for contributing factors and review such things as passing competencies, getting to open spaces, or creating motion on offense (we discuss each of these in detail in Chapters 6, 10, and 16).

If scoring chances are plentiful but goals are not, a review of where to look to score may be in order. Have players focus on the holes around the goalie or the net at the back of the goal. Also have players focus on getting a quicker shot release so that a goalie doesn't have time to set up against their shots.

Team defense is the foundation of any successful team. Strong defense comes from protecting your net and reducing the number of scoring chances against. To do this, all players need to be well versed on defensive play and defensive zone coverage.

One way to identify weakness in your defense is to monitor where goals against you are coming from. For a select number of games, have an assistant or parent mark on a rink drawing where every scoring chance originates against your team each game. See if you note any patterns when you compare the games, such as wingers coming in from the right side and consistently getting shots on net. This monitoring can help you identify where you need to improve some individual skating or team coverage skills to tighten up your defense.

Special teams are just that. Both the power play and the penalty-killing units can be a valuable team strength. The flip side is that they can also be a nightmare if they're not at least functional. Emphasize the basics to make both the power play and penalty kill a strength for your team (refer to Chapter 18). Be sure to dedicate practice time, on a regular basis, for your special teams. You want players to feel comfortable on the ice in these situations. Give players a clear plan, keeping the options simple and limited.

Two to three options are more than enough. On the power play, for example, you might use the "Power-play hot-spot shooting" drill in Chapter 19 but specify the pass pattern, such as starting by getting the puck to a defenseman at the blue line, who passes *deep to a forward* (near the goal line). That forward passes to the center, who is cutting through the slot having started when the defenseman sent off his pass. The plan is for the center to get a shot on goal. If not, she circles the back of the net for a possible wraparound shot as an option to the plan, or, if not available, passes off to the defenseman on the other wing for the second option being that the play starts over from the opposite side.

The most common weakness on power plays is puck movement. Watch for a player who keeps the puck too long, thereby making your power play a 1-on-4 rather than a 5-on-4. At no time during a power play should one of your players attack 1-on-1; he should move the puck looking to create a 2-on-1 instead. If passes are not happening quickly enough, also look for players not moving into spaces quickly enough to become passing options.

Another common weakness in power plays is players looking for the perfect shot opportunity. Reinforce the notion that good is good enough. A goal doesn't have to be pretty to count. A bounce off an opposing defenseman's leg will do. Bottom line: Shoot the puck.

A common weakness to watch for on penalty killing is players not having their sticks on the ice, actively cutting off passing lanes. It's such a simple habit that makes a huge difference in limiting scoring chances. Reinforce throughout all penalty-killing drills that sticks are on the ice and moving (active). Make this a habit.

If the active sticks don't help your penalty killing significantly, look for two other common areas of weakness: straight-line skating and heads on a swivel. Use the penalty-killing drills in Chapter 19, slowing down the drill's pace initially, to check that players re-establish position by straight-line skating and that they use heads-up play. Then speed up the action keeping the focus until these elements become more of a habit for your players.

Assigning Line Matches

As games get more competitive at advanced hockey levels, coaches may want to consider matching lines with the opposition. This tactic puts your best defensive line out against the opponent's best offensive line and tries to have your best scoring line out against their weakest defensive line. As a general rule, when in doubt, don't match lines. Instead, just make sure players are aware of any special concerns with the line they're playing against, such as how to play a particular forward who always *dekes* (fakes) left before moving right or how to get the best of a player who has a wicked slap shot.

If you choose to match lines, do so to provide equitable challenges for your talented and not-so-talented lines or to match lines by approximate size and/or gender. Your priority is to give all kids a positive learning experience — this isn't the Stanley Cup.

Taking Advantage of Team Dynamics

On most teams, and at virtually all levels, players become friends and may bond as a group. You can use these team dynamics as valuable assets in your coaching. When players are friends, they want to do things for the good of the team. A "team first" attitude allows you to use players in a positive sense to keep other players from straying outside the framework you have set up for the team by actions such as exhibiting disruptive behavior or compromising team play. Cultivate mutual respect amongst team members.

A good question to ask a player who exhibits behavior that is outside the team's goals is, "Is this the behavior your teammates should expect from you?" The response is almost always "No," which makes for an easy follow-up for change: "What can they expect from you in the future?"

Team leaders become important to you at advanced levels for utilizing team dynamics. Show respect for them by informing team captains of any plans or changes in plans or by asking them for feedback. By doing this, you open lines of communication and you can usually get their support when issues arise.

Conducting a Coach's Check-up

Advanced-level coaches should check periodically on a few important aspects of their coaching. Are you communicating? How's your team's attitude? Are you keeping up technically with players' improvements?

Communication

Good communication skills help coaches build a level of confidence between themselves, players, and parents. At advanced coaching levels, you can bring this confidence to a higher level.

One of the best ways to improve confidence is for players and parents to see improvement in both individual and team play. Players that have success and teams that win feel better about themselves and their teammates. They also gain an elevated level of confidence in themselves and each other. Use techniques that make improvement visible. For example, use drills to test players in practice, and then be sure you are vocal about any gains made so that the parents and players see it and feel it.

Do the same in game situations by letting players know when they have done something right during a shift on the ice. Any individual corrections that need to be made during a game are best made as soon as the player comes off the ice and has had a moment to catch his breath. Be short and to the point, then finish with a positive: "You'll get it next time out."

While on the bench during game action, make only positive comments about play happening on the ice. Use your comments to also reflect teaching points. For example, say "Great puck movement, Johnny," when one of your players makes a good, quick pass. Conversely, comments like "What are you thinking?" or an agonizing "What did you do that for?" are not constructive for the player or his teammates.

Time for a little sportsmanship

We watched from the stands as the buzzer signaled the end of our 11- year-old nephew's final playoff game. His team lost 4-2. As the team reluctantly headed toward center ice to shake hands with the victors, our team's goalie blasted from his net to the bench, through the door, and off toward the dressing room. The coach, who was in the process of following his team onto the ice, caught the fleeing action out the corner of his eye. He calmly, but swiftly, caught the goalie a few yards down the hall behind the bench, said a few words, then without debate,

both went out to the ice to join the congratulatory line. The incident was so brief, few in the arena probably even noticed; yet we suspected that moment might be remembered for a lifetime. We later asked the coach what he said to rectify the incident so smoothly. He answered, "I told him, you didn't lose this game, Andy; the whole team did. And now your team is showing respect to the other guys just like you want them to show you when you win. Don't you think you should be with your teammates?"

Attitude

Discipline and fair play are fundamental to a constructive team attitude. Their absence is a symptom of poor coaching. You may have witnessed a player lash out at an opponent who got the best of him on a play, with the result being that he hands his opponent a man-advantage opportunity. Or you may have seen a legitimately penalized player throw his stick and gloves into the wall of the penalty box, or a huge player flatten an unthreatening opponent just because he can. You may not have noticed a player take credit for a goal when he knows he didn't touch it. But as coach, you need to catch that.

Aim to have your team be a model of fair play and discipline every time they step on the ice. You want opponents moved to aspire to the way your team acts and reacts — not only when your team is on top but also when they are in the doldrums. Feel proud of your team every day and be proud of how your players are developing as players and people. Players should have pride in themselves, as should you and your staff, every day. Keep these goals front and center for a positive hockey experience for all.

Technical matters

When you keep an open mind to learning as a coach, both you and your players will get a lot more out of your hockey experience. Following are a few examples to consider as you look to expand your coaching horizon:

✔ **Seek out hands-on advice:** Most minor hockey associations organize clinics over the course of the year. Attend as many as possible. You'll often learn something you can use, and the experience is usually good at least as a refresher.

✔ **Do some homework:** You can find plenty of good books to read or tapes to watch that can help with specific aspects of coaching, such as goaltending. Consider, too, books that are not directly related to hockey, but rather come from the business world or from other sports. These books are great sources of creative ideas on dealing with people or what really counts in success.

✔ **Scout coaches as well as players:** In hockey, as in every other sport, you'll find some great coaches. Make it a habit to scout these coaches, especially in person at the rink. Observe how they handle situations that are similar to those you have to deal with. Don't just look at positive situations; you can also learn from situations where a coach handled things poorly. These examples of what not to do in similar circumstances can be great teachers.

✔ **Take on a mentor:** Finally, remember to make use of a mentor if at all possible. If a mentor isn't available, you could organize a coaches' club to provide a sounding board. Then set up a regular time to check in with your mentor or meet with your club. Have questions to ask, think about situations to discuss, and be prepared to listen to feedback and honestly assess how their suggestions might work for you.

Part V

Common Coaching Conundrums

In this part . . .

This part presents tried-and-true solutions to issues that you didn't ask for, but that may arise during your hockey season. Whether you encounter health concerns, injuries, special kids, special parents, or various other situations, this part provides you with some tools for resolving these issues quickly and comfortably.

Chapter 21

Keeping Your Team Healthy and Injury Free

The health concerns of children in your charge are primarily the responsibility of their parents — what they feed them, what equipment they put on, how they deal with them when they're sick. However, kids and parents often look to coaches for advice. Your job as a coach of recreational hockey players is to keep it simple and keep it realistic.

The more urgent health concern that may fall fully in your lap is dealing with injuries or physical mishaps involving players. Injuries do occur with some frequency in hockey. Usually, the problems are relatively minor, such as nicks from sticks, sprains from falls, and the odd bloody nose. Following the rules and having proper equipment can minimize most chances of injury. Players can avoid other mishaps by eating properly, keeping hydrated, and being prepared physically. Keep in mind, though, that at any time a serious injury may occur, no matter how much prevention you preach and practice.

As a coach, you need first to do everything possible to minimize the opportunity for injury. Secondly, you need to know how to recognize and deal with any emergency that does arise. This chapter helps you to develop the health and safety checklists that you can use to get yourself and your team prepared.

Fueling Your Team: What Players Should Eat

You certainly can't dictate what young players eat. They're not professional athletes — and they *are* kids! But that's not to say you can't provide them and their parents with some nuggets of information about what may be helpful and what is harmful to a budding hockey player. Our experience is that most parents and players appreciate getting some nutritional facts so that they're able to separate the facts from the fiction that constantly circulates regarding "right" eating.

A few simple principles underlie healthy eating for young athletes. Advise your players to aim for the following:

- **Eat a wide variety of foods.** Venture beyond burgers or chicken strips and fries every day to include fruits, vegetables, whole grains, breads, dairy, meats, and fish.

- **Eat three to six times throughout the day.** Start with a good breakfast and, at a minimum, have lunch and dinner as well. Healthy snacks between meals are good, such as juice, nuts, or fruit. Healthful snacking keeps hunger at bay in growing bodies and maintains the energy needed for practices and games.

- **Focus on fruits and vegetables, whole grains, and pastas.** These are the primary energy and nutrient-providing foods for exercise. Meat, fish, and dairy are necessary for growing, but players at these ages really only need small (fist-size) portions.

- **Keep fluids handy.** Drink lots of water and choose real juices instead of soda or sugar-added drinks. Hydration is important in a sport like hockey. Water does the best job, hands down.

Healthy eating that provides kids with enough energy to play hockey and grow is incredibly easy. Both the United States and Canada have developed excellent general guides to healthy eating that are available on-line. The U.S. Department of Agriculture's food pyramid is available at www.mypyramid.gov. You can check out Canada's Food Guide at www.hc-sc.gc.ca. Coaches can order or print sufficient copies of the guides to hand out to the team or to the parents at the meeting at the beginning of the year.

One point to emphasize with your team is that players should minimize their intake of sugar foods, such as candy bars and carbonated and sugar-loaded drinks. These foods create huge energy swings. This warning is especially important within an hour of a practice or game because such foods can cause a low-energy phase just when players want high energy most.

Parents may ask about vitamin supplementation, protein powders, and athletic drinks that are marketed for athletes. If kids eat and drink according to the principles and the guidelines given here, they shouldn't need nutritional supplements. We also recommend you discourage the use of protein powders or drinks for "muscle building" in young athletes. Growing muscles and bones need good food, not excessive protein that their bodies have to get rid of. Advise parents to keep their money from going down the toilet. Finally, most athletic drinks are designed for marathon athletic performances. An hour of hockey doesn't qualify. Water is the best and cheaper choice.

You may exercise some influence over what your players eat or drink closer to practice or game times. Advise players that from the hour before and during games and practices, water is the drink of choice for hockey players. Athletic drinks are an unnecessary waste of money at this time and many are laced with sugar, which is not constructive for hockey performance. The one exception may be an all-day tournament in which your team is barely off the ice for an hour before it has to go back on for another game. In that case, a quarter cup (two to three swallows) of water alternating with the same amount of a high-quality, low-sugar athletic drink every 15 minutes all day long is ideal. Between games, fruit smoothies, yogurt, fruit or fruit juices, and a handful of mixed nuts and dried fruit are most suitable along with water.

Preventing Injuries

As coach, you can and should minimize the chances of your players getting injured in the first place. Taking certain preventative measures ahead of time will also help you deal with potential injuries so that they don't become any more serious than necessary.

Establishing a safe base

You can take a few steps at the very beginning of the season to limit some potential for injury from arising:

- ✓ **Know the health history of your players.** Collect confidential information from the parents so that you know which of your players might potentially suffer a medical incident, such as asthma, allergies, diabetes, or seizures. Then do your homework to know how to handle such an occurrence calmly and safely.

- ✓ **Prevent dehydration problems.** Have players bring their own water bottles and establish a practice of having players drink a quarter cup (a few swallows) every 15 minutes throughout practices and games. Do *not* allow sugar or glucose drinks in the bottles (with the possible exception during all-day tournament play, as we note in the preceding section). And at no time should your players take salt tablets.

✔ **Have medical assistance at your fingertips.** Keep a working cellular phone with you at all times or know where the nearest working pay-phone is and always keep a couple of quarters in your kit bag. If 911 is not an option in your area, also keep the local ambulance, hospital, and police numbers with your quarters.

Ensuring a safe environment

Another way to minimize injuries is to take precautions at the rink before practices and games:

✔ **Check equipment.** Do what you can to make sure that players wear proper-fitting protective pads, helmets, and skates. Cheap-quality, worn-out, or loose-fitting equipment is an invitation to injury.

✔ **Check the rink.** Skate around observing the rink boards and glass. See that doors to the ice are closed and that the ice surface is clear of debris, is not soft, and does not contain holes that skate blades could catch in. If a problem exists, fix it.

✔ **Compete against your own size.** As much as possible, match players for size and weight. Ideally the league helps, but players grow at different rates. If you face a team with bigger players, try to get the opposing coach to agree to match lines, at least by size and skill level, especially when contact hockey is introduced. (Refer to Chapter 20 for more information about matching lines.)

✔ **Set rules.** Everyone on the team should know that you don't condone horseplay, you expect cleanliness and hygiene in the locker room and on the bench, and you expect players to stay home with a flu or cold so that they do not spread it to teammates.

Warming up

Warm, flexible joints have not traditionally been a concern with young players because they always used to do plenty of moving before they got to practice. However, with so many kids now sitting with video games, television, and rides to the rink, your players' muscles may be cold and stiff as they step onto the ice. These conditions may predispose them to injury. Therefore, a brief warm-up may be warranted.

Players need ten minutes of whole body exercise, such as skating forward, backwards, and sideways with arm action, to increase heat, followed by a few minutes of loose stretching, such as arm and leg rotations, to prepare the muscles and joints for practices and games. With ice time being at such a premium for minor hockey, you may want to do this off-ice using the same principles, or make your first drill as "whole body" and loose as possible and follow that with some dynamic stretching, particularly for the shoulders and hips.

Working on fitness and conditioning

The more elementary the level of hockey, the less important it is that you spend time on fitness and conditioning for your players. Their hockey activity is their fitness activity, so long as you make sure they don't stand or sit around too much at practices and games. However, as skill level increases, the relevance of fitness increases for players. Players who want to excel in hockey will need a strong fitness habit.

Good fitness training can reduce the risk of injury and can speed up recovery if a player does get injured. Aside from the impact on injury, fitness gives a player more strength to generate power for shooting and skating, and more endurance to be strong longer. So elite hockey players need to be in great shape; youth players need to be safe and feel sufficiently strong.

Basic fitness needs for hockey begin with flexibility. This reduces the chance of strain and sprain-type injuries. After that, some muscle strength and endurance work is useful so that their muscles are strong enough first to grip and skate and then to shoot and check safely. Balanced muscle strength and flexibility help prevent over-use types of injuries, such as bad backs. Aerobics becomes more important as speed and full-length competitive games become part of their hockey level.

Serious fitness training is easiest to do off-ice, but most coaches don't have the time, facilities, or necessity at these levels to conduct serious conditioning sessions. Therefore, we recommend you use an on-ice, fun circuit like the one presented in Figure 21-1 to top up fitness elements in your players. This also provides an opportunity for you to see whether any players have particular weaknesses that need attention. For players who need specific hockey conditioning, a variety of books are available for their reference.

The circuit in Figure 21-1 is designed to make good use of your ice time by combining fitness work with work on some hockey skill elements. The circuit also uses a player's own body weight for strength elements, which makes it safe for all ages.

Discourage young, growing players from experimenting with weight training to increase strength. Weight training can cause more harm than good and is generally unnecessary. For older players who aspire to elite hockey levels, weight training under the supervision of a certified professional who understands hockey is appropriate.

A circuit like the one that follows should be fun for the players. It should also help them develop a fitness activity habit that will serve them well as they advance in hockey — as well as down the road of life.

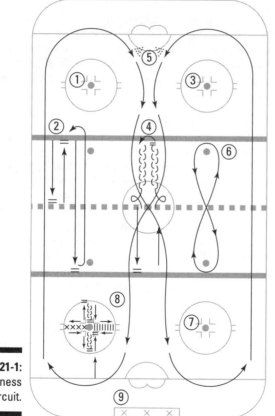

Figure 21-1:
Fun fitness
circuit.

This circuit continues nonstop for 13.5 minutes. To begin, assign each player to an exercise station so that two or three players are at each station. Players must note the number they start at and rotate in numerical order. You signal the start of the circuit.

After one minute at an exercise station, blow the whistle and all players skate at a moderate pace up the middle of the ice and down the outside boards, crossing over at center so that they alternate the direction of their turns. After 30 seconds, blow the whistle again and players move on to and immediately begin the next exercise station in their rotation.

So the circuit alternates one minute of nine different strong exercises with 30 seconds of moderate skating, finishing with a skate. The circuit works on power, strength, and aerobics at the same time as key skating and shooting skills. It is good for all players of all ages. Pace is the factor to change to appropriately challenge the different skill levels. Give breathers (five- to ten-count breaks mid-exercise) or allow a more moderate pace for the little kids so that they focus on their skills. For advanced players, increase the time for lap skating (to 60 seconds) and/or the pace (to strong). Provide loads of encouragement for all.

Mark pylons each with a number 1 to 9. Also write the name of an exercise station based on the following list (or make up your own names) on each pylon. Then set the corresponding pylon at each exercise station as indicated in the rink diagram in Figure 21-1. Players will rotate from pylon station to pylon station performing the following tasks:

1. **Push-ups:** Place hands under shoulders as you lie face-down on the ice. Keep your body straight while you press up until your elbows are straight, then lower back to lying on the ice. Repeat at a steady pace.

2. **Shuttle skate:** Start at the blue line. Going as hard as possible, skate forward to the center line. Stop. Turn facing the boards and skate back to the blue line. Stop. Turn facing the boards and skate to the far blue line. Stop. Skate slowly back to the starting point. If skill allows, use pucks.

3. **Twisting sit-ups:** Lie on your back on the ice with your skate blades flat on the ice (knees bent). Place your hands on your helmet. Curl your right elbow up until it touches your left knee, then return to the starting position. Then curl your left elbow up until it touches your right knee and return to the starting position. Repeat alternating to left and right.

4. **Pivot skate:** Start on the blue line. Skate fast backwards to the center line. Pivot to your left to skate forward to the far blue line. Stop. Skate forward to the center line. Pivot to your left to skate backwards to the starting blue line. Stop. Repeat pivoting to your right for the next lap. Alternate left and right laps.

5. **Rapid shot:** Stand outside the goal crease with seven pucks. Pick a spot low at the back of one side of the net and rapid fire all seven pucks into that spot using a forehand shot with no pause between shots. Be sure your teammate has finished at his side of the net before you retrieve your pucks and repeat using a backhand shot.

6. **Figure-eight skate:** Using the face-off dots between the blue lines, skate a figure eight as fast as possible for three laps. Then do one slow lap. Repeat the sequence. If skill allows, use pucks.

7. **Down-ups:** From a standing position, drop to a crouch, place your hands on the ice, extend your legs straight out to a push-up position, then back to the crouch, and then explode into a maximum jump straight up. Repeat this sequence. Take a five-count breather every five reps if the power of your jump fades.

8. **Cross-circle skate:** Start on the face-off dot. Moving as quickly as possible, skate forward to the edge of the circle. Stop. Skate backwards to the dot. Stop. Side step right to the circle. Stop. Side step back to the dot. Stop. Crossover left to the circle. Stop. Crossover back to the dot. Stop. Skate backwards to the circle. Stop. Skate forward to the dot. Stop. Repeat the sequence.

9. **Dips:** Place chairs, a bench, or the net on its face against the end boards. Sit on the bench placing your hands on the edge of the seat at your hips and extend your legs straight out in front. Shift your hips off the bench and lower them as close to the ice as possible and press back up until they are even with the bench. Repeat.

Being Prepared with Emergency First Aid

What do you do when a player gets injured on your watch? Start with having a plan. You need to know ahead of time exactly what to do. One way to plan for, and to have the confidence that you can handle, any emergency is to take a first-aid course before you start coaching. Community recreation centers or colleges offer such courses frequently.

Secondly, keep a first-aid kit in your hockey bag, which you naturally always have with you at the rink. Make sure that the kit contains a blanket, stretch bandages, ice packs, tweezers, disposable gloves, a triangle bandage, band-aids, a breathing mask or tube, scissors, towel(s), gauze rolls, pads and tape, antiseptic ointment, possibly a mouth opener, and definitely all the parents' phone numbers along with quarters for the phone. Check ahead to find out whether your rink facility has a spine board in the event of a head or neck injury. Know where the facility keeps the board and how to get access.

When an injury occurs, you may or may not see it happen. Regardless, use the following "stop-look-listen-act" protocol:

- **Stop play.** Get to the player and get others away. Don't let anyone move the injured player initially.

- **Look for obvious abnormal signs.** Is the player breathing normally? Is he bleeding? Are his eyes glazed or responsive? Are his joints or bones at odd angles?

✔ **Listen to what happened.** If possible, get a description from the player; if not, talk to her teammates.

✔ **Act.** If the injury is not serious, treat the occasion as you see fit. If you're not sure, call 911. Try to restore the breathing first and stop excessive bleeding, even if you're waiting for professional assistance.

After dealing with an injury, be sure to record the incident and any action you took. In this day of litigation, you're wise to keep accurate records.

Recognizing a Problem and Knowing What to Do

A few rules apply in the event of an emergency at the rink. Make sure, first, that you have your players' medical information cards with you at all times. Then commit the following to memory:

✔ Never move a player if you suspect a back, neck, or head injury.

✔ Save teeth that are knocked out; don't move loose ones.

✔ Loosen clothing as much as possible without moving the player; do *not* remove skates.

✔ If the player is conscious, keep him still and ask questions first.

✔ If the player is unconscious, feels faint, drowsy, or dizzy, is having trouble breathing, or is choking or gurgling, call 911 and prepare to do mouth-to-mouth.

✔ If the player is bleeding severely, call 911 and apply pressure directly on or just above the bleeding (on the heart side).

✔ If the player has an open wound, apply pressure with a sterile gauze pad.

✔ If the player has a nosebleed, sit him down with his head slightly forward and apply a cold cloth over the bridge of the nose as you pinch it closed.

✔ If the player suffers an eye injury, apply ice and get professional help immediately.

✔ If the player suffers a sprain, elevate the limb as you apply ice and possibly pressure, such as keeping the skate boot on.

✔ Recognize potential heat injuries by symptoms of cramps, chills, throbbing head, nausea, and profuse sweating. Immediately remove the hockey gear and cover the player with cool towels or put him under a cool shower and have him drink small gulps of water frequently. If the player becomes dry-skinned even though it's warm, and he's not sweating when he should be, you have an emergency. Call 911 ASAP. You may also see symptoms of high fever and confusion.

Chapter 22

Coping with Challenges

• •

In This Chapter

▶ Managing players with unique challenges

▶ Working with kids with a diversity of skills

▶ Coaching boys and girls together

▶ Handling uncooperative parents

▶ Sharing ice time

▶ Overcoming bad calls

▶ Working with another coach

• •

*E*ven with all your meticulous planning and ardent goal setting, things that you don't anticipate jump up to keep you on your toes. That's coaching. In this chapter, we provide some insight into how coaches who have gone before you have successfully handled some of these little surprises, whether they emanate from the kids, the parents, or your league.

Coaching Special Kids

Ice hockey is a game that can be played in some way by virtually everyone. One great example is sledge hockey, which has wheelchair-bound hockey aficionados playing the game using two short hockey sticks as picks for propulsion.

Beyond physical challenges, attitude is probably a bigger handicap for coaches to deal with. Or you may encounter players who have a good attitude for playing the game, but they can't seem to get coordinated — they're not athletically gifted.

In the following sections, we offer some helpful suggestions should you encounter some of these situations during your coaching tenure.

Physical disabilities

People who can't see or hear or use their limbs in an NHL fashion can play hockey. The elderly can play hockey, as well, given the number of old timers' leagues and tournaments conducted around the world.

If you coach a team that includes players with some physical limitations, first make sure that you and all teammates are aware of the limitations and that everyone understands what to expect and how to work with them. Secondly, teach players to respect their teammates' challenges, and, beyond what is necessarily different, to treat those teammates as they treat any other. This approach goes for you as well. Coaches and players need to focus on what physically challenged players *can* do, what they *can* learn, and *how* they can find ways to compensate for their inabilities, just as you would for teammates who can't seem to hit or shoot effectively.

All players need to have fun, learn, have goals, and see improvement. The principles of coaching don't change with physical challenges, nor do the principles of the game. You may just have to make technical modifications, modify your communication techniques, or adjust a few rules, such as in the following:

- ✔ Tap a deaf player when it's her turn to go on the ice.

- ✔ Don't let anyone blindside a player from the side on which he has no vision in one eye.

- ✔ Encourage the player with the artificial limb to show teammates how it works, then have everyone get on with playing hockey.

- ✔ Set shorter shifts for seniors or adopt a no-hitting rule.

All in the game

A spirited senior league game was in full swing, much to the delight of a big crowd in a small-town Canadian rink. Everyone saw the hit coming at center ice — the winger had his head down. The crushing impact sent the winger crashing to the ice. Then his leg skidded off toward the blue line.

The crowd gasped in horror. Then silence descended. Players skated over to the fallen teammate. One player skated away and picked up the lifeless limb while others helped the winger up onto his remaining leg and assisted him to the bench.

The game resumed with players on the bench keeping their heads down trying to mask their mirth at the unsuspecting crowd's reaction, while Sam, their "physically challenged" teammate, replaced his artificial limb. Moments later, Sam stood. As he tested both legs he said, "That might take the crowd out of the game for a bit, boys. Let's take advantage." Then he was over the boards back in play.

Attitude liabilities

Negative attitudes can be a real challenge in coaching hockey. How do you tone down the disruptive and ratchet up the excessively shy players on your team? You may come upon some of the attitude challenges listed here. Hopefully, some of the proposed solutions will work for you as well.

- ✔ **Whiners and complainers:** Make sure your team is aware of your goals and the team's rules at the outset. Then when a persistent whiner or complainer comes along, you can ask that player to suggest a solution to his concerns, whether it is wanting more ice time or wanting to play on the best line. Because you've stressed team rules and goals from the get-go, when he offers a solution, you can then respond with something like, "How does that fit with the goals of this team?" This usually makes the player become more realistic. However, if a player persists in wanting ice time, for example, that's in excess of what suits the team goals, nothing's wrong with saying, "It looks like this isn't the team for you. Why don't you look around for one that better suits your purposes?" and let him go.

- ✔ **Egocentrics, superstars, and attention-seekers:** One rule applies for all: The team comes first. Sometimes you can tame the big egos before they get too serious by assigning that player tasks to help other team-mates, such as during a drill. Vary the leaders in these situations so that no one player's helmet gets too big. However, if someone breaks the team-comes-first rule persistently, pull that player aside and remind him of the rule and how he fits in that picture. If there's a next time, try a time-out or limit his ice time. Ice time is one of the most valuable com-modities to an ego player. Your players should know what you expect of them, what you expect them to do differently when they need correc-tion, and the consequences of their actions if they don't put the team ahead of themselves.

- ✔ **Bullies:** A hockey team has no room for bullies, whether their manipula-tion is physical or emotional. Emotional bullies are more difficult to spot — they put down and intimidate weaker players rather than hit and shove.

  Watch for players whose equipment goes strangely missing, who stay on the periphery of the group, or who get ignored in plays. Watch for the ring leader (or leaders) ostracizing her and take that person (or group) aside.

  You can send a strong message by saying to the bully, "Who is making you feel so small and stupid that the only way you can feel big is to take your feelings and dump them on someone who is too weak to stand up to you?"

  With bullies, you must also finish on a positive note — something like, "You have more going for you than that. You don't need to pick on some-one else to feel big; you can get good yourself and be big for real rather than faking it. Let's work on making you the best hockey player you can be and you help your teammate get better, too, and you'll have a lot to be proud of. You won't need to pick on anybody to feel like you're a somebody."

✔ **Shy players lacking confidence or friends:** First and foremost, give these players praise for small jobs well done, and do so frequently. Set small challenges for them that you are quite sure they can accomplish and give them a pat on the back when they do. As much as possible, pair shy kids with teammates who are easygoing and helpful. Provide opportunities for them to get to know teammates socially and to cultivate bonds. Find out their interests and include the shy ones in group commentary as much as possible to draw them out.

Athletic inabilities

Some kids simply appear not to be physically gifted when it comes to sports; it's the "two left feet" syndrome. However, every kid still needs to be active, and every kid deserves the right to play hockey if that's what she wants. Try to identify her specific challenge, such as hand-eye coordination, and find solutions for dealing with that. Whatever you do, don't discourage her from playing hockey.

In these cases, a coach or assistant often needs to devote individual time to these players. If you don't have a lot of available time, especially on-ice, give the player one or two things she can do on her own time, off-ice. For example, if a player has poor hand-eye coordination, give her some wall-ball drills that she can do against the garage door. If weak muscles create the difficulty, give the player a couple of callisthenic exercises she can do each morning before going off to school, such as squeezing a tennis ball ten times in each hand to improve grip strength, or jumping from both feet to tap the top of the bedroom door jamb ten times each morning to improve leg strength, or going for a 20-minute bike ride around the park after school twice a week to improve endurance.

Most players who may appear "not gifted" are simply not identified yet as late-bloomers.

Dealing with a Mixed Bag: When Abilities Vary

When coaching young hockey players, you can end up with a team that includes kids who have never played hockey in their lives right alongside the hottest little kid on skates. The challenge for the coach is how to run meaningful practices for all of them. Games are not usually a problem because you are guided by the rule of equal ice time.

When you coach a team with a broad range of skills, you really do need some assistance for at least part of the practice. Ideally, at the beginning of the season, have a segment of practice in which the less skilled players work specifically on the skills they need to improve while the more advanced players work on a level that challenges them. The objective is to get the less skilled players into the ability range of the other players quickly so that the team can come together before some players begin to feel like failures — or you lose some better players to boredom.

Rest assured that, with targeted, individual attention, less skilled players do catch up quite quickly to the more advanced players. Make sure that you balance the individual work with enough whole-team work so that all players feel like they are part of one team.

Coaching Co-ed Hockey

With thousands of small communities providing minor hockey programs for their youth, the numbers of coaches, players, and available ice time will inevitably result in the impracticality of separate guys and girls hockey teams. You may find yourself coaching a co-ed team. Or you may be the co-ed factor. More guys than women coach hockey, making it common for a male to have to coach a female team. These scenarios can come with a few challenges.

Together on one team

Past experience indicates few problems associated with mixing prepubescent girls and guys on one team. Where to dress seems to be the biggest issue. Have players come to the rink mostly dressed if separate dressing rooms are not available, and have a pre-game or practice time when all players come to a common dressing room ready for the coach's talk. Let players know you have the same expectations and that the same rules apply to all, then get on with playing hockey. The few individuals who may have some psychological hang-ups initially will get over them quickly if you focus on hockey, having fun, and treating everyone the same. Don't make gender an issue.

Post puberty, a few more sexual factors come into play. When size, strength, speed, and endurance have more impact on the level of hockey, mixing guys and girls can be more challenging. It can come to a point where only the best girls can play with the guys, which may leave a significant group of females out of the game. In this case, having separate teams may be better. Where numbers don't warrant that, constitute teams to have the same number of guys and girls on each of the teams (such as 12 guys and 3 girls) and coach as you would for a wide range of abilities on one team. Coordinate with other coaches in the league to match lines where appropriate so that a big, strong girl doesn't play against a pre-growth-spurt guy.

You may encounter an occasional male who doesn't handle being second to a girl very well. Reinforce the notion that the team comes first — if a girl can help make the team better, the team should take advantage of it. Besides, everyone is there to get better and enjoy the team experience. Help all players understand that their self-worth is based on their own sense of value, not their skill compared to other players, male or female.

When you are the opposite sex

The biggest challenge for opposite-sex coaches seems to be dressing-room protocol. For your pre-game and post-game talks, have the captain or a parent let you know when the team is suitably ready for you to come in the dressing room. For one-on-ones with a player who needs to be addressed regarding an issue, hold the discussion in a corner of the rink out of earshot of others but in full view.

Never be alone with a player of the opposite sex in the dressing room. If circumstances force you to meet there, take an assistant or a parent with you.

Don't let any other issues for males coaching females or females coaching males become issues. Guys and girls learn the same and want the same things from their hockey experience initially: fun and friendship. A few may want the Olympics or the NHL. Focus on hockey skills and the players' self-worth. Give them skills and a positive life experience that they can take with them wherever they go.

Dealing with Challenging Parents

Expect parents to be biased about their child's abilities and expectations. Their perception versus reality will often not match yours. Also, expect some parents to put themselves above the team: They feel they are paying to have their kid there; they can do as they please, including yell at the referees or at their kid.

Your first step in dealing with challenging parents is to make abundantly clear to all parents your goals, rules, and consequences at the start of the season. Parents must know that your number one rule is that the kids come first, and so all players and the team are your primary concerns. Parents must also know that if they are abusive to officials, kids, or other parents, they will be banned from attending practices or games for the remainder of the season.

When all else fails

Two teams of 7 year olds were battling it out on the ice, as only they can, when the door to one team's bench jammed, and the teams had to wait for the door to be fixed. While the players idled around on the ice, one coach called a boy over to the boards and asked, "Billy, do you know what cooperation means?"

Billy nodded.

The coach continued, "You know that what is important is how we play as a team, not whether we win or lose?"

Again, Billy nodded.

"So you know that means when the whistle goes for a penalty or offside, you shouldn't argue, swear, or start singing "Three Blind Mice"? Does that make sense to you?"

Billy nodded vigorously.

"And when I call you off the ice at the end of your shift so that a teammate can play, it's not good sportsmanship to call me a moron, is it?"

Billy nodded his head with certainty.

"Okay. That's good," said the coach. "Now go over there and explain all that to your mother."

Your second step is patience and diplomacy as you confront issues. In doing so, apply the rule that issues are never discussed until emotions are in check. That could mean 48 hours later. It's your call. Then you, or whoever you have assigned to help you with parent communication, can listen to the person raising the issue and consider with them how the issue meets the team goals and rules. Then take any proposed solutions under advisement, if appropriate, and provide an answer in short order. If you can establish a parent sounding board, that person can help to diffuse issues with parents before they even get to you. Just make sure you are all on the same page regarding team priorities.

Dealing with a Lack of Ice Time

With a scarcity of rinks and an overabundance of people wanting to use them in many communities, ice time can be at quite a premium. Late hours for kids are not desirable. They have lives outside of hockey that include things like being successful in school. Half-ice practices are workable for beginners, but not suitable for more advanced levels. However, if you have no other options for ice, you have two reasonable solutions to supplement players' hockey experiences.

One good option for more advanced players is to design and use drills that serve more than one purpose at a time when you do have ice. For example, you can combine skating, passing, and puck-handling drills with conditioning and power work. Or you can design challenging skating, puck-handling, and shooting efforts in one drill. Note the combination drills presented in Chapter 19.

Another option for teams with limited ice time is to regularly get together off-ice at a gym, field, or empty parking lot. You can work on conditioning, play ball hockey, or do ball skills drills that simulate hockey drills, especially for goalies. Time spent on these types of activities can still help players develop their hockey skills and it definitely helps develop team camaraderie.

Handling Poor Officiating

All coaches suffer games in which the officials seem to be against them. This syndrome is called the "seventh player" syndrome in hockey because you feel like you're playing against a team that has an extra player. However, remember that you're coaching minor hockey. If the officials at this level were perfect, they'd be in the NHL!

When you've had some bad calls in a game and you feel frustration stirring, look straight in the eyes of that young, in-training official and picture that he or she is your son or daughter a few years down the road when they've decided they'd rather officiate than play hockey. You know that they're not going to be perfect at officiating the first or second year, or even the third year out. Just as with the kids you are coaching, these kids can take years to become consistently good officials.

More importantly, as coach, you set an example for your players. "Ouch, that hurts. We'll have to make up for that one," may be the most you should say about a bad call. Then drop it. The key is to be constructive and go on. Your players are going to run into poor officiating and bad breaks now and then for the rest of their (hockey) lives. Having different perspectives is part of the game. Help players accept that most officials truly are out on the ice because they love the game: They're in hockey for fun and participation; they want to learn and improve, just as you and your players do. Work with them.

Once again, you're well off to establish a few rules at the outset:

- ✔ Never let players question an official's call during a game.

- ✔ Coaches and players are to thank officials after every game.

- ✔ Serious concerns about officiating are to be reported to the league in writing and should be left to the league to resolve.

Inform the parents of your rules about handling poor officiating, and explain your rationale for those rules as well. They also serve as examples to the players.

Co-coaching

Selection of team staff should reflect the needs of the team, such as what needs to be done to meet team goals and objectives and who the best person is to do it. In other words, don't accept help simply because it's offered. With many assistants, roles can become insignificant and people can begin to get in each other's way. Less may be better when it comes to coaches.

An assistant coach's role is to assist the head coach. To make this work smoothly, find a coach who complements your skills and has a personality that allows you to work well together. If you are knowledgeable in skating instruction and not great at puck skills, find someone who knows how to coach and instruct puck skills.

Your assistants need to be able to handle responsibility so that you can leave them in charge in your absence. However, they must know that you are ultimately in charge and that you are responsible for overall team leadership. At the same time, you need your assistants to provide honest commentary. For example, if you're off the mark in positive reinforcement, they need to be able to say so. Your job is to be clear and specific about any assistant's role and communicate that before the season starts.

Ultimately, coaches and assistants have to be a team within the team. The keys to a unified coaching front are as follows:

- ✔ Be consistent in philosophy, discipline, and behavior at games and practices.
- ✔ Use each other's strengths.
- ✔ Remember that the assistant is the sounding board for the coach, the parents, and the kids.

Being a good listener is one of the most valuable assets of an assistant or co-coach.

Part VI
The Part of Tens

The 5th Wave   By Rich Tennant

Ice Rink Entrance

"I don't know who you are, kid, but goalie practice was over 2 hours ago! When I'm coach, you can't show up late! Get in here! I'm not through with you!"

In this part . . .

Few things are so important in coaching as the lifelong impact you have on the kids you coach. In this part, we pick three significant occasions for you to optimize your positive influence on kids, with ten items each to help you find opportunities to do so. The three occasions are during practices, midway through the season, and during all the other times you interact with the kids.

Chapter 23

Ten Parts of a Great Practice

*Y*our practices are the foundation of the success of your season and the quality of experience you give the players. Kids deserve great practices. And you'll get much more out of your coaching experience if you take the time to plan great practices. Doing so isn't difficult, but does take a little time. Include the ten items listed in this chapter, and you'll be well on your way to conducting great practices.

Constant Motion

Kids are geared for action when they come to a hockey rink. They don't expect to sit around listening, like in school, and they don't want to stand in line-ups waiting for their turn. Maximize active ice time for all players.

Challenge and Reward

Be aware of your players' changing levels of ability. Then tailor drills so that they challenge the players to do a little bit more than the last time. Nothing breeds success like success, so make sure that players can meet the challenges you set so that they feel like they're achieving something. And they will.

Words of Approval

Everyone likes to hear that they're doing something right. It makes most kids want to do whatever they've done again. Make sure every player on your team gets some individual, positive acknowledgement, preferably every practice, but if you miss somebody, make a note to catch them next practice.

Laughter

Kids want to have fun while they get better at hockey. Use a fun drill. Tell a joke. Sneak a surprise into your practice package. Use comical examples. Laugh with them.

Opportunity to Learn

At every practice, add a new component to at least one drill or skill done last practice. In other words, add one more step to what players can already do. If kids feel like they're learning, they feel like they're getting somewhere, and that builds confidence.

Opportunity to Get Better

Time and attention are two factors that definitely help any player improve. Make sure each player spends time doing, as opposed to watching. They'll get better more quickly that way. Observe each player to catch the little things they can change to make a difference in their play. Then help them discover how to make that change.

Individual Work

No two players have exactly the same strengths and weaknesses. Provide quality individual work, sometimes of your choosing, and sometimes using the player's choice of what she wants help with. Reserve the last ten minutes of practices for individual work or have special sessions to serve this purpose.

Energy

You are a great source of energy for kids. Act alive; be full of enthusiasm. Run practices at a brisk pace, full of positive encouragement. Kids mirror what they see.

Organization

Plan ahead to know what you're doing and what you want to accomplish. Doing so establishes a flow to practice that helps you incorporate the other parts of a great practice so that you don't miss anything important.

Creativity

Use your ingenuity. Kids love the unexpected. Repetitive, boring practices cultivate repetitive, boring players. Winning hockey is creative. To that end, give players the principles, and then give them the freedom to apply those principles creatively in practices and games.

Chapter 24

Ten Things to Ask Yourself Midway through the Season

In This Chapter

▶ Stopping long enough to take stock

▶ Checking that the kids are getting what they need

▶ Determining where to go from here

*T*ime flies when you're a coach. Seasons are often over before you catch your breath. However, we highly recommend you schedule a Sunday morning or sometime roughly mid-season to serve as your time out. Step back. Take a deep breath. And ask yourself, "How am I doin' so far?" It provides the pause that refreshes and that serves both you and the players. Use the ten questions listed here to help you answer "How am I doin' so far?" more specifically.

Are We Having Fun Yet?

If you can't answer this with a resounding "Yes!" for you and the kids, change what you're doing. What's the point if no one is enjoying what they're doing?

Am I Getting Better?

You should be able to glance back to the first couple of weeks and say, "Wow, have I come a long way since then!" Look for something to learn every day: a tip, an observation, an "aha!" that makes you just a little bit sharper than yesterday.

Are the Kids Improving?

Little kids get better in leaps and bounds, even with poor coaching. More advanced improvement is harder to spot, but you should be able to list ten things your players are doing better now than two months ago. Make sure that improvement applies to every kid.

Have I Got the Parents on Side?

If you don't get many complaints and you have few incidents of bad behavior from the stands, you're likely headed in the right direction. If you find you are communicating with parents comfortably before and after games, it's another good sign. If somebody shakes your hand and says, "I really appreciate what you're doing for Joey," you've got parents on side.

Am I Coordinating Well with Assistants?

You should have a sense of good give and take with your assistants and that all the jobs you need to have done are getting done. If you aren't seeing any conflicts in philosophy and approach during practices and games, you're likely on the right track. If kids are getting mixed messages from you and those working with you, it's time for a meeting with your assistants.

Do We Have a Problem That Needs a Solution?

Be honest with yourself. That's why you stop halfway through the season and take a look at how things are going. It's an opportunity to change and make things better. Identify any weak spots and decide on what action you need to take to make it better. Then do it.

Am I Meeting My and Our Team Goals?

Look at the list of goals you made for yourself and the team at the beginning of the season. You should be able to say "Yes" or "We're getting there" to most of them. Catch the ones you're missing out on and decide what you need to do to get them on track.

Am I Running Great Practices?

Practice is the foundation of your success as a team and the experience you give those kids. Turn to Chapter 23 if you mumbled your response to this question. Or turn to Chapter 4, study the content, and try again. You can do it.

What Things Am I Doing Right?

List ten things you like about what you're doing as a coach. Then pat yourself on the back. Don't be shy. You deserve credit for what you're doing well. And you want to keep doing those things. Coaching is a challenge and sometimes it can seem to be a thankless job, but that needn't come from you.

What Do I Still Need to Do to Call This a Successful Season?

If you've asked and honestly answered the previous nine questions, you've probably already started a list in answer to this question. Keep it simple. Pick the one, two, or three items that would have the best impact for the kids and go for it. Then, have a great second half.

Chapter 25

Ten Things You Want Kids to Say about Their Hockey Experience

*W*hen you get caught up in day-to-day coaching and the hectic pace of things going on, you may find it a challenge to keep a broader picture in perspective, such as where does playing minor hockey fit in the broad scheme of things for your players? You owe it to yourself and your players to keep hockey and life in perspective because your brief encounter is but one of thousands along the road of life — both theirs and yours. Yet that encounter can have a profound impact, especially on the kids. Here are ten statements from former minor hockey players that you can keep in your kit bag and refer to periodically to help you keep an eye on the end game.

I Love Hockey

You can give players a lasting love of the game. Teach them good basic hockey skills, help them appreciate a strong sense of team play, and invoke standards for sportsmanship. Do those three things, and you'll leave players with a positive experience that will keep them coming back to the game again and again.

Some of My Minor Hockey Teammates Are Still My Best Friends

You can give players an opportunity to make lasting friendships. Give players the opportunity to learn each other's names and outside interests; give them opportunities to support and count on each other as teammates. That way, you give them a chance to become good friends.

Hockey Taught Me How Far 1 Can Go with a Little Hard Work

You can help instill a positive work ethic. Challenge players, set expectations, and reward accomplishments for them as individuals. Those things help them learn the value and pleasure of hard work.

A Bit of Teamwork Can Accomplish So Much

You can help players learn the value of cooperation, trust, and interdependence. Cultivate an atmosphere of working together and helping each other out, showing examples of how much more can be accomplished with a little help from a friend.

Coach Believed in Me So Much, 1 Had to Start Believing in Myself

You can go a long way toward giving players self-confidence and a sense of self-worth. Give players repeated opportunities to achieve — even little things — and acknowledge their achievements. Reinforce and remind them of what they do well and what is good and unique about them.

I Still Play, and I'm 73

You can help players develop an appreciation for a healthy, active lifestyle. Make fitness and activity feel good. Help players enjoy the freedom of movement, the competency of having strength, and the pleasure of physical capability.

There's Nothing Like Swapping Stories with a Group of Hockey Players

You can give players a ready source of entertainment and sense of belonging wherever they go. Encourage locker-room banter and story telling. Bring in guest hockey players to tell hockey stories. Create experiences that give players their own stories.

Coach Made Us Think and Break Out of the Mold, Which Helped Me Get Where I Am Today

You can give players the freedom to develop independent thought and self-sufficiency. Encourage analytical thinking — and then trying and failing and learning from it. Support determination and commitment, which helps players stand on their own two feet.

Hockey Taught Me That Discipline Is Not a Bad Word

You can give players a healthy respect for rules and authority. Give them opportunities to determine their own rules and to be their own authority when no one is looking. Provide rules and consequences and explain the advantages of having both. Help them set behavioral expectations for themselves and objectively discuss any failures to meet them. Teach players how respect is a two-way street.

I Learned What It Means to Have Passion for What I'm Doing, and It's Made My Life Full and Exciting

You can help players to develop a zest for life. Help players to experience passion — for how they play, how they practice, how they help their teammates, and how they are as people on the ice and away from the rink. Encourage them to explore their passions no matter how temporary.

Index

●●

• J •

• K •

• L •

Notes

Notes

BUSINESS & PERSONAL FINANCE

0-470-83768-3   0-470-83740-3

Also available:
- Accounting For Dummies
  0-7645-7836-7
- Business Plans Kit For Dummies
  0-7645-9794-9
- Canadian Small Business Kit For
  Dummies 0-470-83818-3
- Investing For Canadians For
  Dummies 0-470-83361-0
- Leadership For Dummies
  0-7645-5176-0

- Managing For Dummies
  0-7645-1771-6
- Marketing For Dummies
  0-7645-5600-2
- Money Management All-in-One Desk
  Reference For Canadians For
  Dummies 0-470-83360-2
- Real Estate Investing For Canadians
  For Dummies 0-47083418-8
- Stock Investing For Canadians For
  Dummies 0-470-83342-4

HOME & BUSINESS COMPUTER BASICS

0-7645-7326-8   0-7645-8849-4

Also available:
- Blogging For Dummies
  0-471-77084-1
- Excel 2003 All-in-One Desk Reference
  For Dummies 0-7645-3758-x
- Macs For Dummies 0-7645-5656-8

- Office 2003 All-in-One Desk
  Reference For Dummies
  0-7645-3883-7
- Outlook 2003 For Dummies
  0-7645-3759-8
- PCs For Dummies 0-7645-8958-x
- Upgrading & Fixing PCs For
  Dummies 0-7645-1665-5

FOOD, HOME, GARDEN, HOBBIES, MUSIC & PETS

0-7645-9904-6   0-7645-5232-5

Also available:

- Diabetes Cookbook For Dummies 0-7645-5130-2
- Gardening For Canadians For Dummies 1-894413-37-7
- Holiday Decorating For Dummies 0-7645-2570-0
- Home Improvement All-in-One Desk Reference For Dummies 0-7645-5680-0
- Knitting For Dummies 0-7645-5395-x-

- Piano For Dummies 0-7645-5105-1
- Puppies For Dummies 0-7645-5255-4
- Scrapbooking For Dummies 0-7645-7208-3
- Sudoku For Dummies 0-470-01892-5
- Dog Training For Dummies 0-7645-8418-9
- 30-Minute Meals For Dummies 0-7645-2589-1

INTERNET & DIGITAL MEDIA

0-7645-9802-3   0-471-74739-4

Also available:

- CD & DVD Recording For Dummies 0-7645-5956-7
- eBay For Dummies 0-7645-5654-1
- Electronics For Dummies 0-7645-7660-7
- Fighting Spam For Dummies 0-7645-5965-6
- Genealogy Online For Dummies 0-7645-5964-8

- Google For Dummies 0-7645-4420-9
- Home Recording For Musicians For Dummies 0-7645-8884-2
- The Internet For Dummies 0-7645-8996-2
- Podcasting For Dummies 0-471-74898-6

SPORTS

0-470-83828-0   0-471-77381-6

Also available:

- Baseball For Dummies 0-76457537-6
- Coaching Football For Dummies 0-471-79331-0
- Fishing For Dummies 0-7645-5028-4
- Football For Dummies 0-7645-3936-1

- Golf For Dummies 0-471-76871-5
- Hockey For Dummies 0-470-04619-7
- Lacrosse For Dummies 1-894413-48-2
- Rugby For Dummies 0-470-83405-6
- Tour De France For Dummies 0-7645-8449-9

FITNESS, PARENTING, RELIGION & SPIRITUALITY

0-7645-5418-2

Also available:
- The Bible For Dummies 0-7645-5296-1
- Catholicism For Dummies 0-7645-5391-7

- Fitness For Dummies 0-7645-7851-0
- Pilates For Dummies 0-7645-5397-6
- Teaching Kids to Read For Dummies 0-7645-4043-2
- Weight Training For Dummies 0-7645-76845-6

TRAVEL

0-470-83398-X   0-7645-7386-1

Also available:
- Alaska For Dummies 0-7645-7746-8
- Cancun and the Yucatan For Dummies 0-7645-7828-6
- Cruise Vacations For Dummies 0-7645-9830-9
- Europe For Dummies 0-7645-7529-5
- Ireland For Dummies 0-7645-7749-2
- Las Vegas For Dummies 0-7645-7382-9
- London For Dummies 0-471-74870-6

- New York City For Dummies 0-7645-6945-7
- Nova Scotia, New Brunswick & Prince Edward Island For Dummies 0-470-836739-x
- Paris For Dummies 0-7645-7630-5
- Vancouver & Victoria For Dummies 0-470-83684-9
- Walt Disney World & Orlando For Dummies 0-471-78250-5

NETWORKING, SECURITY, PROGRAMMING & DATABASES

0-7645-3910-8   0-7645-5784-X

Also available:
- Ajax For Dummies 0-471-78597-0
- Access 2003 All-in-One Desk Reference For Dummies 0-7645-3988-4
- Beginning Programming For Dummies 0-7645-4997-9
- C++ For Dummies 0-7645-6852-3
- Firewalls For Dummies 0-7645-4048-3

- Network Security For Dummies 0-7645-1679-5
- Networking For Dummies 0-7645-7583-x
- TCP/IP For Dummies 0-7645-1760-0
- XML For Dummies 0-7645-8845-1
- Wireless All-in-One Desk Reference For Dummies 0-7645-7496-5

HEALTH & SELF-HELP

0-470-83370-X   0-7645-4149-8

Also available:
- Arthritis For Dummies
  0-7645-7074-9
- Asthma For Dummies
  0-7645-4233-8
- Breast Cancer For Dummies
  0-7645-2482-8
- Controlling Cholesterol For
  Dummies 0-7645-5440-9
- Depression For Dummies
  0-7645-3900-0
- Fertility For Dummies
  0-7645-2549-2

- Fibromyalgia For Dummies
  0-7645-5441-7
- Improving Your Memory For
  Dummies 0-7645-5435-2
- Menopause For Dummies
  0-7645-5458-1
- Pregnancy For Dummies
  0-7645-4483-7
- Relationships For Dummies
  0-7645-5384-4
- Thyroid For Dummies
  0-471-78755-8

EDUCATION, HISTORY & REFERENCE

0-470-83656-3   0-7645-2498-4

Also available:
- Algebra For Dummies
  0-7645-5325-9
- British History For Dummies
  0-7645-7021-8
- English Grammar For Dummies
  0-7645-5322-4
- Forensics For Dummies
  0-7645-5580-4
- Freemasons For Dummies
  0-7645-9796-5

- Italian For Dummies 0-7645-5196-5
- Latin For Dummies 0-7645-5431-x
- Science Fair Projects For Dummies
  0-7645-5460-3
- Spanish For Dummies
  0-7645-5194-9
- U.S. History For Dummies
  0-7645-5249-x